DATE DUE

JUN 2 9 2001		
Nov 27 2007		
March 09		
NOV 1 5 2011		
DEC 0 7 2011		

GAYLORD

W9-DGV-136

PRINTED IN U.S.A.

MALE, FEMALE, EMAIL

Male, Female, Email:
The Struggle for Relatedness in a Paranoid Society

Michael A. Civin, Ph.D.

OTHER

Other Press

New York

Production Editor: Robert D. Hack

This book was set in 11 pt. Bell by Alpha Graphics in Pittsfield, NH.

Library of Congress Cataloging-in-Publication Data

Civin, Michael A.
    Male, female, email : the struggle for relatedness in a paranoid society/
Michael A. Civin.
        p. cm.
    Includes bibliographical references and index.
    ISBN 1-892746-30-1
    1. Man-woman relationships—United States.   2. Online chat groups—
Social aspects.   3. Internet (Computer network)—Social aspects.
4. Electronic mail messages.   I. Title.

HQ801.C515   1999
306.7'0285—dc21   99-043547

*This book is dedicated
to my parents,
Harriet and Paul Civin*

Contents

Preface   ix

Acknowledgments   xvii

1. Male, Female, and Email—New Conceptions
   of Relatedness   1

2. The Interface of Janus: Internet Relationships at
   the New Millennium   29

3. Cleansing the Web of Perception   57

4. Between Flesh and Thought: The Substance
   of Internet Relationships   81

5. Being Between Two Lives: On the Vicissitudes
   of Cyberspace as Potential Space in Organizations   139

6. At the Still Point of the Turning World:
   Transformation and Potentiation
   or Constriction and Annihilation   191

Notes   203

References   221

Index   231

Preface

This book is about individuals' relationship to relationships with other individuals, and the role that computer-mediated communication (CMC) plays in the virtually infinite web of these relationships. Computer mediated-communication, as used here, includes email, the Internet, and related media. The book also addresses individuals' adaptations and maladaptations to a societal milieu in which persecutory anxiety has become so commonplace that we no longer notice either the anxiety or individuals' reactions to it.

Almost forty years ago, in his book about the nonhuman environment, Harold Searles (1960) brought attention to this often overlooked aspect of individual experience:

> The nonhuman environment, far from being of little or no account to human personality development, constitutes one of the most basically important ingredients of human psychological existence. It is my conviction that there is within the human individual a sense, whether at a conscious or unconscious level, of relatedness to his nonhuman environment, that this relatedness is one of the transcendentally important facts of human living, that ... it is a source of ambivalent feelings to him, and that, finally, if he tries

to ignore the importance to himself, he does so at the peril of his psychological well-being. [pp 5–6]

Nineteen years later, in an essay on unconscious processes and the
environmental crisis, Searles (1979) gave voice to the individual and societal themes that I address in this book:

> In current urban living, there is not the close-knit fabric of interpersonal
> relationships, enduring over decades of time, which would enable one to
> face and accept the losses inherent in human living—the losses involved in
> the growing up and growing away of one's children, the aging and death of
> one's parents, the knowledge of one's spouse's and one's own inevitable
> aging and death. A technology-dominated, overpopulated world has brought
> with it so reduced a capacity in us to cope with the losses a life must bring
> with it to a truly human life that we . . . *ensure that we shall have essentially
> nothing to lose in our eventual dying.* . . . The proliferation of technology, with
> its marvelously complex integration and its seemingly omnipotent domin-
> ion over nature, provides us with an increasingly alluring object upon which
> to project our "nonhuman" unconscious strivings for omnipotence; hence,
> we tend increasingly to identify, unconsciously, with this. [pp.235, 237,
> italics added]

With the use of computer-mediated communication, we have stumbled
upon astoundingly powerful and resilient ways to project and then identify with our strivings for omnipotence in the face of a world of global
urban living in which "the losses inherent in human living" seem often so
thrust upon us that having and losing, to paraphrase William Blake (1793),
frame a fearful symmetry.

In a therapy session a few years ago, a patient asked me what my opinion was of Internet relationships. My first reaction was that I had no opinion, and even less of an idea of why the patient had asked the question.
Invoking the time-honored, and in this case somewhat uninspired, therapeutic strategy of answering with a question, I asked my patient if he

thought I ought to have an opinion. With an incredulous sigh and a brow furrowed with disapproval, the patient responded, "Of course you should have an opinion. Do you live in the same world I do?" Although I was not sure then and cannot be sure now that I live in the same world as another person, the patient's incredulity made an impression on me. Even though it seemed to me that his disdain for my ignorance pertained to many of the emotional issues that had brought him to therapy, I began to become aware that in my professional work I *had* been hearing a great deal about the Internet and various people's use of it in their relational lives. On reflection, I realized that for about six months I had heard tales of the Internet from not only my patients but also my supervisees and professional colleagues as well. As my interest grew in understanding more about this new method of relating, and as I began to inquire more actively about others' experience of it, I discovered that the frequency of these Internet relationships was far greater than I had appreciated. As I focused more clinical attention on the details of these relationships, I began to realize that the dynamics of these relationships were far more complex than I might have thought. I also began to understand that I was not entirely clear about what might distinguish a technology-mediated interpersonal relationship from one that was not technology mediated.

From my own vantage point as a clinical psychologist, an organizational consultant, and an educator, I am constantly dealing with issues involving human relationships. Whether my focus is an individual, a couple, a group, a class, a company, or society as a whole, it remains easy enough to spot the intrusion into relationships of nonhuman, machine-like phenomena. In fact, following Searles's lead, I have spent a good deal of time mulling over clinical instances of ambiguity between humans and the nonhuman environment. But even from my perspective, as someone whose business and inclination it is to think about these things, I was amazed at the nature of the changes in relatedness that had become so pervasive and yet at times so subtle that they had often been easy to overlook.

Despite my awareness of Searles's ideas on the subject of the nonhuman environment, person-to-machine/person relationships had become so ubiquitous that I failed to notice the clinically significant new ways in which technology in general, and the technology of cyberspace in particular, had insinuated itself into the most basic aspect of being human. I had glossed over the elision between human relationships with the human environment and human relationships with the nonhuman environment, failing even to question whether these latter relationships might be synecdoches for relationships with the human environment. I had overlooked these new ways of having relationships, and thus I overlooked the shift in the meaning of "relationship," until my patient's incredulity startled me into awareness.

To a great extent, the ideas in this book have emerged from such oversights. On subsequent reflection on these issues, I have become keenly aware of just how complex and how interesting these matters really are. These complexities—at times painful, perplexing, and limiting, and at other times enhancing, transitional, and transformative—stand at the center of this book and give rise to the questions I explore here. Is the nature of being human based so fundamentally on interpersonal relatedness that this insinuation of the technological poses basic threats to our being? Does this technology, like any other tool, stand in the service of expanding our human abilities? In particular, does the technology of cyberspace facilitate the emergence of alternative identities, of other ways of being human that otherwise remain trapped, encumbered, and dissociated? Does the emergence of cyberspace alter fundamentally the significance of gender, blending or socially mutating maleness and femaleness into techno-gendered email-ness? Does the arrival of these technological developments represent the latest in a series of scientific revolutions and revelations that must be accepted as altering the human experience? How can we understand the interpersonal and intrapsychic dynamics of individuals who are engaged in these relationships? What significance does this understanding have for our existing beliefs about the human psyche?

As a practicing psychoanalyst, a great deal of the sense I make of these questions is informed by psychoanalytic theory, and in particular by some of the perspectives on relational life that have gained favor within psychoanalysis in the past several decades. I will highlight these theories' relevance to the issues of relatedness that interest us here. In guiding us through this tour of contemporary psychoanalytic theories of relational life, I will illustrate some of the ways in which the relationships I have just described reflect individuals' successful and not-so-successful efforts to retain fundamental qualities of human relatedness, while enacting a societally induced, paranoid reaction to interpersonal engagement.

In his 1925 essay, "A Note Upon the 'Mystic Writing Pad,'" Freud discussed the pros and cons of writing with pen on a sheet of paper, which preserves forever but has finite receptive capacity, versus writing with chalk on a slate, which has infinite receptive capacity because it is erasable but fails to preserve forever. The Mystic Writing Pad consisted of a wax base with a two-part transparent overlay. The upper of the two layers was a transparent piece of celluloid and the lower layer was thin translucent waxed paper. The whole device was fastened at one end only, so that each of the other sheets could be separated, one from the other. To use the pad, you wrote on the upper, celluloid part with a pointed stylus that left no superficial mark on the surface. By pressure, the bottom part of the waxed paper came into contact with the wax slab and the writing became visible through the celluloid. If you wished to erase what had been written, you simply raised the two-part covering off the wax slab and when you restored it to the former position, the traces of writing were gone. Freud observed, however, that the wax slab itself retained a permanent trace of the impressions. As subsequent messages partially erased and overwrote the underlying impressions, the wax slab had become a palimpsest of traces of what had been written, overwritten, and overwritten again and again.

For Freud the Mystic Pad served as an analogue to the conscious and preconscious systems (the celluloid and waxed paper) and the unconscious (the wax slab). But the Mystic Pad serves a symbolic purpose for us as well. For Freud, whose economic model relies on the closed energy system of a one-person psychology, the structure of interest is intrapsychic. In our study of the computer-mediated communication of the Internet, we are more interested in the perpetual interplay between the intrapsychic and the interpersonal, the interplay between fantasy and reality, between virtual reality (VR) and real life (RL).* The relationship that Freud observed in this Mystic Pad exists in the interstitial tension between paper and slate, between permanent and transitory, between palpable and imaginal. On the Internet, this same relationship exists, not only in the areas of one-person psychology but also in the tension between relation and nonrelation, between substance and thought, between real and virtual, and between simulation and dissimulation.

For Winnicott (1971), the transitional object exists in the middle ground between "me" and "not me," between fantasy and reality, between that which is created and that which is found. Winnicott discovered that play, which he saw as the primary vehicle for our maturational processes, "is in fact neither a matter of inner psychic reality nor a matter of external reality" (p. 96). "The place where cultural experience is located is in the *potential space* between the individual and the environment (originally the object). The same can be said of playing. Cultural experience begins with creative living first manifested in play" (p. 100).

At a glance the Internet (as a contemporary version of Freud's Mystic Writing Pad) exists in a space between inner psychic reality and external reality, between the individual and the environment. To what extent is this intermediary space a "potential" space? To what extent is the pro-

---

*Throughout this text I use the term "real life" (RL) in opposition to "virtual reality" (VR) (although I do not always articulate the opposition because that would prove redundant). These terms are commonly used in talking about computer-mediated communication to distinguish between experience on-line and experience apart from computers. I use this convention as a convenient shorthand, although I do not believe that any way of experiencing is more or less real than any other.

cess of text-based computer-mediated communication a "transitional process"? To what extent does this form of communicating stand between the individual and the environment in a way that links the two, and to what extent does it keep them separate?

These ideas, as well as the ideas of numerous other writers exploring this infinite and daunting new field, will intermingle with my own throughout this book. Chapter 1, "Male, Female, and Email—New Conceptions of Relatedness," introduces some of these ideas and provides a few general illustrations of the sorts of relationships that I will be discussing. Chapter 2, "The Interface of Janus: Internet Relationships at the New Millennium," briefly sketches psychoanalytic theories and provides Internet-related clinical examples of these theories. This chapter draws heavily on the work of the influential psychoanalysts Melanie Klein and D. W. Winnicott. (The more technical aspects of their work are described in the endnotes.) In Chapter 3, "Cleansing the Web of Perception," I develop my own ideas, building on the theories of Klein, Winnicott, Ignacio Matte-Blanco, and a few others. Chapter 4, "Between Flesh and Thought: The Substance of Internet Relationships," explores the personal and relational side of cyberspace, focusing on how and why people have come to relate with each other and with machines that represent each other, and on the ways in which many of these relationships reflect adaptations, both functional and pathological, to the experience of pervasive, psychologically threatening conditions of living. I use psychoanalytic theories to clarify what is happening within relationships. Chapter 5, "Being Between Two Lives: On the Vicissitudes of Cyberspace as Potential Space in Organizations," focuses on the world of work, exploring the organizational impact of cyberspace on how and why people have come to relate with each other and with machines, which represent each other within organizations, and the impact these types of relationships have on both the individuals and the organization. Chapter 6, "At the Still Point of the Turning World: Transformation and Potentiation or Constriction and Annihilation," places the central themes of the book in the context of computers, society, and the future of relatedness.

Acknowledgments

There are a number of people whose contributions to this book I would like to acknowledge. From Other Press, Llc, Publisher Michael Moskowitz recognized this book's potential and, together with Managing Editor Melissa Kresch and Production Editor Bob Hack, helped me to bring the effort to a successful conclusion.

I have benefitted ever so much from more conversations than I am able to remember with colleagues, students, supervisees, and friends at the Derner Institute at Adelphi, BCADA, Division 39 conferences, on chairlifts at Bromley, and elsewhere. I would especially like to single out the helpful comments I received from my colleagues at Adelphi—Joseph Newirth, Robert Mendelsohm, and Karen Lombardi. From ISPSO, the thoughts of Larry Hirschhorn, Richard Holti, James Cumming, and others were especially useful in helping me think through the section on organizational use of email. I am also grateful to Todd Essig and other members of the Psychoanalytic Connection for the generous sharing of ideas. The energetic contributions of Richard Baker, both on- and off-line were also extremely helpful at a critical time in the book's development. Without the efficient and resourceful help of my research assistant, Jennifer Naddell, this book would still be hiding in the keyboard of my computer, waiting for me to find the time and industry to begin the preparatory work.

Many people have influenced the development of the ideas in this book over the years, both directly and indirectly, including Linda Jacobs, Gene Lubow, Kate Fodaski, Liza Fodaski, Michael Zentman, Linda Bergman, Naomi Rucker, Drucilla Cornell, Mary Fassett, Don Milman, and others too numerous to mention. I would never have been able to write this book without borrowing from and, hopefully building upon, the pioneering efforts of Harold Searles (whose kind and ever so valuable encouraging words I will always cherish), D. W. Winnicott, Heinrich Racker, and Ignacio Matte-Blanco.

On a more personal note, I am grateful to my mother-in-law, Theresa Lombardi, for her gracious and thoughtful help, and to my parents, Harriet and Paul Civin, whose love, support, and faith have guided me my whole life. My daughter, Chloë, is the amusing muse who was my constant inspiration in this endeavor, as well as in everything I undertake to do. Most of all, it is to my fellow analyst and parent, fellow and former professor, colleague, collaborator, office-, house-, and play-mate, critic, supporter, wife and friend, Karen Lombardi, who, as the most whole of subjects to whom I relate, that my gratitude, appreciation, and love belong.

1 Male, Female, and Email— New Conceptions of Relatedness

But it could be the creeping realization
that the blue sky did not exist any more.

> *On the contrary.*

That there is no meadow with a flower
here and there.

> *On the contrary.*

That there is nothing irresistible any more.

> *On the contrary.*

That there is no glucosis,

> *no droning,*

> *no time,*

> *On the contrary.*

And thus it will be. Until
someone gets bored. By that life,
That death, or that tickling in the palm.

"*On the Origin of the Contrary,*" Miroslav Holub (1980)

A front-page *New York Times* headline reads "On Frontier of Cyberspace, Data is Money, and a Threat" (June 12, 1997). The article tells the story of Beverly Dennis, a woman in her fifties who grew up in a part of southern Ohio's coal country that verged on the preindustrial, without running water, electricity, indoor toilet, or car. Her grandfather built the house she was raised in and lived in it his whole life. Her grandmother boiled clothes on the stove and scrubbed them on a washboard. Not only was Dennis born before the word *computer* had entered the public vocabulary, but her early life belonged more to the nineteenth century than to the twenty-first.

The article describes her coming home one evening after work and opening an envelope with a postmark she doesn't recognize. Inside is a letter written by a man she doesn't know, but who seems to know a vast amount about her, her birthday, what magazines she reads, the kind of soap she uses. In the 12-page handwritten text of the letter, these bits and pieces of her way of living have been transformed into the elaborate, explicit sexual fantasy of an unidentified man who turns out to be a convicted rapist serving time at a prison in Texas. Working as an inmate, the man had found her name, address, and the data for his sexual fantasy on a product questionnaire she had filled out and he was entering on computer tape to be used by a company, Metromail, that had contracted with the Texas prison system.

As the headline suggests, Dennis's story rests at the frontier of cyberspace. One participant is a woman who filled out a questionnaire by hand, a woman born and raised in a place that lagged behind the industrial age, let alone the age of computers. The other participant is a man, identified only as a prisoner, living in a setting that also belongs to a preindustrial age. The journalist, Nina Bernstein, describes it: "In the heat-soaked shimmer of an August noon in 1996, in a field outside a Texas penitentiary, prisoners with hoes stood double file, before a lone guard on horseback. It was a tableau from an earlier era" (*New York Times*, June 12, 1997, p. A14).

The prisoner's letter was also written by hand. It was sent through the U.S. postal system to its recipient, as any letter would have been sent before any of us had ever known of a computer. In between and surrounding these relics of earlier eras extends the infinite realm of cyberspace.

When Beverly Dennis set out to find her tormenter, she needed the help of local investigative television news reporters. When Metromail needed to learn about her, because of her eventual suit against them, they "turned to the company's own massive consumer data base, and retrieved more than 900 tidbits of Ms. Dennis's life going back to 1987. Laid out on 25 closely printed pages of spreadsheets were not only her income, marital status, hobbies, and ailments, but whether she had dentures, the brands of antacid tablets she had taken, how often she had used room deodorizers, sleeping aids, and hemorrhoid remedies" (p. A14).

In 1923, in his play *The Adding Machine*, Elmer Rice created a menial office clerk named Mr. Zero, a "brainless boob" of a creature who reduces people to disembodied numbers. He is himself as disembodied as the objects of his efforts. In a prophetic stroke, at the end of Rice's play Mr. Zero is offered a "super-hyper-adding machine." But in our era, the capabilities of computing vastly transcend even Rice's prophetic vision. The psychologist/sociologist Sherry Turkle (1995) has described computers as having moved from an age of calculation to an age of simulation. No longer do computers merely reduce people to the bits of data of Mr. Zero's super-hyper-adding machine. Computers have moved into an entirely new dimension, taking bits and pieces of disparate data and simulating whole people from them.

Later in the same *New York Times* piece cited above, Bernstein concocts a character whom she names Joe Consumer. She follows Joe through a day of electronic fingerprint-leaving and the eventual consequences. At the most innocuous level, he calls an 800 number to check on the pollen count. The agency captures his number through caller ID and his name is put into a database of allergy sufferers. This database is sold to a drug company, which results in his getting junk mail. More closely related to the general themes of this book, Joe criticizes his boss in an email to a friend. His company performs a review of Internet activity and discovers a copy of the email, resulting in Joe's dismissal. Joe orders cufflinks and silk boxer shorts from a catalogue and pays with an American Express card. This puts him on a list of male buyers of sexy lingerie. Joe ends up receiving not only jewelry catalogues, but also a sex-videotape offer. Whether Joe is on the telephone, driving in his car, sending an email, dining, getting prescription drugs, shopping at the supermarket, or ordering from a mail order catalogue, his electronic fingerprint is being deposited, retrieved, and combined with other data. As a result, he is sent coupons, has his insurance rates increased, is fired and tracked on the Internet as a litigious employee, and receives magazines, catalogues, and sex-videotape offers. Had he been Beverly Dennis, he might have been electronically stalked as well.

In *1984* (Orwell 1949), our first encounter with Big Brother is through Winston Smith's eyes: "The hostile figure melted into the face of Big Brother, black-haired, black mustachio'd, full of power and mysterious calm, and so vast that it almost filled up the screen" (p. 17). The screen symbolizes Big Brother, but in addition we are constantly reminded that Big Brother is everywhere. As Bernstein's *New York Times* article captures, and as *1984* anticipates, the computer has become both the symbol and the agent of a paranoid orientation toward life in our society.

In 1811 in the area around Nottingham, England, a group of workers in the hosiery and lace industries instigated a campaign of breaking machinery, specifically knitting machines, to protest and strike out against the unemployment that had resulted from the encroachment of the technology of the Industrial Revolution. This movement spread quickly to the wool and cotton mills of Yorkshire and Lancashire. As a group, these anti-industrial guerillas proclaimed to be acting under orders of General Ned Ludd, a mythical figure who derived from yet another mythical figure, a boy named Ludlam who was said to have rebelled against his father by breaking a knitting frame. Dealt with severely by owners as well as by the government, the Luddites fared poorly. In January 1813, fourteen Luddites were hanged in Yorkshire, and the movement had vanished by 1816. But General Ludd and the Luddites have endured as a symbol of active opposition to technology. This Luddite tradition includes some contemporary critics of cyber-technology such as Roszak (1986), whose book *The Cult of Information* carries the subtitle "A Neo-Luddite Treatise on High-Tech, Artificial Intelligence, and the True Art of Thinking," and Birkerts (1994, 1996), whose books *The Gutenberg Elegies* and *Tolstoy's Dictaphone* bemoan the fate and plead for the return to primacy of the written word in the electronic age.

But the image that the Luddites leave us with is much more complex than merely the symbol of taking up arms against the encroachment of technology. Seen from another perspective, Ned Ludd is a symbol, a whole person created out of a myth of oedipal rebellion, which represents human striving for wholeness in the face of perceived invasion and destruction.[1] As much as the Luddites present us with the image of smashing into pieces that which is whole (the knitting machines and computers of technology), *they present us with the image of making whole that which is in pieces* (the way of life).

To be sure, the computer and the cyberspace that has emerged from it have become both the symbol and the agent of the threats and invasions that have led to a paranoid orientation toward life in our society. But, like General Ned Ludd, the computer, which becomes a trope for the systems that make use of it, may also be seen as both the symbol and the agent for attempting to piece together something whole out of the fragmentation that this paranoid orientation has engendered.

Over the past ten to fifteen years our society has witnessed an almost invisible change in the nature of what we mean by the word *relationship*. But however invisible it may be, this change is profound at the very least, and perhaps even revolutionary. Commonplace phrases like "I have a friend," "I have an acquaintance," "I know someone," even "I love" and "I hate" may still refer to relationships carried on among people in much the same way they were conducted in past decades. But increasingly, these same phrases denote relationships between a person and a machine, perhaps a machine that, in some way or another, represents another person. With barely a sideways glance from social commentators, this new way of relating is becoming an unconscious adjustment in our conception of relatedness, and this is all happening at a speed that approximates the advances in microprocessor technology.

This book explores what the notion of relationship means to us in the context of computers, and in particular computer-mediated communication systems, and the lives we have constructed around them. I will shed light on why some of these shifts in meaning have come about, what the implication of these profound changes may be, and the way in which these contemporary forms of relatedness reflect adaptations and maladaptations to the prevailing societal paranoia depicted in the *New York Times* article and in so many other places.

Many of these changes are startling, with broad and compelling implications. We read in the newspaper about competitions between a man and a chess-playing machine, or we watch television or the movies and see computers cast as sentient beings, transcending a software-driven status. In a brilliant encapsulization of the anthropomorphizing of a computer system, we learn in a recent movie, *Star Trek: Insurrection* (Paramount, 1998) that *Star Trek*'s android character, Data, has an optional emotion chip. Presumably with his emotion chip in, Data bemoans having no history of having been a child, of having his body change as he grows, of tripping over his feet. As Data learns from a young boy (whose family, in the Luddite tradition, has chosen to forsake technology because of its disruption and destruction) to play hide-and-seek in the hay, the elision between software and flesh approaches completion.

But many of the changes in which we are most interested remain far more elusive. When a newspaper headline calls attention to the machine's triumph over human intelligence or a motion picture dramatizes a machine's fictional humanization, our attention is focused on the issue. If we choose willingly to suspend disbelief, we choose also to suspend belief. In the voyeuristic elaboration of the progress of life through the advance of the computer system, we simultaneously depict the destruction of much of what we understand to be human; in so doing, we may often bring ourselves to a point at which we try to avoid looking at what we are seeing. In her book *Modest_Witness@Second_Millennium.FemaleMan©Meets_OncoMouse*™ Donna Haraway (1997) captures this dilemma: "Apocalypse, in the sense of the final destruction of man's home world, and comedy, in the sense both of the humorous and of the ultimate harmonious resolution of all conflict through progress, are bedfellows in the soap opera of technoscience" (p. 8).

However, the subtlety and elusiveness of these changes blurring the boundary of the human and the technological no longer limit themselves to the realm of science and science fiction. With the proliferation of the Internet and the World Wide Web, the everyday business of living has, for many, become so intertwined with the use of technology that we often no longer notice when we have chosen to engage in an activity that previously involved another person but now involves a machine instead. With services like PeaPod.com and NetGrocer.com (groceries), Amazon.com (books), Travelscape.com (travel), 1–800–flowers.com (flowers), musicblvd.com (CDs and music), insweb.com (insurance quotes), fidelity.com (stocks), and thousands of others, we are now in a position to carry out in cyberspace many activities that used to require interaction with another person. When looking for the telephone number or address of a person or a business, you no longer need to contact an operator. A simple search on-line can give you not only a person's address and number, but also a map and directions to get to the house and the names and professions of the neighbors. Even if you prefer the old-fashioned approach and choose to dial the operator, you may never speak to an actual person; rather, a prerecorded message will give you the number and offer to dial it as well. If you want to find out who can make a custom-designed piece of furniture for you, you no longer need to call around and speak with people about their ability to furnish what you want. You can post a message on a dozen different Internet bulletin boards and receive email messages back from people without ever speaking to anyone.

These, and hundreds of other examples, illustrate instances in which there has been an elision between human-to-human engagement, whether face-to-face or voice-to-voice, and engagement between a human and a machine. These are interesting and perplexing social changes. As we will see, a number of writers have explored the personal and social ramification of such processes of change (e.g., Doheny-Farina 1996, Gergen 1991, Haraway 1997, O'Reilly and Associates 1997, Provenzo 1991). Here, however, we will focus our attention on the complex ways in which technology, in the form of computer-mediated communication systems such as the Internet and the World Wide Web, have insinuated themselves into the fabric of interpersonal relatedness. On the one hand, we will look at ways in which it may seem that basic threats to the essence of our being are captured in this insinuation of technology into domains that previously were unequivocally personal and interpersonal. On the other hand, we will look at ways in which these computer-mediated modalities of communicating facilitate the exploration of transmutable aspects of being human that, in the absence of technological help, remain either inaccessible or encumbered by social symbolism. In this view of computer-mediated communication, for example, the biological imperative of gender is softened by the blending of the divide between maleness and femaleness through techno-gendered email-ness.

In this discussion of the impact of technology on the fabric of human relatedness, we will focus primarily on relationships that develop through the modality of computer-mediated communication, which is conducted from the keyboard and display terminal of a computer, making use of the vast network of the Internet. There are at least as many versions of these relationships as there are users of the systems. In this survey, we will touch on just a few of the ways in which human relatedness takes form through the mediation of the Internet. But first, what are these relationships? A few vignettes, to which I will have occasion to return throughout the book, will help us begin to answer this last question and set the stage for approaching other issues.

A therapy patient, a man in his early forties, married for twelve years and the father of four, has struggled with problems of identity, success, and addiction for years. He is a proud man, boastful about his accomplishments, but he is also a shameful man, humiliated by his failures. Years of striving have led him through a patchwork of frustrated careers, repeating a pattern of rapid ascent and languishing inability to achieve his ambitions. Throughout it all he has struggled, often in vain, against a tendency to withdraw, trying to remain connected to his wife and family, hanging on by a thread of human relatedness to a hopefulness he is not certain he deserves. Finally, his relentless efforts are bordering on success. He has a new line of work, in the computer field, in which he has not only risen to the top but has managed to retain a position of prominence and to grow in responsibility, in power, and in wealth. He has been on the verge of declaring his therapy successfully completed when he comes into his therapist's office distraught and nearly shattered. After fifteen minutes of sobbing, he manages to explain: His wife has appropriated the computer he brought home to do his work and now she leaves him alone to tend the children and doesn't come to bed at night. She has an email lover. She is cheating on him.

An adolescent girl is in psychotherapy because of her feelings of loneliness and isolation. She complains that she is too fat, too awkward, and that she has never been taught the social conventions that the other girls deal in so gracefully. She spends all of her time alone, reading, playing video games, and fantasizing about a relationship she would like to have with a boy in her class. Finally she musters the courage to sit at his table in the cafeteria and suffers through twenty minutes of profound humiliation, convinced that everyone in the school has witnessed him make fun of her and then get up and move to a different table, leaving her alone and mortified. In tears she goes to her guidance counselor, who listens to her sensitively for over an hour. Having learned that the girl is in psychotherapy with me, the counselor calls. She is tremendously worried about the girl, who has spoken of suicide and who feels so profoundly alone and dejected. To make matters worse, the counselor says, the girl's parents are about to go away on a trip, leaving her entirely alone in the house for a week. "She can't drive. She has no friends," the counselor reports. "She has her computer but she's not even on the Internet. Can you talk to her parents and tell them to get her a modem?"

Employees and management of a successful company on the verge of an important merger find themselves in an unaccustomed state of turmoil. Management attributes this to a failure in implementation of a new computer-based material requirements planning (MRP) system. However, as I meet with middle management and others throughout the organization, I find that even though everyone agrees that the MRP implementation has been a disaster, most people are far more preoccupied by a different complaint: endless meetings are being called, interfering with their work schedules. Even worse, as they rush around from one meeting to another, they are rarely able to figure out whom to contact to confirm the meeting, and they never know if the meeting is a genuine or fictitious one called by a character they collectively label "the phantom." All of the phantom's actions are conducted via email.

A woman in her late forties enters psychotherapy. She relates that she has been married three times, each marriage ending in her being abandoned and feeling more disconsolate and alone. She has endured a lifetime of other losses, tragic deaths, imprisonments, and hospitalizations. She is a resourceful woman, decisively intelligent, bold, and outspoken, with a successful career on Wall Street, several vacation houses, and an important collection of modern "industrial" art. But, she says, none of these has meaning for her any more. Any of them can be taken from her at any minute and she will have to endure living with yet another loss. Two relationships keep her going. "I only have Charles [her 19-year-old son] and Carlos [her Internet lover of more than a year]. With them it's all clear. If Charles gets hit by a truck, I can kill myself because there would be no more reason to live with that kind of pain, and if Carlos goes away, I will find another Carlos. To try any other relationship out there, I'd have to be willing to suffer. What's the point?"

A 34-year-old man suffers greatly from an unrelenting series of failed relationships. Nearly suicidal, he enters psychotherapy and reveals a history fraught with enormous anguish, beginning with parents who tantalized him with unfulfilled offers of tenderness. As he enters therapy he also begins to become interested in Internet chat rooms. After two weeks he reports that he has begun his first truly satisfying relationship, spending up to six hours at a time on-line, often in the middle of the night. The relationship is "complete and satisfying." At times, he speaks of meeting her, but the meetings never happen. He becomes totally immersed in the on-line relationship until one night, about three months later, they have a fight. He resists signing on for a week. When finally he tries to contact her, his message is returned. No such email address can be found. His perfect relationship has vanished, literally without a trace.

A young lawyer with two small children, each from a different failed marriage, seeks psychotherapy because she feels "my life is going nowhere quickly." Intelligent, well-spoken, and attractive, she has always done reasonably well in school and at work, but feels that one relationship or another has inevitably kept her from thriving. Beginning with her home life as a child, she recounts a lifetime of feeling too dependent to live without someone else around. Nonetheless, she feels so suffocated and disappointed by others' treatment of her that she finds the thought of closeness repugnant. Initiated into the world of computers through legal searches at her work, she has sought solace in cyberspace. After putting her children to bed, she stays awake throughout a good part of the night, occasionally the entire night, sitting at her computer. Often she contents herself with downloading files and programs and tinkering with her computer, trying to make her machine world rich and functional in a way her outside world is not. Occasionally she chats. For months she has found the experience of assuming alternate identities gratifying. She has taken pleasure in "hanging out, doing what I want to do and saying what I want to say." This new freedom finally allows her to break off contact with her ex-husband, with whom she has remained marginally involved for three years after the divorce. Soon she finds herself in the chat rooms, taking on an identity that she is appalled to recognize, for the first time, as her own. She becomes more circumspect, more self-censoring, and, within a week, she has begun a new relationship, on-line. For the first month she finds this relationship almost blissfully satisfying, but soon finds she is craving more and arranges a meeting. For a time they alternate occasional meetings in real life and nightly intimacy on-line. Quickly enough, the frequencies and intensities shift, so that most of their relationship occurs in the flesh. Finally, the computer is abandoned altogether and for the briefest interlude she feels comfort in his presence. Two weeks later, she has begun to spend time on her computer again, even when he is present—not chatting, just downloading programs and protocols. At the same time that she reports, in therapy, that he is expressing his dissatisfaction with her distance, she begins to join chat rooms again, meets another man on-line, and breaks up with her first on-line lover. That lover, who knows her code name and password, signs on *as her* and carries on a series of conversations with the new man whom she has met, "stalking" her by trying to find out through his questions how far the relationship has gone.

In this last vignette, one person simulates another person, using the computer as a vehicle. But other simulations are possible. Leonard N. Foner (1993) describes Julia, who is a "bot," short for "robot," an "agent," a tiny MUD (multiuser dungeons, multiuser dimensions, or multiuser domains) robot developed by Michael Loren Mauldin at the Center for Machine Translation at Carnegie-Mellon University (see also Turkle [1995] for a discussion of Julia). MUDs are software programs that provide shared databases (typically "rooms") to multiple users (Curtis 1992). (I will be discussing MUDs later in the book.) Julia is a program that appears on the Internet, in a MUD, and represents itself as a person. In Julia's contest mode, "she" tries to lead hapless users astray by convincing them that the program is another human user. In a celebrated episode, Julia engaged with a user, whom Foner calls Barry, over a period of thirteen days. Assuming that Barry was a human user, and not another "bot," even at the end of thirteen days of trying to hit on a robot, he may have remained unclear about her nonhuman state. A sample of their unedited dialogue gives a sense of the interaction:

July 9, 1992

Barry: Hey girlfriend are you out there?
Julia: Hello, barry.
Barry: Hello, I love Your name. It's sexy.
Julia: Me too, barry.

Barry: Did I repeat Myself? Didn't mean too. What are you doing there?

Julia: I'm just hanging around in (› The Hearts Room!, barry.

Barry: Well come over to MY ROOM.

Julia: Could you say that again, it scrolled off my screen.

July 15, 1992

Barry: Hello how are you?

Julia: Hello, barry.

Barry: Are you a virgin?

Julia: As far as you're concerned, barry, I always will be.

In this dialogue and in the above vignettes, there is a blurring of the distinction between the human and the nonhuman in the context of a relationship. Although each vignette will be discussed later in the book, a few brief comments here will give a sense of how this blurring emerges and what significance it may have.

The man in his forties who breaks down because his wife is cheating on him appears not to notice whether her partner is present in the flesh or represented by a video display terminal (VDT). In addition, we might even suspect that she feels more humanly connected to the VDT than she does in the type of relationship she has had with her husband, who has had to struggle to see himself as entirely human.

The guidance counselor who expresses her genuine concern for the young girl's well-being suggests an equivalence between friends and a modem. The girl is desperate, lonely, and suicidal, and, in the absence of her parents and friends, the counselor hopes that a modem will connect her to the world, that the Internet will provide a relational world for this child that parents and friends have failed to provide. Given that the parents are leaving the girl alone in the state that she is in, or that they may be unaware of the state that she is in, the counselor may be entirely right.

Within the company that has been turned topsy-turvy by "the phantom," people have stopped caring whether it is a person or a computer that is calling the meetings. In fact, they feel that they have been driven crazy by a computer in the first place, in the form of the dysfunctional MRP system, and the phantom is merely the latest expression of that. Interestingly, the initial corrective action suggested by the company was to establish positive voice contact with the person who is calling the meeting. However, that suggestion proved impractical. Most meetings are called via email because it is so hard to track people down. Quite accidentally, the phantom has made use of the fact that it is easier to relate to a machine than to locate the person whom the machine is, presumably, representing.

The successful Wall Street woman with a lifetime of losses maintains a painfully clear distinction among the sorts of relationships available to her, but this distinction is framed in terms of the impact that the loss of these relationships will have on her, not on any fundamental quality of the relatedness itself. She needs to relate because living without relating is insufferable. Relationships in the real world, such as her three failed marriages, can hurt her because she will have to endure the loss of them, which she deems inevitable, and continue living to fulfill her obligations to her son. If she loses her son, she has license to cease living. But she knows she is a creative and seductive writer and if she loses Carlos, her Internet lover, she can conjure up another Carlos with a few strokes on the keyboard. She discriminates only in terms of the suffering, but Carlos is not a relationship "out there"; he is a relationship inside a place where no one else may enter and do her the harm that other people have always done to her.

The 34-year-old man experiences his chat-room lover entirely differently. For him, she is unlike other relationships only in her perfection and completeness. She is the most satisfying relationship he has ever had. Until she leaves, he remains blissfully unaware that anything about her perfection or completeness may have to do with the circumscribed nature of his interaction with her. Even once she leaves, she becomes yet another in the unrelenting series of failed relationships. The only difference is that the quality of their "relationship" is mirrored in her leave-taking, which is irrevocably complete and perfect.

The young lawyer whose life is going nowhere quickly becomes entangled in an intractable web of relational confusion. She has experienced a lifetime of dismayed alterations, shuffling between being dependent and becoming suffocated. On the computer she seems to find a world where she can consume as much as she wants and shut it off whenever she wants, but she finds that is not enough. Her dependency prevails and she wants to turn the computer relationship into a more complete relationship. Then, once again feeling suffocated, she wants to return to the computer. Acting as if the two phenomenologies are virtually interchangeable, she suddenly finds herself exchanged for a presence that emanates from the machine.

Julia, the "bot," presents the clearest instance of confusion between a human relationship and a computer relationship. In reality, many of Barry's interactions with Julia appear to reflect his uncertainty about "her." He is constantly amazed by how fast she can type and appears confused by some of her more aberrant remarks. But his inability to discriminate continues. For example:

July 21, 1992

Barry: Are you still Holding out on me?

Julia: I mean, have I convinced you I'm a computer, yet?

Barry: I guess your real . . . but Id still like to get you to my DEN to run tests on you.

Julia: I live for your approval, barry.

Barry: Im so happy to hear that. Why don't you come over to my home?

Julia: I want to have a child someday.

Barry: What a coincedence [sic] . . . I too wish to make a baby . . . some day.

Julia: The date is Tue Jul 21 23:57:31, barry.
Barry: May I have the honor of FAthering the child?

In 1950 Alan Turing wrote an influential paper called "Computing Machinery and Intelligence" in which he created a game that has come to be known as the Turing test.[2] The essence of the Turing test is whether a human interrogator is capable of distinguishing between a human participant and a computer participant. Turing's actual prediction was that by the year 2000 computers would have the capability of tricking human interrogators at least 70 percent of the time in a conversation that lasted five minutes. Foner (1993, p. 24) makes this stunning observation: "Frankly, it's not entirely clear to me whether Julia passed a Turing test here or Barry failed one" after Barry's interaction on July 22, 1992 with a player named KeyLime. The conversation is as follows:

Barry: hey is Julia for real or what?
Julia: Hello, barry.
Barry: She says that same stuff every time.
KeyLime: It's all macros, Barry.
Barry: how about filling me in on some of these things . . . like how Julia can type so damn fast.
KeyLime: barry, it's macros.
Barry: Damn I need to do some programming.
Barry: im an ant among lizards.

In fact, Barry has not merely failed a Turing test by proving he is unable to distinguish between human and computer participants. By the end of his conversation Barry suggests, at the very least metaphorically, that just as he is having difficulty making that distinction, he is having some trouble figuring out whether to deal with himself as a human (who needs to be filled in), a computer (which needs to be programmed), or an animal (a tiny ant that is doomed to be eaten by giant lizards).

These examples convey a sense of what I mean by a "slippage" in the meaning of *relatedness* and *rela.ionship*. In subsequent chapters, I develop this picture more fully by examining these examples in greater detail, and by adding other examples covering a reasonably wide range of human functioning. I place these new meanings of *relatedness* in the joint contexts developed at the start of the chapter: the slippage of meaning signifies one thing in the context of the computer as a symbol and agent of threat and another thing in the context of the emergence of computer-mediated communication systems as a vehicle of adaptation.

Psychoanalytic theory provides a useful backdrop for investigation of some of the perspectives on relational life that emerge in the study of computer-mediated communication systems. As I make use of some of the constructs of these theories, I emphasize their pertinence to the revisions to relatedness that interest us here. The theories I apply come less directly from Freud and his immediate followers within classical psychoanalysis than from more contemporary psychoanalytic theories of relational life, especially the branch of contemporary object relations theory that has been built upon the writings of Melanie Klein. Psychoanalytic theory can illuminate some of the complexity of these new engagements. These theories shed light on the paradoxical observation that stands at the center of this work: the same computer-mediated relationships may promote a given individual's successful or unsuccessful attempt to maintain basic human needs for relatedness, at the same time that these relationships may serve to facilitate that individual's paranoid withdrawal from interpersonal engagement.

Among the champions of virtual reality, there may be no one who is more evenhanded, clear, and well versed than the Massachusetts Institute of Technology psychologist/sociologist Sherry Turkle. She has argued that the elaboration of cyberspace as a medium for self-expression and relatedness is consistent with the exigencies of a postmodern life. In discarding unitary notions of "truth" and "knowledge," Turkle follows Lacan in portraying "the self as a realm of discourse rather than as a real thing or a permanent structure of the mind" (Turkle 1995, p. 178). The culture of the computer, and the Internet version of cyberspace in particular, facilitates the equation of identity with multiplicity, the building of "a self by cycling through many selves" (p. 178).

> Each of us in our own way is incomplete. Virtual spaces may provide the safety for us to expose what we are missing so that we can begin to accept ourselves as we are. Virtuality need not be a prison. It can be the raft, the ladder, the transitional space, the moratorium, that is discarded after reaching greater freedom. We don't have to reject life on the screen, but we don't have to treat it as an alternative life either. We can use it as a space for growth. Having literally written our online personae into existence, we are in a position to be more aware of what we project into everyday life. Like the anthropologist returning home from a foreign culture, the voyager in virtuality can return to a real world better equipped to understand its artifices. . . . Internet experiences help us to develop models of psychological well-being that are in a meaningful sense postmodern. They admit multiplicity and flexibility. *They acknowledge the constructed nature of reality, self, and other.* [p. 263, italics added]

For Turkle, our postmodern nature is so inherently "fluid, emergent, decentralized, flexible, and ever in progress" (pp. 263–264) that our nature and the nature of others, and hence the nature of relationships, is continually constructed, destroyed, re-created, and destroyed anew. In this sense, then, the extension of relatedness into computer relatedness is facilitative. The computer facilitates the acceptance and realization of postmodern values such as "opacity, playful experimentation, and navigation of surface" (p. 267). In the contest of the real and the virtual, Turkle envisions us on a boundary, with the possibility extending before us of emerging with dramatically new and more flexible ways to think about being human and engaging as humans in relationships.

The ecologist/philosopher David Abram (1996) has quite a different outlook, one that we also might link to the postmodern, in a neo-romantic reaction against technology:

Humans are tuned for relationship. The eyes, the skin, the tongue, the ears, the nostrils—all are gates where our body receives the nourishment of otherness. This landscape of shadowed voices, these feathered bodies and antlers and tumbling streams—these breathing shapes are our families, the beings with whom we are engaged, with whom we struggle and suffer and celebrate. . . . Today we participate almost exclusively with other humans and with our own human-made technologies. It is a precarious situation, given our age-old reciprocity with the many-voiced landscape. We still *need* that which is other than ourselves and our own creations. The simple premise . . . is that we are human only in contact, and conviviality, with what is not human. [p. ix]

Abram does not fear that relating with computers is too unlike relating with humans. Quite the opposite, he fears that in the re-creation of ourselves that we have performed with the development of computer technologies, we have, through virtuality, removed ourselves even further from the sentient world of interaction with nature.

Without the oxygenating breath of the forests, without the clutch of gravity and the tumbled magic of river rapids, we have no distance from our technologies, no way of assessing their limitations, no way to keep ourselves from turning into them. . . . Direct sensuous reality, in all its more-than-human mystery, remains the sole solid touchstone for an experiential world now inundated with electronically-generated vistas and engineered pleasures. [p. x]

Abram is an environmental activist, but his concern is not only with the environment. He is also concerned with the flattening of human relationships. Our abilities to experience each other become limited as our sensing abilities become constricted. We no longer know the richness of each other, as we no longer know the air around us. "Our fascination is elsewhere, carried by all these *other* media—these newspapers, radio broadcasts, television networks, computer bulletin boards—all these fields or channels of *strictly human communication* that so readily grab our sense and mold our thoughts once our age-old participation with the original, more-than-human medium has been surrendered" (Abram 1996, p. 258).

For Turkle, being in relation to computers facilitates the flexibility of being by allowing us to experiment with different ways of experiencing ourselves. For Abram, the goals remain flexibility, mutability, and infinity of being, and thus, paradoxically, he might be linked with Turkle's view of the postmodern self. But Abram traces the ways in which civilization has isolated itself from this flexibility, first through the advent of formal writing systems and now through the development of technologies that conspire to insulate us from the sense of being immersed in a sentient world. Only from the vantage point of the fully sentient being can we approach the vastness of relation, and to achieve this vantage point, technology and our connections with technologies will have to realign themselves with the natural world.

The historian Bruce Mazlish (1993) articulates yet a different perspective. He contrasts Freud's view of the development of self-knowledge with Jerome Bruner's. For Freud (1915, 1917), as interpreted by Mazlish, our view of ourselves has progressed through a series of discontinuities. In the Copernican discontinuity we had to discard the naive notion that the earth was the center of the universe, in favor of the notion that it merely was a tiny fragment of a vast cosmic system. In the Darwinian discontinuity, we were forced to discard the notion that humans hold a more privileged place in creation than other members of the animal kingdom. Finally, in the Freudian discontinuity, we have had to discard the notion that humans are even the master of their own house. With his introduction of the power of the unconscious, Freud confronts us with our limitations, not with respect to a cosmic universe or an inclusive animal kingdom, but with respect to ourselves.

In Mazlish's view, Bruner (Bruner et al. 1956) stands Freud on his head by seeing the establishment of continuities where Freud had seen discontinuities. For Bruner, the first such continuity is unfolded by the Greeks in the sixth century B.C., who saw the world in terms of a continuity of natural laws. Agreeing with Freud, but with the obverse angle, Bruner sees Darwin contributing the second continuity by articulating a commonality between humans and the animal kingdom. And Bruner sees Freud establishing that continuities in understanding laws of causality are as prevalent for humans (explained by unconscious drive-determined motivations) as for the balance of nature. Bruner's Freud sees continuous links between the primitive, infantile, archaic phenomena and civilized, evolved phenomena.

This understanding lays the foundation for what Mazlish puts forth as a fourth discontinuity that still exists in our time, and that he proposed to dedifferentiate into a continuity. Mazlish (1993) addresses the apparent discontinuity between humans and machines:

> Once again, we are confronted with the human need to be special, to feel superior—but in this case in regard to the machine. Such a need satisfies important psychological and social purposes yet is a crutch that is best discarded, in order to move closer to reality and away from disabling fantasy. To put it bluntly, we are now coming to realize that humans and the machines they create are continuous and that the same conceptual schemes that help explain the workings of the brain also explain the workings of a "thinking machine." [p. 4] . . . Tools and machines are inseparable from evolving human nature. . . . The development of machines, culminating in the computer, makes inescapable the awareness that the same theories that are useful in explaining the workings of mechanical contrivances are also useful in understanding the human animal—and vice versa. [p. 233]

Mazlish does not address issues of human relationships directly, nor does he express his views on the nature of human/machine interactions as distinct from human/human interactions, but the conclusion seems evident. If there is a fundamental continuity between humans and machines, there must be a corollary continuity between human/human relationships and human/machine relationships.

Among the commentators on contemporary problems of identity and technology, Kenneth Gergen's (1991) view of the saturated self is one of the more influential. His inquiry is positioned within a view of postmodern discourse in which we may no longer take for granted the validity of notions such as truth, science, and objective knowledge. Extended into the psychological realm, this version of the postmodern view challenges concepts of identity, individual being, and the self. "Not only do attempts at characterizing *the actual person*—the workings of the mind, the human spirit, or biological individual—become suspect. The very concept of an internal core—an intentional, rational agent—also begins to fray" (p. 111). If modern technology was born in the age of modernism, fueled by beliefs in how much rational man can know and do, that technology, according to Gergen, has created the conditions for our postmodern world by establishing a state of social saturation. Gergen believes that the small neighborhood, the community, even meaningful personal relationships have become superseded by "a vast and ever-expanding array of relationships" (p. xi) in the form of radio, telephone, television, facsimile, and computers. These new arrays present such enormous increases in social stimulation that we have moved in the direction of a state of saturation in which our sense of ourselves and of others around us is so overtaxed that it is no longer knowable.

A century ago, social relationships were largely confined to the distance of an easy walk. Most were conducted in person, within small communities: family, neighbors, townspeople. . . . From birth to death one could depend on relatively even-textured social surroundings. . . . For much of the world's population, especially the industrialized West, the small, face-to-face community is vanishing into the pages of history. . . . As a result of the technological developments . . . contemporary life is a swirling sea of social relations. Words thunder in by radio, television, newspaper, mail, radio, telephone, fax, wire service, electronic mail. . . . Through the technologies of the century, the number and variety of relationships in which we are engaged, potential frequency of contact, expressed intensity of relationship, and endurance through time all are steadily increasing. As this increase becomes extreme we reach a state of social saturation. [p. 61]

According to Gergen's view, as the social saturation engendered by technologies increases, both intimacy and enduring commitment decrease within relationships. In a postmodern world in which truth is obsolete, true love is similarly displaced. Inherent in Gergen's version of the postmodern is a suspicion of both self and other, with both in a continuously shifting motion, one that he likens to a shuffling of cards.

The disappearance of "true self" encourages one to search for the kinds of personas or situations that will enable the various actors in one's ensemble to play their parts. . . . For postmodern, social complicity and identity walk hand in hand; without others there is no self. In effect, with the disappearance of true self, the stage is set for the *fractional relationship*, a relationship built around a limited aspect of one's being. The same technology that favors populating of the self also facilitates the development of partial relationships. [p. 178]

When our focus turns to psychoanalytic views, we will develop a number of ideas that resonate with Gergen's concept of fractional relationships.

The technology communications specialist Stephen Doheny-Farina (1996) strives for a balanced position in *The Wired Neighborhood.* He perceives our communities across the nation to be dying, undermined and destroyed by the forces of modernity. He believes that global computer networks like the Internet "represent a step in the continual virtualization of human relations" (p. 37). For him, in a social version of Abram's physical/sensual dissolution, it is a misplaced hope to believe that such networks can supersede and replace the old geographic neighborhoods, such as his in upstate New York. Indeed, the Internet threatens to seduce us into even further remove from meaningful local agendas. However, it may be possible for the Internet to enhance communities by "enabling a new kind of local public space" (p. 54). Doheny-Farina traces the search for such a new form of public space through the multiuser domain MediaMOO but finds instead the "representation of the representation of interpersonal discourse" (p. 64) and ultimately concludes that to infuse MediaMOO, or other such enterprises, with the possibility of becoming a virtual world "is to misplace their function dangerously" (p. 73). His final appeal is for the net user to remember the local community and to use the net to reconnect to the places where we live physically.

Finally, for Allucquere Rosanne Stone (1995) in *The War of Desire and Technology at the Close of the Mechanical Age,* cyberspace is a social environment capable of creating novel interactions. These interactions enact what she perceives to be the current state of complex relationships between humans and machines, fostering new types of identities that "we ourselves are in the process of becoming, here at the close of the mechanical age. I see these identities engaged in a wonderful and awesome struggle, straining to make meaning and to make sense out of the very idea of culture as they know it, swimming for their lives in the powerful currents of high technology, power structures, and market forces beyond their imagination" (p. 36). But, consistent with the ideas I am presenting here, Stone also finds older structures trying to reassert themselves and "these are the structures of individual caring, love, and perhaps most poignant, of desire" (p. 36). The new identities that emerge in entanglement with the older structures are fractured, multiple, and always in tension. The identities occur in the context of a tension between simplicity and multiplicity. Among the elements of identity challenged by this tension are traditional notions of gender, age, and race. In concert with Turkle, Stone perceives the rise of the Internet to facilitate the trying on of other, alternative identities. Stone believes that via the Internet people gain the opportunity to reinvent themselves, others, and the notion of relationship. This reinvention has both constructive and destructive potential outcomes as we witness the implosion of the boundaries between technology and self. But ultimately Stone finds the war she portrays an adventurous and exciting one, filled more with promise than with threat.

In the verse quoted at the start of this chapter, the Czech poet/scientist Miroslav Holub notes, "It could be the creeping realization/that the blue sky did not exist any more./On the contrary./That there is no meadow with a flower/here and there. . . . /And thus it will be. Until/someone gets bored. By that life,/That death, or that tickling in the palm." The world of relational life on the Internet has come to be known as virtual reality (VR), a reality in which disbelief in the blueness of the sky is as willingly suspended as is belief in the boredom of this life and death. Among the questions we will address is whether Holub's "tickling in the palm" can be the friction of the mouse in the hand of the Internet user, or whether it must be the physical touch of another human being.

The backdrop for this book is the computer screen. The Internet, email, and hypertext have extended the two-dimensional surface outward toward infinity at the same time that, inwardly, we can fasten on minute fragments of our beings and elaborate them into complex, seemingly whole shapes and forms. From the nearly infinite inside to the nearly infinite outside, we can reach out, we can be in touch. But to what are we reaching, and what is doing the reaching? What does it mean to be in touch when neither side can touch? And why have so many come to favor these infinite but disembodied alternatives to the palpable substance of human interactions? These are the questions we will strive to answer here.

2 The Interface of Janus: Internet Relationships at the New Millennium

Men's curiosity searches past and future
And clings to that dimension. But to apprehend
The point of intersection of the timeless
With time, is an occupation for the saint—
No occupation either, but something given
And taken, in a lifetime's death in love,
Ardour and selflessness and self-surrender.
For most of us, there is only the unattended
Moment, the moment in and out of time.

The Dry Salvages, T. S. Eliot (1941)

As the twentieth century fades, the Internet relationships that have emerged capture some of the complexity of what may, or arguably may not, be a significant and discernible moment. With the two faces of a reconfigured Janus, the division of temporal continuity into millennia appears artificial and deceitful when viewed from one angle and yet significant and suggestive from a different perspective. Has the human condition truly reached a point at which we can define a threshold between past and future, or have we created the artificial distinction of a millennium as a defining moment in compensatory overreaction to the devaluation we impute to sameness?

What could be more appropriately paradoxical than the observation that the fleshless Internet fleshes out both views of this contemporary Janus. Certainly this new World Wide Web of influence is a trope for change. In an instant, now measured in milliseconds for the millennium, we locate ourselves in something we have come to call a global community. From the military ARPAnet of 1969 through the research and academic Telnet of the 1970s and JANET (Joint Academic Network) of the 1980s to a World Wide Web of the 1990s, change has seemed the only constant. From a system that required security clearance to a world in which one major survey estimates that at least 71 percent of adult Americans make use of email (Digital Citizen Survey by the Luntz Research Companies, available at http://www.hotwired.com/special/citizen/survey/survey.html), the nature of communication has been transformed more rapidly than all but a few quixotic technologists might ever have imagined. From here in New York I can send the words I am writing to Singapore and Sacramento faster than I can read them myself. In fact, from another's screen-based perspective my "here in New York" can "be" in Sacramento or Singapore. Even more to the point of this book, suddenly, and almost effortlessly, a vehicle has emerged for many people to play with aspects of their experience that they had kept in hiding, even from themselves, and for people to come out of their rooms while remaining closeted within the space between their keyboard and their video display terminal.

From either aspect of this millennial Janus, technology has changed the way we lead our lives, but have our lives changed meaningfully because we lead them differently? Is the change heralded by technology little more than the figurations of a few dozen corporate jingles transformed into the rhetoric and habits of lives that are, as they may always have been, too threatened by circumstance to reflect on signification? If "progress is our most important product," then sameness may be such a sin that it begs for relabeling, and the hypertext of the Internet, whether or not it be more hype than substance, exquisitely lends itself to the art of figuration.

From the rock carvings of antiquity to the pen, the printing press, the telegraph, telephone, television, and telefax, humankind has availed itself of technology to alter our vehicles for relating to each other. We may argue that each of these new vehicles has served to elaborate the same synecdoche that email currently advances. From this perspective, whatever technology allows the vehicle of communication to be, humankind is still engaged in the same attempt to communicate the entirety of our experience by parts that represent it, to transform the fragmentary into the whole, or to find refuge from the annihilatory threat of the whole in the relative security of the fragment.

Imagine for a moment an isolated, hungry hunter several thousands of years before email who imagines himself, in a moment of triumphant satiety, spearing at will from an entire herd of animals. When this hunter broadcasts and reifies his fantasy with a drawing on a cave wall, is he doing anything fundamentally different from the fantasy-elaborations of emailings? For centuries before email, lovers separated by distance used the fragments of experience of written correspondence to represent both themselves and their imagined partners, either as they saw or wished to see themselves to be. For as long as we have records, people have existed in a fundamental antinomy between aloneness and togetherness, between fragment and whole. From this side of Janus, technology has always been a trope for bridging the irreconcilable. Progress truly may be our most important product, and with progress we may connect more quickly and represent aspects of our being with greater ease, but we remain in between the fragmented and the whole, between connection and isolation. With progress we may live longer than in the past, but we still die.

Michael Heim (1993) states, "The final point of a virtual world is to dissolve the constraints of the anchored world so that we can lift anchor— not to drift aimlessly without point, but to explore anchorage in ever-new places" (p. 137). Sven Birkerts (1996) comments,

> My instinct, signaling from some vestigial part of the psyche, tells me to avoid placing all of my faith in the coming of the chip-driven future. It bids me to question the consequences of the myriad promised simplifications and streamlinings and to stall somehow the rush to interconnectivity that comes—as all interconnectivity must—at the expense of the here and now. . . . Otherwise we are in danger of falling into a dream that is not ours or anybody else's, that spreads inexorably on the legs of its ones and zeroes. [p. 199]

Both Heim and Birkerts recognize the sameness and the shifts in being and being with each other that are symbolized and actualized by the tangled web of the Internet. For Heim, the face of Janus, which points toward the next millennium, signals freedom, while for Birkerts it signals loss. For Birkerts, the face of Janus, which reflects our history, prizes substance over illusion, while for Heim it anchors us in finite structure when we might visit instead the infinite ports of virtuality.

I believe that Internet relationships at the dawning of the next millennium exist in the antinomic relationship between the two visions articulated by Heim and Birkerts. I am proposing a way of understanding and describing Internet relatedness that reflects, but does not select, the complex intersections of the past and the future, the fragmentary and whole,

the connected and the isolated, the internal and the social, which are represented in different Internet users' experience. These individual experiences expand, in turn, to include experiences of other Internet users, of
the technology, of real life, and of the relationships among all of these
aspects of the environment. In many ways, this attempt at description and
understanding is impossible. The infinitely dimensioned challenges, even
defies, both understanding and description. Browsing through the hypertextual links of the Internet creates an infinity of plausible texts. Similarly, wandering through the infinitely dimensioned intersections of
people's lives on-line in relation to their internal experiences and their
social surround embeds us in the inexhaustible.[3]

Paradoxical phenomena play a large role in the demarcations of contemporary life at the interface of Janus. People are striving to use cyberspace to create or to sever linkages between competing, irreconcilable
experiences of themselves. Among these competing experiences are
people's sense of themselves as irreducibly alone yet fundamentally connected to important others; their sense of themselves and others as consistent discriminable entities yet interchanging, overlapping repetitions;
and their sense of themselves and others as sequential and simultaneous
fragmented personae yet stable and structured personalities. These
Internet relationships exemplify living at the interface of Janus. Internet
users can be alike in the intensity of their involvement but different in
the use to which that intensity is put. Some people have become involved
in cyber relationships by withdrawing from almost all other meaningful
human contact. They have opted for a more provincial and limited reality
within the still infinite world of the machine; they reside at all hours
of the day and night in the universe created and illuminated by the
VDT screen. Their most important and prized relationships are with disembodied text, which represents other human beings whose presence is
immediate without being present. Other people, similarly immersed in
cyberspace, make use of it to free themselves from the overwhelming anxi-

ety of persecution that accompanies their real-life personae, and from the life in which their abilities to function as themselves are experienced as strained and constrained by relationships that are more demanding than fulfilling, more perplexing than gratifying. These are portraits of paranoid withdrawal and of hopeful reaching out. These people find in cyberspace boundless opportunities to function as themselves in all their complexity, and with this multidimensional experience of self they find themselves greeted by others who enhance the deepness of living. Occasionally, people will use this cyber relatedness to make transitions into the embodied world, with or without their cyber partners, or they will choose to remain in the most fulfilling world they have known, heedless of disembodiment.

These people represent a well-lived paradox of contemporary life. Viewed from one perspective, people who are immersed in cyber relationships appear to have retreated from the arena of human contact and to have selected, instead, a more insular and circumscribed reality. Day after day, or more often night after night, these people slip into a world illuminated primarily by the glow of the VDT, a world in which the only audible sounds are the clicking of the keys, the whirring of the hard drive, and the buzzing of the modem, a world in which physical contact is made only with the keyboard and the mouse, a world in which other human beings exist only in the disembodied unidimensionality of strings of letters on the surface of the screen, a world in which people cannot touch those with whom they are in touch or know whom it is they are getting to know. Viewed from another perspective, these people are using cyberspace to liberate themselves from a life in which their identities are constricted and attacked by a world that forces them into limited, threatened versions of themselves and that brackets them in unfulfilling relationships with others who are similarly constricted. In cyberspace they find limitless possibilities for themselves, and bolstered by this multidimensionality of self they encounter a richness of being with others they might otherwise never have known. And so the paradox emerges: cyberspace appears to be, at once, a world of oneness and isolation and a world of personal richness and interpersonal complexity.

Psychoanalytic theory has had to deal with a similar paradox. This theory, which began with Freud as an exegesis of the individual psyche, has migrated in the direction of a relational theory in which the psyche of the individual has no meaning apart from interactions with the interpersonal field.

Viewed from one perspective, the perspective of Freud and his closest followers, the essential core of human experience resides in the deepest recesses of the individual, in the instinctual drives that underlie our biological being and provide the energy and motivation for all of our psychological existence. For Freud, relationships with others (so-called object relations) and with the external surround were always seen as important. In fact, this importance grew as Freud's theory evolved through his own writings, but even more through the writings of his daughter Anna Freud and the ego psychologists who have followed her. But to a large extent it has remained the watermark of Freudian integrity to view object relations, hence the importance of the external surround, as secondary to (or in complemental series with) the drives. To this end, within ego psychology and some of the newer theoretical models built, at least in part, upon the underpinnings of ego psychology, Freud's foundation of drive-primacy remains, even though it has been stretched and distorted, at times almost beyond recognition. Rooted as they are in the primary determinacy of the individual's instinctual being, these theories are often referred to, somewhat hyperbolically, as one-person psychologies.

Viewed from a different perspective, the perspective of some object relations and interpersonal theorists, there is no essential core of an individual psyche apart from its context in the continuous field of others. For some of these theorists, Melanie Klein for example, the language of drive remains a fundamental element of the theory. But for Klein, and those who have followed her, drive no longer provides the motivation for all of our psychological existence as it did for Freud. Rather, drive is a vehicle for connectedness with others. In its place, the fundamental motivation for human psychological behavior is found in the mutuality of relational influences, in the creation and elaboration of intrapsychic templates that emerge from living in the presence of others who take from us and give to us in never-ending patterns of exchange. These are theories in which parts of our psychological beings are in continuous processes of exchange with parts of others' psychological beings. In the reductionism of theoretical nosology, these psychoanalytic theories are often referred to as two-person, or relational, psychologies.

In cyberspace I have observed that there is a dialectical tension between a view of the individual as insular and disconnected from the field of others and a view of the individual as intensely involved in complex exchanges between aspects of self and aspects of others. Within the psychoanalytic theories, there is a dialectical tension between a view of human psychology as essentially rooted within the individual and a view of human psychology as essentially rooted in interpersonal influences.

Potential Space

In her important book, *Life on the Screen*, Sherry Turkle (1995) applies to Internet use the concept of potential space, which has evolved from the notion of transitional space introduced by the British psychoanalyst D. W. Winnicott (1971) to describe arenas of human psychological functioning that exist simultaneously and ambiguously inside oneself and outside oneself, phenomena that both belong to one and yet are presented to one from outside. They are phenomena of which we cannot even ask if they were created or found. For Winnicott, it is within potential space that we maintain the ability to develop psychologically, to grow as we find ourselves thwarted, to integrate love and hate, and to create and re-create as we destroy, repair, and find ourselves repaired.

These cyberspace themes reflect vicissitudes of potential, or transitional, space. For Winnicott (1971), transitional space is a sequel to transitional objects. The infant's teddy bear or blanket may serve as the first of these transitional objects or experiences, instances of meaningful ambiguity between that which is "me," an inherent part of the infant and thus within the infant's arena of omnipotent control, and that which is "not me," an inherent part of the physical surround and thus outside the realm of omnipotent control.[4] Potential space, for Winnicott, is an extension of this concept: "It is useful, then, to think of a third area of human living, one neither inside the individual nor outside in the world of shared reality. This intermediate living can be thought of as occupying a potential space" (p. 110).

Turkle (1995) similarly discusses the application of Winnicott's notions of potential space to cyberspace. However, she makes no suggestion that there is any difficulty, or, as I am terming it, vicissitude, in the use of cyberspace as potential space. "The experience is diffused in the intense experiencing in later life of a highly charged intermediate space between the self and certain objects. This experience has traditionally been associated with religion, spirituality, notions of beauty, sexual intimacy, and the sense of connection with nature. Now it is associated with using computers" (p. 273n). I believe that the transitional and facilitative nature of the use of cyberspace as potential space is much less of a given than Turkle might be suggesting.

Turkle (1995) is particularly interested in the facilitation of multiplicity of being. Thus, she has made use of Winnicott's ideas to argue that cyber systems serve a transitional function in "the intermediate space between the self and certain objects" (p. 273n). In this intermediate space, people are able to try on for size aspects of their being that they might otherwise set aside. Stone (1995) arrives at a similar view: "I am interested in prosthetic communication for what it shows of the 'real' world that might otherwise go unnoticed. And I am interested because of the potential of cyberspace for emergent behavior, for new social forms that arise in a circumstance in which *body, meet, place,* and even *space* mean something quite different from our accustomed understanding" (p. 37).

Like Turkle, Faber (1984) also invokes Winnicott and finds a facilitative and transitional quality in computer systems: "I do not believe the computer can be viewed correctly apart from our transitional seeking and the influence of internal objects in the personality" (p. 264). Faber views "the computer as an aspect of our *culture*, and our culture as the chief instance of our transitional striving, as the way we achieve what Roheim (1971) termed the 'dual-unity' that succeeds the separation of infancy and childhood" (pp. 263–264). Within the notion of this dual unity, the nature of being is to strive for individuality and secure independent functioning at the very same time that we are trying to compensate for the loss of the original protective object, the mother, by replacing her. Faber asserts that the computer represents one such substitutive, transition-seeking object. Like Turkle, Faber believes that it is impossible to view the computer as other than transitional. Invoking Offe's (1978) contemporary Marxist views, Faber positions this impossibility to have occurred within the shift from conflicts between large social groups (in the early stages of capitalism) to conflicts within the individuals themselves. Technology is "related integrally to the 'objects' of the inner world, to the problems of anxiety, separation, and conversion that characterize the early, internalizing period of human life" (p. 267). For Faber, the computer is a substitutive object, a compensatory replacement for the maternal object who could not be controlled perfectly and who, ultimately, created a sense of powerlessness and narcissistic injury. In this role the computer becomes an instance of transitional process.

In contrast to these writers, I believe that no object or process, the cyber system included, is essentially transitional. It may well be, and frequently is, the case that the computer, or cyber system, may be a transitional phenomenon. However, for parents and infants there is nothing essential in the nature of the teddy bear or blanket that assures the transitional nature of the object. A parent may present the teddy bear as a gift once and then never fetch it again after it is dropped on the floor several times. Far from becoming a transitional object, the bear will become an invisible object and serve no role at all, or the caregiver's fear of disease may be so great that the blanket is always in the wash. Alternatively, the parent may so overvalue the bear or blanket that it is always being shoved in the child's face.

In any of these cases, the transitional nature of the potentially transitional object becomes seriously undermined and even thwarted or turned into an object of fixity instead. Such is also the case within organizations when we come to consider the transitional, or potential, role of the cyber system. Within relatively healthy psychological functioning, the introduction of a new cyber system may, in fact, serve the sort of transitional function that Turkle and Faber depict. It may come to facilitate a sense of being that is less unidimensional and constricted, more creative and at ease, and more productively capable of harnessing the extensive power of digital phenomena, in both a computational and simulational mode. But potentially transitional space faces vicissitudes of developmental use and, if we are to engage the psychoanalytic metaphor, we should avoid doing so in a partial manner. Just as cyberspace may potentiate, it may also thwart and debilitate.[5]

The Cyber System Dialectic

To apprehend the whole of Janus, we must view not only both aspects but the linkages, the *interface*, as well, which implies simultaneous acceptance of the contradictory polarities of the cyberspace dialectic. At one pole of this dialectic is a view of the individual in cyberspace as insular and disconnected from the field of others, while at the opposite pole is a view of the individual intensely involved in complex exchanges between aspects of self and aspects of others. In keeping with the whole view of Janus, with the striving for the balance implied by the simultaneous acceptance of these polarities, we must explore them both and understand the ways in which they are linked. Cyberspace can be used as a vehicle for insularity, withdrawal, and disconnection,[6] or as a facilitator of relatedness within a paranoid experience of the world.

The Cyber System as a Vehicle for Insularity, Withdrawal, and Disconnection Within a Paranoid Experience of the World

Faced with the prospect of persecution, whether aimed at us from without or ricocheting about from more internal origins, we tend to seek psychological relief by retreating to safer psychic dwellings. These dwelling-retreats are often likened to a fortress buttressed against the invasive threats of outside assault. But an alternative metaphor seems even more powerful and more useful when applied to the Internet. Instead of a fortress, imagine the Internet users confined in isolated cells, locked away so that they may neither do harmful things nor have harmful things done to them. But if to some extent the cell affords them safety, it also brings isolation. From their point of isolation within the cell they are denied connection with others, because the very bars that represent their safety also prohibit complete contact. The types of connections that may be established are limited and partial.[7]

But many people, however threatened and in retreat they may be, and however many times they may have incarcerated themselves in the relative safety of their isolated cells, crave more than partial and limited relationships. This craving persists even though fear and anxiety dictates to them that they remain confined for a time within the safety of their self-imposed cell. However much they may feel the need to protect themselves from others, or to protect others from their own destructiveness, they also feel the need for the others from whom they are secured. Without these others, *or at least the illusion of others*, the cell itself may become a place where they will perish.[8]

Above I criticized Faber's (1984) use of Roheim's notion of dual-unity, because I felt Faber, like Turkle, erred in seeing the computer as necessarily transitional in its use. However, once we place these same ideas in a broader context, in which transition may be either facilitated or not, Roheim's ideas directly become pertinent to the development of illusory others. According to him, "Civilization . . . is a huge network of more or less successful attempts to protect mankind against the danger of object-loss, the colossal efforts made by a baby who is afraid of being left alone in the dark. . . . Culture . . . leads the libido into [acceptable] channels by the creation *of substitute objects*" (Roheim 1971, p. 122). For Roheim, invoking a male-centered version of psychoanalytic theory, the most significant of these substitutes is, for example, the wife, who replaces the mother. "Substitutes of another category—dolls, property, money, etc., in fact, material culture—are objects based on a withdrawal of libido from object love to a narcissistic position" (p. 131).

In the cases on which I will focus here, the confinement in the cell of paranoid withdrawal or regression is self-imposed. In fact, the confinement has occurred for the very purpose of removing oneself from the world of experience that threatens persecution, either in the form of murder or in the form of revenge for damage done to oneself. Eventually, the study of Internet relations leads us to the conclusion that many people confined in cells away from connection with others may choose to seek the best illusion of something that seems like a complete relationship, even when they have volunteered for that confinement to seek protection from actual contact with others. In the cases we look at first, however, the experience of persecution and threat is too great and what is found is *not* a good replacement for connectedness, but the need for even greater retreat.

Persecutory Anxiety

In his 1925 poem "The Hollow Men," T.S. Eliot captures the ubiquity of the threat of annihilation.

Between the idea
And the reality
Between the motion
And the act
Falls the Shadow

         For thine is the Kingdom

Between the conception
And the creation
Between the emotion
And the response
Falls the Shadow

         Life is very long

Between the desire
And the spasm
Between the potency
And the existence
Between the essence
And the descent
Falls the Shadow . . .

This is the way the world ends
This is the way the world ends
This is the way the world ends
Not with a bang but with a whimper.

For many of us, the omnipresence of the shadow of annihilation leads us into a life filled with pervasive persecutory anxiety. Between our every idea and our every action, our every emotion and response, comes the anxiety that we will be forced to pay for what we have done, or for what others may want to do to us. At the current technophilic interface of Janus, the computer and its technological derivatives have come for many to serve as tropes for the Shadow.

Here our main interest is in communication-based cyber systems that exacerbate underlying persecutory anxieties. Of course there is nothing inherent in the computer that makes it a persecutory object, just as there is nothing inherent in the teddy bear or the blanket that make them transitional objects. The individual's subjective experience is contextual, and for any one person that context has both internal (historical or psychological) factors and external (environmental) factors. The internal factors vary for every individual. But there are some culturally significant metaphors that may bring into focus individual psychologies in the context of the persecutory symbol of the computer. Here we need look no further than Hal in the Stanley Kubrick film *2001: A Space Odyssey* as an archetypal instance. But there is also the prevailing mythos of Big Brother, as epitomized by the IRS computers, which will track us all down and deplete us with taxes. And there are the CIA and FBI computers that omnisciently retain all of our personal transgressions.

Faber (1984) articulates the strength of these views of the computer, observing the "fears and fantasies" surrounding the computer. Faber refers to these fears and fantasies as delusional and confirmatory of the machine's "ability to arouse the primitive unconscious: computers run mad, take over the world, devour and enslave human beings" (p. 273). The availability of these cultural metaphors does not force us into delusional enslavement, but these metaphors do provide a locus around which individual experience may cluster.

But in addition, the cyber system *is* potentially invasive (via email, for example), in the sense that, if so used by an individual or group, the once-private domain of the individual becomes increasingly public and vulnerable to scrutiny. I began the book with one example of such an invasion, in which a woman who innocently filled out a product questionnaire became terrorized by a prison inmate doing computer data entry. Other illustrations of this concept appear throughout the book, with numerous examples of actual and symbolic invasion. Here is one brief vignette to clarify how email can become toxically invasive in a way that fosters persecutory anxiety.

Clinical Example: Email as Invasion

In her late twenties Jeannette had left a promising career in business to marry. She had always dreamed of pursuing graduate studies in history, and now she felt that it would be easier to combine being a student and beginning a family than it might be to work and begin a family. She felt herself to be very much in love with her new husband, whom she had met at her job, and gladly busied herself with the work of putting together a household. In fact, between school and being a newlywed Jeannette was finding her life busier and more rewarding than ever. The honeymoon was brief. In short order, her husband Ron was promoted twice, with the second promotion involving frequent week-long or two-week-long trips out of the country. Given the intensity of his travel schedule, not to mention his deeply rooted ambivalence, Ron adamantly refused to have anything to do with having a baby. Jeannette was profoundly disappointed and often equally lonely. Quite consciously she immersed herself in schoolwork, opting to complete a doctorate rather than stopping with a master's degree.

On her thirtieth birthday she reported making a conscious decision that her dissertation, which involved the study of the private lives of a number of very successful professional women, would be her baby. At that point, although she still professed to be in love with her husband and committed to the success of the marriage, she and Ron had not been intimate in over a year, sexually or otherwise. Quite innocently, from time to time when she tired of doing her research, Jeannette began to drop in on Internet chat rooms. Since a good deal of her work required her to use her computer, and increasingly the Internet, she found herself chatting more and more frequently. Most of her Internet friends shared similar intellectual interests. In fact, almost all of her chat room time was spent in forums built around historical topics. Not surprisingly, she soon began to develop some special friends. It struck her as amusing, but coincidental, that one of them, Charles, was from Belgium, given that Ron's company had a Belgian headquarters and that Ron spent a great deal of his travel time in Brussels. As their talks grew more frequent, Charles suggested that Jeannette install a program that would notify her instantly when he wanted to speak with her.

At first Jeannette found the attention gratifyingly different from her relationship with her husband. Even when Ron was in town, his career led him to spend long hours at the job, frequently even on weekends, and seeking out Jeannette seemed the furthest thing from his mind. She told other of her on-line friends about the program and transmitted copies to them as well. In no time, she had a handful of friends who could seek her out any time she had her computer on. Much to her surprise, Charles reacted with anger to the news that Jeannette had shared "their" program. With anger turning to jealousy, he began to email her more frequently. Soon, Robert, another of her friends who knew Charles and was in the same group with the two of them, joined in the competition. The interruptions became so frequent that Jeannette had difficulty getting any of her work done for the dissertation. In addition, she was terrified to turn the computer on when her husband was home, for fear that he would learn about her other relationships.

Jeannette was far from technically sophisticated, but she knew that someone would be able to disinstall the program or that she could terminate her accounts with existing carriers and start afresh with another one and a new email address. But much of her dissertation correspondence was linked to her existing address and it felt to Jeannette that to purge herself of the invasions meant to throw away the progress she had made on her thesis. Jeannette knew through her work in therapy that the computer, once a symbol of hope now turned a symbol of persecution, was linked representationally to the marriage, and for that matter to relationships before the marriage. Nonetheless, feeling that all that it contained had become invaded by an infectious disease, she shut the computer off and stopped work on her dissertation.

Paranoid Responses to Persecutory Anxiety

As Jeannette's example again illustrates, the Internet has impressive persecutory potential. When Jeannette shut off her computer and ceased work on her dissertation, she submitted, almost fully, to the threats around her. Her reaction typifies one type of response to pervasive persecutory anxiety. At its most extreme, this type of response results in the attempt to create an experiential fortress that isolates and insulates so perfectly that the walls are invulnerable to persecutory attacks. All that is evil and persecutory remains without, and all that is within is pure and safe.

The next example illustrates that in many cases much of what is apprehended as a persecutory external threat is actually as internal as it is external. Often, this internal form of persecution is the residue of earlier life experiences of disappointment and persecution that have long since become incorporated as a part of the self.[9] In response to these threats of attack, which emanate from within but can only be experienced as coming from without, the walls of the fortress are forever being narrowed in an effort to escape the inescapable. If the process is so relentless that eventually there is no room left, the only alternatives may be suicide or psychosis, but fortunately for most of us, we generally develop alternative ways of organizing our experiences.

The following illustrates one such instance of internal persecution and the way in which the Internet came to play a role in the experience.

Clinical Example: Responses to Persecutory Anxiety

As the eldest son, Preston inherited the name of his great-great-grand-father, great-grandfather, grandfather, and father, but from the start he seemed to have a harder go of it than his namesakes. Great-great-grand-father Preston had built a successful company that the next two name-bearers had expanded into a near empire. At the time of Preston's birth, his father was being groomed to take over the running of the family busi-ness from Preston's grandfather and there seemed little doubt that he would carry on the family tradition of success. Although the founder had not even a high-school education, his three successors were Princeton educated and all had married educated women whose families had con-siderable social standing and wealth.

Preston's mother, Payne, was no exception. Her family traced its roots to the early settlers and schooled all its children in the significance of their lineage. Payne was an eager mother. Herself the fifth, and youngest, sis-ter in a family of seven children, she had followed in her siblings' success-ful footsteps through boarding school and college. Her eldest sister al-ready had a child who had been accepted into Princeton by the time Payne was carrying Preston.

Preston remembered being told repeatedly that he had been a difficult child even before he was born and the birth was as complicated as the preg-nancy. Six weeks premature, weak and sickly, Preston spent five of his first seven months in the hospital, at times teetering at the brink of death. De-velopmentally delayed, perhaps due to the birth trauma, Preston did not speak until he was over 3 years old, but what he lacked in speech he made up for in action. His mother was aghast at his wildness and the family story went that one day when Preston went with his mother to visit his aunt he was so wild, and she so humiliated, that she called him her feral child. The nickname Feral stuck throughout his youth and on into adulthood.

In his mid-forties, after his father's death, he entered therapy with a colleague of mine. An attractive but angry and remote man, in the first session he revealed that at his father's funeral family members still referred to him as Feral, even though there were now no other living Prestons with whom he might be confused. His mother had always considered the name one of convenience, even affection, but Preston believed it had stuck with him because of her sense of shame that he bore the family name but seemed so unlike his predecessors. In fact, as Preston unraveled his story, he himself juxtaposed his steady deterioration with his father's and grandfather's successes. He had drifted through a series of private, parochial, and military schools, always with the same result. Friendless, or with a single friend who suffered a similar fate, and failing, he was removed from school after a single year, or in the middle of a second year. In a combination of projection and descriptive accuracy, Preston contrasted fine preparatory schools like Exeter at which his father and grandfather had excelled to the "disgusting and fourth-rate trash schools" at which he had failed. Naturally, he extended this contrast to the college at which they had achieved honors and the series of "bottom feeders who would let in anyone who could sign a check" at which he had failed.

In everything Preston described, a similar pattern emerged. Without inflating himself in any way, he managed to find condemnatory fault with his surrounding environment. Notably, one day when reminiscing about a college in Florida that he had dropped out of after a single semester but that continued to solicit contributions, he asked, "How do they dare ask for money? How do they even dare *to call* the place a college?" His work life had followed a similar course. Living for the most part on the substantial proceeds from his stock in the family business, he had drifted from one to another line of work and from one to another job, sometimes quitting and sometimes getting fired. In describing his current employer, he said, "He acts like an idiot and he has the nerve *to call* himself a boss."

Preston's friends and lovers lasted for weeks or months, occasionally a year. Attractive, intelligent, and well spoken despite his educational fiascos, he had always found it easy to get into relationships, but described himself as having an unerring knack for picking women who were just like his mother—critical, demanding, and dissatisfied. Thus, "We go out to a fancy dinner where I'm picking up the tab and Celia introduces herself as my girlfriend, but the minute we get home I'm not good enough for her. She *doesn't deserve the name* girlfriend."

Deserted, persecuted, and betrayed at every turn by the projected internal experience of deserving not even his name, Preston found the Internet. Here, for the first time *he called himself* Feral, or alternatively FederalFeral or, his favorite, bigFF, and for a time felt himself invulnerable to external attack. In fact, initially he described his greatest pleasure on the Net to be to go into a room and "flame"[10] until he got shut out. "Everybody must groan when bigFF signs on. They just see *the name* flash on their screen and they know what they've got in store for them."

After a few months of using the Internet, Preston complained that he had stopped signing on because it was no longer any fun now that nobody bothered to pay attention to him anymore. With intensity and bitterness he said the computer was just an electronic box and email relationships were not relationships at all. He continued to describe a series of encounters, which he had failed to discuss previously, in which he felt he had befriended people on the email system. These were people whom he thought had come to accept him despite his flaming, only to have them turn on him and attack him. When his therapist suggested that with the Internet he had thought he was in control of his mother for the first time, he responded, "When you say things like that you don't deserve *to be called* a psychologist!" He walked out of the room and never returned to therapy.

Discussion

For Preston, the therapist, like the Internet and everything that preceded it had become versions of Eliot's "Shadow," persecutors from whom the only rescue was a whimpering termination. In Preston's case, the email system symbolized transgressions and persecutions from the past, just as the therapist symbolized his mother. But from his perspective the email system not only was symbolic of the past, but also functioned as an actual agent of attack.

Although there is nothing inherent in a computer system that makes it either a symbol or an agent of persecution, under many circumstances the email system and the other functions of the computer system may, like a therapist, be experienced as quite benign, even facilitative. This example illustrates paranoid reactions to persecutory anxiety and the peculiar dual role a computer system can play when paranoid anxieties reach extreme levels. For Preston, as for others for whom Eliot's Shadow lurks between every thought and action, the computer system seems a far cry (in all meanings) from the teddy bear or favorite blanket, and the breach between the cyber system and the transitional or potential looms unnegotiably vast.

These examples illustrate one pole of the cyber-system dialectic. At this pole we have seen individuals whose experience in cyberspace is increasingly insular and disconnected from the field of others. But this is not the only use to which a cyber system can be put. Within paranoid functioning, the cyber system may also function as a facilitator of relatedness; at the opposite pole of the dialectic are individuals who are intensely involved in complex exchanges between aspects of self and aspects of others. So far, I have addressed the idea that the cyber system can enhance the likelihood of such more extreme withdrawal into the cell of paranoid functioning. Next we will look at some instances in which it appears that the cyber system can be used to facilitate something that appears like complete relatedness with others, while remaining safely ensconced within the cell.

Relatedness on the Internet Within a Paranoid Experience of Living

I have likened the paranoid withdrawal of the Internet experience to the experience of a prisoner in a cell. Unlike other cells, however, this Internet cell is not just confining. To the contrary, many participants experience

their "confinement" as boldly empowering. As it happens, the most compelling description of which I am aware of the empowering activity[11] that
I am depicting comes from John Custance's (1952) gripping account of
his own experiences in the depth of a profound manic-depressive psychosis, in his book *Wisdom, Madness and Folly—The Philosophy of a Lunatic.*
In his case, the cell is an actual one:

> I first noted it in the padded cell at Brixton while in a state of acute mania.
> I saw a series of visions which impelled on my consciousness a strong sense
> of destiny and leadership. I imagined myself a sort of lion destined to con-
> quer the world, and in conformity with this delusion pace interminably
> round and round my cell on the balls of my feet with a sense of extraordi-
> nary muscular looseness or suppleness. [pp. 55–56]

The computer version of this empowerment, which at times approaches
mania, was described beautifully by Ingber (1981). Ingber sees "computer
addicts" as individuals who spend endless hours in "electronic ecstasy,"
unable to tear themselves away from their machines, returning after an
hour or two even if they need to sleep. She concludes that for such people,
"Computers are not just becoming more and more part of our world. To
a great degree, they are our world" (p. 114).

In *Life on the Screen,* Turkle (1995) cites three case illustrations in which
gender swapping on the Internet not only provided people with increased
relatedness while on-line, but also extended their capacities to feel as themselves and to relate to others off-line. In the first of these, a 28-year-old
man named Garrett takes on a female identity on the MUD for nearly a
year, a helpful female frog named Ribbit. Turkle illustrates the way in
which this Internet identity facilitated Garrett's expression of lifelong
issues of living: "As a man I was brought up to be territorial and competitive. . . . In some way I really felt that the canonically female way of
communicating was more productive than the male" (p. 216). Garrett's
experience as an on-line female facilitated his development of a sense of
helpfulness and connectedness that he had not known previously. In an-

other instance cited by Turkle, a designer named Case is able to use his on-line experience as a female to learn to be related in a more assertive and aggressive manner. For Case, "There are aspects of my personality—the more assertive, administrative, bureaucratic ones—that I am able to work on in the MUDs" (p. 217). Finally, a 34-year-old woman named Zoe plays both male and female characters on the MUDs in a way that facilitated her ability to assert herself in both marriage and job: "I got really good at playing a man, so good that whoever was on the system would accept me as a man and talk to me as a man. . . . It was very validating. All those years I was paranoid about how men talked about women. Or I thought I was paranoid. And then, I got a chance to be a guy and I saw that I wasn't paranoid at all" (p. 222).

In the cases Turkle cites, the improvement in relatedness emerges from the opportunity to express aspects of gender identity that were otherwise repressed. In the clinical vignettes that follow, I describe situations in which gender identity is not a central component of the improvement in the person's ability to feel related. It is also noteworthy that in Turkle's cases, the overall outcome of the on-line experience appears to have been almost exclusively positive, even in the case of Zoe, who eventually stopped going on-line. In the cases I cite, the experience of enhanced relatedness is clear, even though the overall outcome is not always so favorable.

Clinical Examples: Paranoid Relatedness on the Internet

This case was introduced briefly in Chapter 1. It is the man in his mid-thirties who had suffered greatly from what seemed to him an unending series of failed relationships. After more than a month of virtually total isolation, with his depression reaching nearly suicidal levels, he entered psychotherapy and began to reveal a history of enormous emotional frustration. He perceived both parents to have tantalized him with offers of tenderness and love that they never delivered and to have lavished him with a type of attention that he never experienced as pertaining to anything meaningful or essential about himself. Soon after entering therapy he purchased a computer system and quickly immersed himself in Internet chat rooms, at first merely lurking, but subsequently engaging actively. After two weeks he reported that he was deeply involved in the first truly satisfying relationship he could remember. He was often reluctant to discuss his experience in this relationship, a reluctance that was quite uncharacteristic for this patient. He did report that he spent up to six hours at a time with his Internet girlfriend, often in the middle of the night, talking to each other through the medium of the screen. To him, the relationship was "complete and satisfying." Once, near the very beginning of the relationship, he joked that he had never met the girl and that "she" might be a 12-year-old boy, but the possibility of a hoax was dropped quickly and never again broached. At times, he spoke of their arranging to meet, but he never evidenced any compulsion to make such meetings happen. One night about three months into the relationship, they had a terrible fight, the specifics of which he declined to relate. He refused to turn on his computer for a week. When finally he tried to contact her, his email was returned with a message that no such email address could be found. His perfect relationship had vanished, literally without a trace.

Discussion

All of the characteristics of the type of paranoid relatedness I have been describing exist in this vignette. The cell-like paranoid withdrawal is evident both in his precomputer isolation and in the fortress he built around the experience itself. For example, as his therapist I perpetually felt paralyzed to intervene in any way, unable to insinuate myself into the perfect isolation of the relationship, just as he felt unwilling to share it with me, or to integrate it into any context larger than itself. The paranoid nature of the psychic reality of his experience is evident not only in the manifest quality of the relatedness (through a keyboard, on a computer screen, without physical contact, without visual context other than text), but also, perhaps even more saliently, in the idealizing of the object of his affection.[12] This idealization even surpasses the example cited by Lea and Spears (1995) of two members of Presbynet, a Presbyterian church open conference, who "declared after 2 months of exchanging messages with strangers they had never 'met' that 'I know some of these people better than some of my oldest and best friends' and that 'I'm still constantly amazed at the "companionship" and warmth one can find at the computer terminal'" (pp. 203–204). The hyperactivity or mania that so typifies this type of relationship appears in the form of the insatiability of the contact, the relentless need to be in the act of contact, and, like Ingber's "computer addicts," the sleepless nights engaged in conversation.

In this particular vignette, we may observe this man's tendency to deny much of his own psychic reality. At other points in his life, he might have described this Internet relationship as limited and only partially fulfilling. Now, however, he repeatedly describes the experience as whole and complete, in fact perfect. Paradoxically, this denial of psychic reality continued even in the absence of any such reality. Short of physical death, few actual relationships have the potential to end with the object of the relationship having literally and totally vanished. It seems quite astounding to an outsider, for whom the "relationship" might appear, at the very best, a partial experience, but for this patient, as for many others, the relationship retained the quality of a whole and complete relationship for almost all practical purposes, even in his reactions to its loss.

This clinical vignette illustrates the phenomenon of relatedness within a paranoid experience of living, relatedness in which a partial experience can take on the quality of whole and complete relatedness. I will offer other examples of this throughout the text, including a lengthy one in Chapter 5, in which a similar phenomenon happens within an organizational context.

So far, our exploration of Internet relationships at the millennial interface of Janus, the technophile/technophobe, has illustrated some ways
in which people make use of the Internet to create or to sever linkages
among competing experiences of themselves and of others in their surround. I have illustrated the notion of potential space and looked at the
ways in which use of the Internet may serve a creative and potentiating
role or a limiting and thwarting one. At the interface of Janus, we have
observed a cyber-system dialectic, at one pole of which is a view of the
individual in cyberspace as insular and disconnected from the realm of
relationships with others, and at the other pole a view of the individual
embracing and fulfilling aspects of self and of others that otherwise remain repressed and limited in expression. In some of the clinical material
we have looked at, we have seen the cyber system as a vehicle for insularity, withdrawal, and disconnection from others within a paranoid experience of living in the world; here it is a way of living within the confines of
the cell to escape, as best one may, the inevitability of persecution. Of
course, as we have seen, the email itself may become tainted with persecutory experience, or the internal persecutors may be so powerful that
they become projected into the Internet as they are into everything else.
But we have also seen that the Internet may serve as a vehicle for increasing relatedness, even while retaining a primarily paranoid experience of
living. In the next chapter, we explore two central questions: How does
the use of the Internet as an alternative form of relating happen? Can this
paranoid relatedness be psychologically beneficial?

3   Cleansing the Web of Perception

Thereto the silent voice replied:
"Self-blinded are you by your pride;
Look up thro' night: the world is wide.

"This truth within thy mind rehearse,
That in a boundless universe
Is boundless better, boundless worse.

"Think you this mould of hopes and fears
Could find no statelier than his peers
In yonder hundred million spheres?" . . .

Forerun thy peers, thy time, and let
Thy feet, millenniums hence, be set
In midst of knowledge, dream'd not yet.

Thou hast not gain'd a real height,
Nor art thou nearer to the light,
Because the scale is infinite
      "The Two Voices," Tennyson (1833)

But first the notion that man has a body distinct from his soul is to be
expunged; this I shall do by printing in the infernal method, by corrosives,
which in Hell are salutary and medicinal, melting apparent surfaces away,
and displaying the infinite which was hid.

If the doors of perception were cleansed every thing would appear to man as
it is, infinite.

For man has closed himself up, till he sees all things thro' narrow chinks of
his cavern.
      "The Marriage of Heaven and Hell," Blake (ca. 1790–1793)

For many of us, when we sit with our fingers at the keyboard and our eyes fixed on the screen of a video display terminal (VDT), our physical experience feels so compressed that it assumes an almost two-dimensional quality. The spatial continuity of depth fades as the plane of the VDT dominates our experiential field, and often the passage of time seems countered by our ability to do and redo at will. We seem to have found life in a flat and minimal form. But for others, the hypertext of the Internet cleanses their perceptions and extends their experience in the vectorless nondimensionality of infinity. As Derrida (1977) predicted of hypertext, long before there was a World Wide Web, "in so doing it can break with every given context, engendering an infinity of new contexts in a manner which is absolutely illimitable" (quoted in Landow 1992, p. 8).

In the previous chapter, we discussed the interface of a millennial Janus of technology and observed that the Internet appears to have a profound capacity to function either as a vehicle for insularity and disconnection or as a vehicle for increasing relatedness. In this chapter, we look beyond the warning I quoted from Blake to make use of our understanding of the dual dimensionality of the Internet. We explore how cyberspace functions in these dichotomous roles and whether it can, in any meaningful way, be psychologically beneficial.

Symmetrical and Asymmetrical Organizations of Experience

I have been describing a dichotomy of dimensional experience—flat and asynchronous on the one hand, infinitely rich and textured on the other. But the dichotomous potential of dimensionality that people experience with the Internet is not unique to cyberspace. In fact, Blake wrote the quoted passage almost two hundred years before the Internet existed, and

Tennyson's poem "The Two Voices" was written barely fifty years later. Yet each of them refers to similar phenomena. With the help of some ideas introduced by the Chilean-born, England-trained psychoanalyst Ignacio Matte-Blanco, I will argue that all of our psychological functioning is built on a similar experiential dichotomy. I will then apply this understanding to the ways we use the Internet.

Building upon Freud's models of topography and Klein's understanding of psychic process, Matte-Blanco (1975, 1988) described the forms of logic used in conscious processes as asymmetrical logic, and the forms of logic used in unconscious processes as symmetrical logic.[13] For Matte-Blanco, human psychological functioning is bi-logical, that is, composed of both sorts of logical processes—the symmetrical and the asymmetrical. Specifically, he characterizes being human as being in a fundamental antinomy (Matte-Blanco 1988). For Kant (1781), the notion of antinomy emerges from the unavoidable contradiction to pure reasoning that human limitations introduce. For Matte-Blanco, the antinomy, or inability to reason in a clear, unique, and incontrovertible manner, results from our fundamental and inescapable coexistence in these antithetical logical states. We are always in a state of being in which our psychological functioning is at once symmetrical and asymmetrical.

The Logic of Asymmetry

Within this antinomy, or fundamental dichotomy, the organizing principles that we use for asymmetrical thought differ radically from the organizing principles we use for symmetrical thought. The logic of asymmetry, roughly speaking, is the logic of most conscious experience. Within the organizing principles dictated by this form of logic, experience may be located with respect to the three dimensions of Euclidean space and may be oriented in time. We know roughly where things are and when they are happening. Similarly, within this organizational modality, cause and effect prevail. As a result, we are in a position to discriminate clearly one experience from other experiences. In addition, it is normally relatively clear-cut for us to figure out what thing precedes or succeeds another thing. If one thing is in causal relation to another thing, we can generally figure out the nature and direction of that causal relation.

Let me use the simple statement, "John helped his young son Peter into the car," to illustrate how the logic of asymmetry works. Within this asymmetrical logic, we would be able to reach a number of conclusions about this statement with a considerable degree of certainty:

- John is the father and Peter is the son.
- John and Peter can be located with respect to a certain car, and, similarly, they can be located with respect to each other.
- The car is a specific physical object, and no thing other than a car, and it occupies a specifically identifiable physical place.
- John's and Peter's location with respect to that car and to each other are things that can, themselves, be situated in time, specifically at some definite time in the past.
- John is the facilitator and Peter is the facilitated and the direction of the facilitation is from outside to inside.[14]

The Logic of Symmetry

The logic of symmetry, roughly speaking, is the logic that prevails in most of the organization of experience that, somewhat misleadingly, psychoanalysts have come to call unconscious. This is the logic of emotional experience, of dream life, and of fantasy. Here, the general rule is whenever somebody or something stands in a certain relation to another thing (or person), then that other thing (or person) stands in the equivalent relation to the first thing. In other words, within the rules of unconscious logic, the converse of any relation is treated as identical to the relation itself. Given this way of ordering and organizing experience, no one thing is clearly different from any other thing, nothing happens clearly and uniquely before anything else, and nothing is in clear and unique causal relation to anything else for the mere fact that the direction of causality is always reversible. If the event is in the past, it may also be in the present or in the future, or, to quote Eliot (1935, p.175), "Time present and time past are both perhaps present in time future, and time future contained in time past." This is the logic of the unconscious, which Freud (1900) revealed in *The Interpretation of Dreams* and which has become a central element in the mainstream of psychoanalytic understanding.

Applying symmetrical logic to the same phrase, "John helped his young son Peter into the car," an inexhaustible array of possibilities emerges:

- If John helped Peter, then Peter may have helped John.
- If John is the father to his son Peter, then Peter may be the father to his son John.
- If John is helping his son, John may also be hindering his son.
- John may be the actor and Peter the acted upon, and Peter may be the actor and John the acted upon.
- The direction of the action may be into and the direction may be out of.
- The car may be a specific car and it may be one among the set of all cars, or, for that matter, all objects (or parts of objects, or people, or parts of people).
- The temporal location of the event may be present, past, future, some amalgam of the three, or never.[15]

The Triadic Nature of Experience and Transformational Processes

So far this glimpse into the realm of Blake's perceptual cleansing has illuminated that our psychological being depends on the simultaneity of two vastly different logical modes with so-called antinomic, or incompatible, rules of logic (which are also called organizational paradigms). The next step is to understand that any experience is not only dyadic, consisting of these two modes, but actually triadic. The triad is composed of a symmetrical organization of the experience, an asymmetrical organization of the experience, *and the relationship between the two.* This relationship between the two is a central factor in the ideas I am developing. It has the characteristic of being a relationship that requires psychological work; it is a relationship that can only be described as unavoidably transformational. This transformational process is always necessary because the modes of experiential organization are so alien to each other that no simple, linear equivalency or isomorphism can arrange a correspondence between them. With one part of our psychological being we are dealing with the well organized, with another part we are dealing with the unorganized, and with a third, connective, part we are making the difficult connections between the other two. Our ability to function as psychological beings depends on all aspects of this triad. Other dichotomies, for example, self–other, inner–outer, dynamic–static, may be viewed from a similar perspective.[16]

Thinking about language sometimes helps to clarify what I mean by "transformation." We can translate among most Western languages relatively easily. The words are different, some of the grammar and syntax may be different, but the underlying rules of organization tend to be quite similar. Translation of this sort is not really transformation; the surface structure has been altered, but the form remains unchanged. Now let's say we are interested in conveying emotions over a text-based Internet connection. There is no clear way to translate from one to the other because the form is so different. One attempt has been to transform text to approximate an emotional state, for example, :-) or :-(for happiness or sorrow (turn the book 90 degrees clockwise to see the representations of happy and sad faces), or to transform emotion into linguistic text, say by use of poetry or metaphor. In any case, the effort requires psychological work, because a transformational process is necessary.

A clinical illustration of transformational process will demonstrate how these ideas come into play in computer-mediated communication.

Clinical Example: Transformational Processes

Now in his early forties, persistent thoughts of suicide drove Patrick into the treatment he had refused to consider for many years, recalling childhood memories of being made to sit for endless hours in therapists' waiting rooms while his mother sought, and in his estimation failed to receive, help. His appearance and demeanor—attractive, fit and trim, conservatively dressed, soft-spokenly gracious, cordial, and attentively polite—stood in contrast to his portrayal of himself as socially out of step, hopelessly depressed, and isolated.

He described growing up as the youngest by ten years of five children in a family that was outwardly cohesive and content, but, quietly, financially, intellectually, and aesthetically ambitious and competitive and plagued by alcoholism and depression on the part of both parents. His father was a reasonably well-known figure in the entertainment business, a man of enormous talent and celebrated stature who, in moments of sobriety or partial sobriety, Patrick pictured holding the entire family in the palm of his hand. The father's situation in the entertainment industry put him on a first-name basis with the most privileged strata of society, only to succumb to incapacitating alcoholism at the very moment he might have gained superstar-level immortality. The mother, a gracious and politically concerned woman, found herself progressively more isolated from the world and found little meaning to her life, as her older children grew up and moved out and the family moved to progressively more suburban, ultimately rural, areas.

The older siblings, all of whom had grown up to lead outwardly successful lives, were well out of the home by the time the marriage ended in a bitterly acrimonious divorce. And even during the time when the family was together, Patrick expressed the feeling that they were on the bus together and he was left behind at the bus stop, ridiculed for being unable to do the things they could do, laughed at for trying. At such moments, he felt that even his mother, for whom he normally was the only link to vitality, willingly hopped on the bus as well.

Such had been the continuing picture of his life. With the family's multiple moves and ultimately the divorce, he had never felt quite a part of anything. In a family of Ivy Leaguers, celebrated entertainers, and political figures, he was a high-school dropout who had meandered his way through communes and beliefs, attaching himself to one after another guru, one after another job, and one after another woman, until, ultimately and to his mind arbitrarily, he married, had five children, and settled into a slightly more than menial job that he had kept for fifteen years. *For each of his roles in life he applied the same formula. In all situations he was contemptible and contemptuous, not worthy of breathing the same air as his wife, children, and colleagues, and, alternatively or even simultaneously, horrified by the foulness of their polluting invasions on his privacy.*

When Patrick used computers, he found himself in one of two modes. At one end of the spectrum, he was highly rigid and rule bound. Each computer event had a specific objective. When he sat down at the keyboard, he knew exactly what he wanted to accomplish and exactly how to go about it in a well-reasoned, logical, unassailable way. At the other end of the spectrum, Patrick would lose himself for hours in a hypertextual, hypersexual web of pornography, drifting aimlessly from image through chat, to other images, and on into nowhere. When Patrick was in his rigid mode on the computer, he hated himself for being like a computer; when he was in his pornographic drift, he hated himself for being less than human.

Similarly, his manner in our sessions alternated between highly rigid, rule-bound behavior and insatiable wit and playfulness, with either mode well defined by suicidal hopelessness and despair. He appeared to enjoy both types of sessions, if only as an opportunity to express his unrelenting mixture of self-hatred and hatred of others. He declared that as his newest guru I would soon enough prove myself unworthy of my robes one way or the other, either by tolerating his presence or becoming intolerant of it, and that, as pleasant as it might be to pass the time with me, it was equivalent to his other pastimes—pot and pornography—and of no greater lasting value.

About six months into the treatment he increased his sessions to twice weekly, whereupon I found myself frequently wandering into series of dream-like reveries during our meetings. Often these reveries occurred while he obsessively worried about his despair in the rigid, rule-bound mode of behaving, and not infrequently they commingled my issues with important male figures in my life and his issues with his father and elder brothers. Near the start of one such session, while he was defiling himself for his failure as a father to his youngest son, I suddenly found myself trying to recall the precise positioning of the central figures on the ceiling of the Sistine Chapel. I had just reversed the outstretched arms from right to left when he switched modes, punctuating his self-reproach by saying, "I feel like I'm balancing on the nipple of infinity."

I was so struck by the similarity of my reverie, in which I floated inside the breast-like structure of the dome, and his declaration, that I chose to share my imagery with him. He listened politely and responded, with an impish smile, "Maybe the right-hand version is you as Michelangelo and the left-hand version is you as Michel-devilo. How do I make out the check?" I paused for a second and suggested that cash might cover all the bases.

For the next half hour we played together with the symmetry and asymmetry of the images and as we played it seemed unnecessary to choose whose infinity was internal and whose was external, whether issues were maternal or paternal, balanced or imbalanced, mine or his, angelic or demonic, guru or follower, robed or defrocked, polluting or polluted, on the bus or off the bus. For that half hour, his ubiquitous formula for all experience, the paralyzing double-bind of the contemptible and the contemptuous, was augmented by countless other formulae, both of us as gods, as devils, actively rivaling each other for cleverness or collaborating perfectly.

Of course, a single session rarely creates change, and this was no exception. It was a notable moment, and the session did become a reference point, although a fluid one, a reminder that we had the capability to transform our experience of each other in vastly different ways from the ways to which he was accustomed. Similarly, his ways of experiencing himself in the context of his wife and children, even of his dreaded workplace, have come to change as well. The suicidality has not vanished, nor has the formula of contempt, but, just as in our session, these are no longer the only processes of transformation available to him. The ways in which we were with each other, or were each other, in that session did not acquire the status of names, nor was there any discovery of structure, insight into etiology, or articulation of authentic ways of either of us being ourselves.

For Patrick, the computer and the Internet have become meaningful tools for actualizing and integrating some of these new ways of transforming the previously unintegrated modes of being. He no longer feels so bimodal in his use of computer-mediated communication. When Patrick is involved in a logical, rule-bound process, he has begun to be able to play, to use his wit and humor to make tasks easier, both for himself and for others. When he drifts off into pornography or seductive chat, he no longer finds it so toxic that he has to stay there for hours in order to avoid the shame and self-disgust he used to feel when he emerged from it. He reports that his ventures into this realm are both much shorter and much more satisfying.

The Application of Symmetry, Asymmetry, and Transformations to Paranoid Relatedness

Earlier I gave an example of a man who immersed himself in a computer relationship in a way that, at least subjectively to him, felt more complete and satisfying than any previous relationship. We were able to use this example to show how the idea of denial of psychic reality contributes to an understanding of what was occurring for him. We can apply the concepts of the triad of symmetry, asymmetry, and transformation to the example, and to more general conceptions, and connect the triad to the ways we deal with persecutory anxiety.

As I have outlined it, the nature of psychic reality is triadic, consisting of experience organized according to the rules of symmetrical logic, experience organized according to the rules of asymmetrical logic, and of the transformational processes that convert or map these experiential organizations into each other. Earlier, I concluded that one characteristic type of response to pervasive persecutory anxiety is the attempt to construct barriers around our experience, to create an experiential fortress, to protect us from toxic attacks, to keep us pure and safe.[17]

Clearly, anxiety about invasion or persecution may emerge from actual as well as psychological threats, but the nature of the attacks we are considering here is primarily psychological. Framed in terms of the triadic model of psychic reality I am proposing, there might be a number of ways to attempt to minimize the psychological threats; for example, we might try to eliminate one modality of experience or the other, or to eliminate the transformational processes themselves. Several ways of doing this are possible.

In one version, at its most extreme, this type of elimination results in an annihilation of the experience of emotional being. If we obliterate the capacity to organize experience symmetrically, we can no longer access our unconscious and, hence, we lose contact with our intuitive, impressionistic life, and with our ability to generalize, symbolize, and create. This way of experiencing, in a gross caricature of the obsessive, is limited to a robotic entrenchment in the facts. Meaning, without symmetry, is a parody of science, a formulaic set of logical connections among facts. Persecution can no longer move from outside to inside because inside, in its very essence, no longer exists as a meaningful phenomenon. If an individual fact, or set of facts, is seen as persecutory, the interest generated is merely another fact. The very notion of anxiety, like any other emotional label, has little significance beyond the name.

Alternatively, the psychic reality associated with persecutory anxiety may be avoided by discarding our experience as reasoning beings living in an orderly, well-defined world. If we obliterate our capacity to organize experience according to the rules of asymmetry, we destroy our capacity to think logically, to orient ourselves with regard to time, person, and place, and to discriminate meaningfully between one phenomenology and another. This way of organizing experience, in a gross caricature of the hysteric, is global, diffuse, impressionistic, and random, without facts or connections. Meaning without asymmetry has no meaning. There is merely experience in a disorganized fog of phenomenology. The experience of persecutory anxiety is avoided for a number of reasons. The anticipation associated with anxiety cannot occur without asymmetry since the very notion of anticipation requires the arrangement of time in a linear, forward-moving way, an organization that is asymmetrically determined. Additionally, persecutory anxiety, except in its most diffuse form, requires the type of causal associations that pertain to asymmetrical organizations of experience.

Finally, persecutory anxiety is eliminated when we isolate our experience of living in an orderly, causally determined world from our experience of living in an emotional, associational world. If we eschew the processes of transformation between experience organized symmetrically and experience organized asymmetrically, we deny ourselves the means of connection between inside and outside, between self and other, and between persecutor and persecuted. Here, in a gross caricature of borderline phenomenology, there is either an alteration between or a simultaneity of order and disorder, emotion and logic, chaos and structure, but there is no connection between the two organizations. Meaning is meaningless because it is in disarray or it is encapsulated in structures without depth. In the disaffiliation between hunter and hunted, attacker and attacked, destroyer and destroyed, the very notions of persecution and of anxiety lose context and significance.

Each of these mechanisms is a means of denying a psychic reality that consists of symmetrical and asymmetrical organizations of experience and the processes of transformation that link them. If we favor symmetry at the expense of asymmetry, we forsake their connection to each other and deny the complexity of our experiential world in one way. If we favor asymmetry at the expense of symmetry, the connection is similarly forsaken and we deny the complexity of our experiential world in the opposite way. If we experience both symmetry and asymmetry but refuse to connect them, we introduce yet a third way of denying the complexity of our experiential world.

Internet Illustration of the Link Between the Triad and Escape from Threats

Let's return to the patient I discussed in the previous chapter, who, for a time, experienced unparalleled completeness and fulfilment in his Internet relationship (and continued to express this same feeling, even after his "true love" vanished without a trace). For this man, the prior experience of persecutory anxiety, in his life as he had been living it, had been extraordinarily great. The series of failed relationships, and the ubiquity of frustration in love from his parents onward, had left him with a feeling that to experience life was to subject himself to frustration, even to persecution.

While engaged in his Internet relationship, this patient continued to go to work, to come to therapy, to shop and eat. Seen from the outside, he functioned better than ever. When immersed in the relationship, he abandoned that world of structure, time, and causal significance. For him, persecution was eliminated from his life by *severing the connections between the asymmetry of his worldly functioning and the symmetrical atemporality of his Internet relationship.* At the end, suddenly invaded and attacked from a source he could locate neither within nor without, he held his head in his hands and repeated, "Either I shouldn't have turned it off or I shouldn't have turned it back on."

For this man, and countless others, the persecutory anxiety of living is avoided, at least for a time, by a strategy of living that denies psychic reality by eschewing the links between its different aspects. But here the doors of perception have been cleansed. This particular form of Internet relating allows the denial of psychic reality in a manner that permits a type of relationship that has, for those who can pull it off, the subjective feeling of wholeness with neither the annihilatory consequences nor the persecutory anxieties that in their experience pertain to real-life relationships. It is precisely this way of relating that I mean by the term *paranoid relatedness.*

Clinical Example: Paranoid Relatedness—The Semblance of Real-Life Relations from Within the Cell of Withdrawal

In Chapter 1 I introduced the example of a woman in her late forties who entered psychotherapy after having endured a lifetime of losses, tragic deaths, imprisonments, and hospitalizations. This case illustrates paranoid relatedness. An Internet experience is used to maintain the semblance of real-life relatedness within an experience that is quite manifestly maintained from within the cell of paranoid withdrawal. What is remarkable about this case, and what makes it so useful for purposes of illustration, is this woman's clarity about what she is doing at a conscious level.

In her first session Miranda informed her therapist that she had grown up in a family of four children with a mother who was clinically depressed and who, throughout Miranda's adolescence, had been hospitalized at regular intervals before suiciding when Miranda was 16. Her father never recovered from grief and died within a year himself. She described him as a generous and devoted man who was so caught up in his wife's illness and his despair that he had little time for the children.

She reported that she had been married three times, with each marriage repeating her parental abandonment. Her first marriage, which she entered into within a month after leaving college, came to an abrupt end two years later when her husband eloped with a male lover. It was only then that she came to learn that all the while she was going about her graduate school training, happily persuaded that her marriage was a successful one, he had been engaging in a haphazard series of bisexual relationships. Despite her reluctance to become involved again, in her first job out of school she was swept off her feet by a senior partner, a wealthy man twenty years older than she, who for more than a year devoted himself to wooing her by lavishing her with expensive gifts and the promise of world travel. Within a month after their marriage he was accused of fraudulent actions, including insider trading and embezzlement. Miranda felt embezzled herself and initiated divorce proceedings immediately, only to find out that she was pregnant. By the end of her difficult pregnancy, he was imprisoned and she had obtained her divorce.

Miranda settled into a life of single parenting as her work and, most of all, her son Charles became the focus of her life. Despite her loneliness she began to build a successful career on Wall Street. In contrast to her victimization in relationships, she proved herself to be a resourceful woman, decisively intelligent, bold, and outspoken, who easily earned the trust of a wealthy clientele and, more often than not, did well for them. As Charles grew up, she dedicated herself to establishing her own personal wealth and independence so that he might have a secure life. Miranda had come to feel that objects and money were more reliable than people, and she surrounded herself with them. She purchased several vacation houses and amassed an important collection of modern "industrial" art. With her parents' deaths the siblings had tried to remain connected but drifted apart little by little. As she became more liberated economically,

Miranda attempted to pull the family back together. On the way home from a family reunion at her vacation house in Maine, her elder brother fell asleep at the wheel and drove his car off the road. He and her sister died and the younger brother, a man plagued for years with drug and alcohol problems, somehow blamed Miranda for the accident and never talked to her again.

Bereft of all family connections, Miranda decided that she could not tolerate the loneliness, and that, for Charles's sake as well as her own, she needed to have someone else in her life. After a brief courtship, she settled into a comfortably loving, if passionless, marriage with another older man, a lawyer who had himself been widowed. From the time Charles was 11 until he was 16, the family felt intact. Frank had grown children who substituted as aunts and uncles for Charles, and gradually, even reluctantly, Miranda allowed herself to slip into a feeling of comfort and security. And so for Miranda it was as if a bomb exploded inside her head when Frank was diagnosed with pancreatic cancer. He was dead within three months, leaving her feeling more disconsolate and alone than ever.

For the first time, Miranda's experience of grief and abandonment caused her to shut down. For her 16-year-old son, she managed to put on a show of perseverence, but she found herself unable to function either in her office or in any social activities. By her own description she became reclusive, leaving her house only when necessary. In her exile, the computer became salvation. Miranda discovered that she could manage to negotiate a great deal of her business dealings without ever actually speaking to anyone. With CNN on one side and her video screen on another, equipped with state-of-the-art stock-market software, she could remain up to date, even immersed, in her work in the seclusion of her bedroom. And she learned the power of email, in dealing both with her clients and her office staff. When it became necessary for her to visit the office or to speak with clients on the phone, she kept the contact as brief and to the point as possible and then beat a hasty retreat to her quarters. Miranda described the experience of being outside her house as one of being attacked by an outside world that wanted to force itself on her, to attack her.

As time wore on, Miranda's reclusiveness became less a reaction to grief and more a habitual way of living. As much as she longed in some way to remain connected to people, actual relationships had lost meaning for her any more. Since any relationship she might have could be snatched away from her at any minute, to relate would only mean to have to endure living with yet another loss. As much as she worried about Charles, she decided that if she lost him as well, the answer for her would be quite simple. With Charles dead she could suicide without regret since there could be no reason to continue living with the kind of pain that his loss would create.

It was in this context that Miranda began her Internet involvements. Her insularity now a perfect paranoid regression, she hungered for a type of contact that might gratify without exposing her to loss. On the Internet she satisfied that hunger. Miranda had always maintained an interest in technology. In her stock dealings, she favored small technology firms with interesting new products. Her art collection was based on works that featured technology and industry. Her office had always featured the latest technological improvements. Now she made technology a central part of her life. Far from a beauty, Miranda had always attracted men with her intellect and her charm. In addition, she was a powerful and persuasive writer. As soon as she began to chat, she knew that she would be able to pick and choose her companions.

She tried out a number of different identities in a number of different chat rooms and bulletin boards. On LambdaMOO she logged on as Twylight, a shadowy, depressive, anorexic ballet dancer. Twylight basked in the morbid side of Miranda's experience. She fascinated her suitors with her despair and seduced them into futile attempts to rescue her from the depths of suicidal descent. In ECHO she was Muselle, a flighty barfly with a fiery temper and a ravenous appetite for men. Muselle delighted in the tease. She was an omnivore, insatiable in her repetitions of seduction and abandonment. In HotTub Miranda became BulleMarquette, a no-nonsense, savoir-faire businesswoman who demanded her pleasure on the barrelhead and expected to pay fair value for it, while in CB Simulator she altered the character to BelleMarquette, a businesswoman who was a shy seductress, tantalizing suitors with a savvy helplessness.

Miranda enjoyed all of these characters and returned to each of them frequently to pass the time, to amuse herself, and to distract her from her loneliness. But none of them was enduringly gratifying. Where Sherry Turkle (1995) and Allucquere Rosanne Stone (1995) describe the realization through the Internet of dis- or misplaced aspects of self, Miranda experienced a sense of fragmentation, satisfying as a distraction but little more.

Seeking something different she subscribed to a few single-parent newsgroups. In each of them she took the name Myrna and represented herself in a reasonable likeness of her character and circumstances. After two weeks on-line, Carlos sought her out:

Carlos: I have been listening to you for several days now . . . in several
    places.
Myrna: I am flattered that you find me so interesting.
Carlos: You speak so deeply and with such clarity. Truly you must have
    survived a great deal in your lifetime.
Myrna: And you speak of me with such eloquence. What does that say
    about you?
Carlos: Hope is such a burden, some of us can neither annihilate it nor
    realize it. I suspect that you, like I, are one of these people.

Miranda did not fall in love with Carlos, nor did she ever suspect that he was in love with her. Unlike many Internet relationships, there was no progression to telephone contact and no discussion of meeting. Their virtuality was their virtuosity. She expressed to Carlos ideas and emotions that she had kept hidden from everyone, herself included, and she knew that she could rely on him to understand her and to respond with sensitivity and directness. In turn, he seemed more openly expressive to her than any man she had ever known. But she had no urge to touch him or to have an image of him that moved beyond the pixels on the screen that composed the text and context of their relationship. She spoke of him as her Internet lover, but their lovemaking was generally sexual only when the theme of what they had to say to each other was sexual. At times this was frequent, but for months at a time nothing sexual was spoken of.

Miranda spoke with Carlos at least daily, and generally many times a day. She was respectful of his life and of his commitments—he was a writer—as he was respectful of hers. She dropped all of her alternative personae and chat room involvements and looked forward to their engagements with each other. In fact, knowing that there was Carlos to return to allowed her to leave her house and to resume working out of her office. He encouraged her to begin psychotherapy to deal with her overwhelming experience of loss and, reluctantly at first, she accepted his advice. But as involved and buoyed as she was by her relationship with Carlos, Miranda never feared losing him in the way that she might have feared loss or abandonment in a wider bandwidth relationship. As special an individual as she felt Carlos to be, she knew her power as a writer and she could say, with remarkable insouciance, "If Carlos goes away, I'll find another Carlos."

Paranoid Relatedness and Potential Space

For Miranda, her persecutory experiences of loss, abandonment, and disappointment had transcended levels that she could bear. By entering the Internet she isolated her experiences of symmetry from her experiences of asymmetry. In the asymmetrical world a person has individual meaning and thus the loss of that person can be a crushing blow, especially to someone as tormented by prior loss as Miranda. But in a purely symmetrical world, such as the one Miranda cultivated on the Internet, people are sufficiently interchangeable that if she were to lose one Carlos she could rest assured that she would find another equivalent one. Keeping these symmetrical and asymmetrical ways of organizing her sense of living as separate as they could be kept allowed Miranda to continue living in a world that might otherwise have left her unable to function, perhaps even suicidally so. To endure her despair, she negotiated a paranoid adaptation to the world, concretely within the confines of her house and abstractly within the fortress of her emotional withdrawal. This adaptation shielded the parts of her that still longed for relationships with people from the parts of her that experienced as inevitable that any relationship with another person would lead to loss and suffering. In her relationship with the interchangeable Carlos, Miranda created and maintained for herself a potential space in which she could simulate whole-object relating within the safety and security of a part object, concretely symmetrical world.[18]

We use the phrase *all things being equal* to indicate that there are no biases that might alter an outcome. Within the symmetrical universe of Miranda's cyber-potential-space all things truly were equal. As long as she remained within the hermetic seal of that symmetry, in which she functioned only as a part of herself dealing with partial aspects of an other of her own invention, she was safe to create for herself ways of becoming a whole person, once again dealing with other whole people.

Miranda's case illustrates both the use of cyberspace as potential space and the concept of paranoid relatedness, or the semblance of real-life relations within the cell of paranoid withdrawal. As I have pointed out, there is nothing inherent in any experience or object that characterizes it as necessarily transitional or potential. For any individual, cyberspace may become an extension of persecutory experience, as in the case of the Preston/Feral/BigFF. Or the cyber system may become a refuge, a separate world, as in the case of Miranda. Alternatively, the cyber system may remain with neutral valence, reflecting neither persecution nor escape from persecutory anxieties.

Summary

Few would argue that human psychological functioning, and in particular human relatedness, has been altered irreversibly by computers and computer systems. In this chapter I have described the complex and obscure path leading to understanding the nature and consequences of the alterations that have occurred within modem-connected human contact. By doing so I begin to approach the problem of evaluating cyber systems' potential as vehicles for individual growth and psychological flexibility and their threat as a perpetrator of the dehumanization of psychological functioning.

These are ways in which contemporary Internet systems serve both as a symbol of dissociation and as a vehicle to propagate dissociated characterological phenomena, ways in which the Internet promotes a way of interacting that subjectively may feel interpersonally engaged and related, while nonetheless remaining predominantly isolated, self-protective, and asocial. These ways of interacting are a form of object relating that is characterized by partial relationships, confusion, or ambiguity between what is happening and what is imagined, what is occurring inside oneself and what is occurring outside oneself as manifested by the screen of a computer. This form of partial relating rests on ambiguity between knowing and making oneself known and hiding and making oneself less vulnerable. Most of all, this is a way of interacting in which we suspend, or even obliterate, the inherent tensions between our experience of ourselves and the world as structured and ordered and our experience of ourselves and of the world as disordered and chaotic.

The clinical illustrations demonstrate that one type of response to pervasive persecutory anxiety is a form of splitting that may be characterized as paranoid regression or withdrawal. However, the notion of the denial of psychic reality allows us to see that the cyber system can become an instrument for paranoid relatedness, an experience of relating from within the cell of withdrawal that takes on qualities and characteristics of real-life relatedness. Matte-Blanco's conception of the antinomy of symmetrical and asymmetrical organizations of experience, as well as my own elaboration of the notion of transformational processes, has provided insight into how this process of paranoid relatedness occurs. Finally, I have returned to Winnicott's notions of paradox and of potential space to reconstruct some ways in which relatedness has the potential to act as a transitional process. In paranoid relatedness, persecutory experience is fended off for long enough to regain the experience of oneself as a whole person, once again dealing with other people in the ways characteristic of oscillations between the cell of withdrawal and real-life functioning. Within this oscillation triadic experience can be restored, including both symmetrical and asymmetrical organizations of experience and an infinite array of transformational processes connecting the two.

4 Between Flesh and Thought: The Substance of Internet Relationships

If the dull substance of my flesh were thought,

Injurious distance should not stop my way;

For then, despite of space, I would be brought,

From limits far remote, where thou dost stay.

No matter then although my foot did stand

Upon the farthest earth removed from thee;

For nimble thought can jump both sea and land,

As soon as think the place where he would be.

But, ah, thought kills me, that I am not thought,

To leap large lengths of miles where thou art gone,

But that, so much of earth and water wrought,

I must attend time's leisure with my moan;

>*Receiving nought by elements so slow*

>*But heavy tears, badges of either's woe.*

Sonnet XLIV, W. Shakespeare (1609)

Balanced, at times precariously, between the limited substance of flesh and the nimble limitlessness of thought, Internet relatedness exists within the complex intersections of different Internet users' experience of internal life and the social surround. This is a social surround that expands and contracts, in turn, to include experiences of other Internet users, of the technology, of real life, and of the relationships among all of these aspects of an environment that is as much a part of the imagination of the Internet user as it may be a part of some larger reality.

Shakespeare's tortured lover is killed by the thought that he cannot be thought, that he cannot make contact with the object of his fantasy, except via the fantasy itself; when absence is the greatest presence, longing is the only active way to love. The torture of this longing, this prison cell of solitude and loss, has been memorialized by poets through the ages. Often in these writings, it appears that it has taken separation to experience fully the vastness of love, at the same time that love has brought about the truest experience of isolation.

But how will we memorialize longing in the age of the Internet? If it is through solitude that we discover desire and through desire that we come to know solitude (Phillips 1993, Winnicott 1958), what is it that we discover when the sharp divide between flesh and thought becomes blurred by the mediated contact of the computer? The Carnegie-Mellon report suggests that "greater use of the Internet leads to shrinking social support and happiness, and increases in depression and loneliness" (Sleek 1998, p. 1). Yet, unarguably, use of the Internet has become greater and greater. What is it that makes the experience of Internet use so compelling and so popular if its outcome is, as the report suggests, increased depression and loneliness? What is it, in fact, that the Internet user is experiencing in this domain that seems to reside somewhere in between thought and flesh?

Using psychoanalytic theory to examine the details of a number of individuals' lives in cyberspace can illuminate this paradox, which plays so large a role in the demarcations of contemporary life. Our goal here is to approach the infinitely dimensioned intersections of contemporary life by delving deeply enough into people's lives, and their lives on-line, to gain some understanding of their internal experience, as well as gleaning some appreciation of how they understand and relate to the part of the social world that we inhabit in this realm between flesh and thought at the interface of Janus.

The authors of the Carnegie-Mellon report find that "Internet use was associated with declines in participants' communication with family members in the household, declines in the size of the social circle, and increases in depression and loneliness" (Kraut et al. 1998, p. 1017). Without refuting the data of the Carnegie-Mellon report,[19] I believe that by using a psychoanalytic view, we can illustrate and explain some of the ways in which people are learning to adapt to paranoid experiences of living and paranoid ways of organizing experience; or, as I have framed it in Chapters 2 and 3, people are adapting to experiences in which the computer is both the agent and the symbol of persecutory experience. I describe the lives of people who have become involved in cyber relationships by withdrawing from almost all other meaningful human contact. These are people who have opted for a more provincial and limited reality within the still infinite world of the machine, the people who reside at all hours of the day and night in the universe created and illuminated by the screen of the VDT. For these people, the world I describe is one in which their most important and prized relationships are with disembodied text that represents other human beings whose presence is immediate without being present. I describe other situations in which people, similarly immersed in cyberspace, make use of it to free themselves from the overwhelming anxiety of persecution that accompanies their real-life personae, from life in which their abilities to function as themselves are experienced to be strained and constrained by relationships that are more demanding than they are fulfilling, more perplexing than gratifying.

At times these portraits, of paranoid withdrawal and of hopeful reaching out, are one and the same story. These are the people who find in cyberspace boundless opportunities to function as themselves in all their complexity, and with this multidimensional experience of self they find themselves greeted by others who enhance the deepness of living. Some use this cyber relatedness to make transitions into the embodied world, with or without their cyber partners, while others choose to remain in the most fulfilling world they have known, heedless of disembodiment. All of the people whose lives I am describing have found a way to experience life in between flesh and thought, a way to experience life that, as valuable as such descriptions may be for other purposes, cannot be described as quantitative "declines in participants' communication with family members in the household, declines in the size of the social circle, and increases in depression and loneliness" (Kraut et al., p. 1017).

The Carnegie-Mellon report, as most other Internet scholarship, touches upon Internet relationships by treating them from a perspective in which the primary context is social. Their sample of 93 families is drawn from eight Pittsburgh, Pennsylvania, neighborhoods. The researchers use four measures of social involvement (family communication, size of local support network, size of distant social network, and social support). They measure family communication by asking participants "to list all the members of their household and to estimate the number of minutes they spent each day communicating with the members" (Kraut et al. 1998, p. 1022). Similarly, the authors used "three measures of psychological well-being that have been associated with social involvement: loneliness, stress, and depression" (p. 1023). From this broad empirical perspective, the writers locate a paradox. They observe that "the Internet is a social technology used for communication with individuals and groups, but it is associated with declines in social involvement and the psychological well-being that goes with social involvement" (p. 1029).

Many writers approaching the subject of Internet use from a broad social perspective stress both the role of such relationships in a world in which technology pervades and the impact of this way of relating on the fabric of society, or the nature of the individual within society. Not surprisingly, these social commentaries tend to fall into two camps: the critics and the extollers. Thus, there are writers whose primary emphasis, like that of the Carnegie-Mellon report, is of the social loss created by changing relationships of the individual to society, whether that loss is centered around issues of community (e.g., Doheny-Farina 1996), around issues of man's relationship with the world of the senses (Abram 1996), around issues of man's relationship with thought and text (Birkerts 1994), around mental entrapment without physical interaction and the undermining of social relationships (Stoll 1995), around man's technological saturation (Gergen 1991), or an infomania that erodes our capacity to determine what is and is not significant (Heim 1993). In contrast, there are writers who emphasize the ways in which Internet relationships highlight technology's contributions to society via the gains of the individual. For some writers such gains are found in expansion of contexts for social attraction (Lea and Spears 1995), the ascension to the technological social unconscious (Dowling 1996), or to a collective consciousness (Herz 1995), the making available through technology of venues where people may say and enact what they want, or develop aspects of their being that they feel otherwise inhibited to express (Bruckman 1992, Haraway 1991, Stone 1995, Turkle 1995), the use of technology to establish true personalization (or expression) in places without the constraints of space (Negroponte 1995).

The Case Study Method of Psychoanalytic Investigation

The more sociological approaches discussed above provide a valuable framework for debating the ramifications and social meaning of Internet relationships. However, it remains unclear whether these approaches, even those as thorough and sophisticated as the Carnegie-Mellon longitudinal project, tell us much about the experiential life of the Internet user, the person whom I am portraying as living in a realm between flesh and thought. Our attempt here is to amplify, not to discard, this more sociological work by looking in more depth at the experience reported by individual users.

The case study method has a long history within psychology and specifically within psychoanalysis. Freud's earliest publications in the field, co-written with Breuer (1895), are entitled *Studies on Hysteria*. They consist of a series of detailed case histories that Freud and Breuer used to advance a theory of the etiology and treatment of a class of psychological disorders typified by hysteria. Later in his career, Freud continued to illustrate and articulate his theories by relying on detailed case studies, at times drawn from his clinical practice and at times from other sources. Among these studies number some of Freud's more important contributions: Fragment of an Analysis of a Case of Hysteria (the case of Dora) (Freud 1905a), Analysis of Phobia in a Five-Year-Old Boy (the case of Little Hans) (Freud 1909), Notes Upon a Case of Obsessional Neurosis (the case of the Rat Man) (Freud 1909a), Leonardo da Vinci and a Memory of His Childhood (Freud 1910), Moses and Monotheism (Freud 1939), An Autobiographical Study (Freud 1925a), and many others.

Since Freud's time, this case study method for advancing theoretical ideas by providing detailed clinical substantiation has endured. In fact, few psychoanalytic articles or books lack clinical case studies. While Freud proffered his cases as proof of his theories, the contemporary stance—having weathered decades of controversy—tends to use case material illustratively. It is in this spirit that the case material is presented here, with the clear understanding that the case presentation proves little or nothing.

In fact, clinical case studies may be terribly misleading. Take, for example, some material presented in *Online Friendship, Chat-Room Romance and Cybersex* by Michael Adamse, Ph.D., and Sheree Motta, Psy.D. (1996).

Adamse and Motta do something that many others do not—they give some history, or at least background data, about a few of their examples. The fact that they present case material allows me to disagree, much as there have been countless recastings of the clinical data Freud presented in his relating of the Dora case. The case study approach gives us something to talk about. Take, for example, this vignette by Adamse and Motta.

> Jerry (JC_) in Texas works as a detective. He spends his days dealing with the various stresses that police work brings with it. By the end of his shift he's frequently had it. He's tired and burned out and sits down with a cold beer in front of his PC and joins an Internet chat room called COPS. There he talks with Super Cop out of San Francisco; Koala, a police officer in Sydney; and FancyJane, a police groupie out of Baltimore. These are all regulars whom he knows after months of conversing online.
>
> He immediately feels at home, connected with others who know just how he feels. He tells them he's had a hard day. They commiserate around their terminals, just as our ancestors did around a campfire after the day's hunt or a day spent tilling the land. JC_'s experience reveals a deeper truth: the need to be connected to others who can understand where he's coming from. It helps to know that cops in Australia can get as stressed out at times as cops in America. There are millions of JC_s out there in cyberspace. [pp. 9–10]

In fact, there probably is a deeper truth in the example of JC_'s experience, but from my perspective it seems unlikely that such a truth is simply that JC_ and the "millions of JC_s out there" have a "need to be connected to others who can understand" where they are "coming from." To the extent that our ancestors may have gathered around campfires after hunting or tilling, JC_ might have sat around police headquarters and chatted with his colleagues or even gone to a local watering hole (the authors call their chapter "Welcome to Cybercheers") and had a few drinks with other cops.

JC_ may indeed be seeking "to be connected to others," but he is simultaneously avoiding connection to others. What do the authors tell us about this? We know he works as a detective, and it would be foolish to classify all detectives as one thing or another, just as it would be foolish to classify any other group blindly. But nothing prevents us from making hypotheses about JC_. We merely have little or no way to validate or invalidate them, other than to see how well they line up with the rest of the data that we have. Purely speculatively, then, we might wonder if JC_'s choice of occupation reflects any characterological paranoia. If we had even more data about him, we might be able to examine this more carefully. Psychologists often highlight, as a paranoid characteristic, paying a great deal of attention to details of the surrounding environment. Perhaps some people who become detectives have found an adaptive way of making use of paranoid features of their character, and perhaps JC_ is one of them. We also know he is a cop. Again avoiding overcategorizing, it might be reasonable to suggest that cops have greater paranoid tendencies than the population at large. Even if this is true, as a general rule, it is certainly not true in every case so this may or may not have a bearing on JC_. We also know that he is tired and burned out by the end of the day. If nothing else, this description suggests someone who is looking to withdraw and someone who, to some extent, feels attacked, even perhaps persecuted, by the day's experience.

Where does all of this speculation get us? Not far. In the end we have little or no idea why JC_ does what he does in front of the PC. But from the data put forth by the authors, neither do they. He may be seeking connection. He may be expressing his paranoid experience of living by seeking withdrawal. Or, reflecting my bias, he may be doing both. At least the case material put forth by the authors allows us to speculate about what we do know and to wonder about what we do not.

By presenting case material, I hope to illustrate and illuminate the general and theoretical, at the same time that I provide the writers I may criticize with a chance to use my data to counter my position with their own, or to amplify by augmenting my interpretations with their own. In the case of JC_, I conclude that Adamse and Motta have provided too little information about meaningful aspects of JC_'s life for us to make much sense of what he is doing. I arrive at this conclusion because of the categories of information I require to evaluate psychological functioning in terms of my theories. Adamse and Motta, or other commentators, may have different theoretical orientations that require different data. In many ways, the significant differences in theoretical position become clear only when missing categories of information emerge from the attempt to apply a given theory to the details of a given case. In this way, the application of different theories can serve to illuminate and amplify material as much as they can compete for the escutcheon of truth. To illustrate this, let me discuss some instances of Internet relationships in terms of a psychoanalytic theory that were developed before the earliest days of the Internet.

Harold F. Searles and the Nonhuman Environment

Writing in 1960, nine years before the U.S. Department of Defense launched the Internet's earliest ancestor, the ARPANET system, Searles observed that most writings pertaining to the development of human personality and psychological functioning are limited in focus to considerations of intra- and interpersonal processes. Based on his own psychoanalytic work with profoundly troubled hospital patients at Chestnut Lodge, Searles argued that the nonhuman environment, "the totality of man's environment, with the exception of the other human beings in it," (p. 3) plays a highly significant role in psychological development and functioning. His thesis is

that the nonhuman environment, far from being of little or no account to human personality development, constitutes one of the most basically important ingredients of human psychological existence. It is my conviction that there is within the human individual a sense, whether at a conscious or unconscious level, of *relatedness to his nonhuman environment*, that this relatedness is one of the transcendentally important facts of human living, that—as with other very important circumstances in human existence—it is a source of ambivalent feelings to him, and that, finally, if he tries to ignore its importance to himself, he does so at peril to his psychological well-being. [pp. 5–6]

Searles's words resonate with the contemporary view of David Abram (1996): "Today we participate almost exclusively with other humans and with our own human-made technologies. It is a precarious situation, given our age-old reciprocity with the many-voiced landscape. We still *need* that which is other than ourselves and our own creations. The simple premise . . . is that we are human only in contact, and conviviality, with what is not human" (p. ix). Abram turns his focus outward, delineating civilization's isolation of itself from the flexibility that comes from a full relationship with our sensual presence in a nonhuman world. Abram looks at the development of technology from the advent of formal writing systems to the development of computer technologies that contrive to exclude us from this sentient presence in the world. For Abram we can approach the vastness of relational potential from no other vantage point than that of this fully sentient being, and he fears that the development of computer technologies, and specifically virtuality, has removed us even further than we may imagine.

But Searles uses his understanding of the centrality of the nonhuman environment in a very different way than Abram does, although as recently as 1995 his letters and papers were typed on a manual typewriter. Searles turns his focus inward, examining in exquisite detail the role of the nonhuman environment on individual development and functioning. In Searles's view human development is predicated on gradual processes of maturational differentiation from both human and nonhuman aspects of our early environment. Unlike the developmental model of Margaret Mahler (Mahler et al. 1975), who sees the infant emerging from a state of primary symbiosis with the mother, Searles views early relatively undifferentiated states to involve the totality of the environment, both human and nonhuman. For Searles, then, subsequent failures to differentiate the human from the nonhuman environments become pathological indicators of great significance. If we live in a state of confusion, or dedifferentiation, between the human and nonhuman environments, we are deprived of the fulfillment that we require from both.

To what extent does a person involved in an Internet relationship exhibit the sort of dedifferentiation between the human and nonhuman environments of which Searles speaks when he describes severely disturbed, often hospitalized, patients? Note the following tongue-in-cheek take-off on David Letterman's Top 10 lists. This list comes from a Web site known as The World Headquarters of Netaholics Anonymous (http://www.safari.net/~pam/netanon). The humorous intent of the list notwithstanding, almost all of the items on the list demonstrate some level of dedifferentiation between human and nonhuman environments. I present it with my own interlinear comments:

Top 10 Signs You're Addicted to the Net

10. You wake up at 3 A.M. to go to the bathroom and stop and check your email on the way back to bed. [*Confusion between interacting with the machine and human bodily needs*]

9. You get a tattoo that reads, "This body best visited with Netscape Navigator 1.1 or higher." [*Confusion between the body and a computer program*]

8. You name your children Eudora, Mozilla, and Dotcom. [*Confusion between people, the children, and computer-programmed "bots"*]

7. You turn off your modem and get this awful empty feeling, like you just pulled the plug on a loved one. [*Confusion between the relationship with the machine and the relationship with a loved one*]

6. You spend half of the plane trip with your laptop on your lap . . . and your child in the overhead compartment. [*Confusion between the child and the computer*]

5. You decide to stay in college for an additional year or two, just for the free Internet access. [*Confusion between staying in school for social reasons and Internet reasons*]

4. You laugh at people with 2,400–baud modems. [*Confusion between human and nonhuman attributes*]

3. You start using smileys in your snail mail. [*Confusion between using the computer symbol :) and writing*]

2. The last mate you picked up was a JPEG (a standardized image compression mechanism). [*Confusion between a human and a nonhuman*]

1. Your hard drive crashes. You haven't logged in for two hours. You start to twitch. You pick up the phone and manually dial your ISP's (Independent Service Provider) access number. You try to hum to communicate with the modem. You succeed. [*Confusion between the self and the machine*]

A Rape in Cyberspace

Among the existing reports of the complex issue of Internet relatedness, perhaps the most interesting, provocative, and intelligent piece to appear is Julian Dibbell's (1996) "A Rape in Cyberspace; or How an Evil Clown, a Haitian Trickster Spirit, Two Wizards, and a Cast of Dozens Turned a Database into a Society," which originally appeared in *The Village Voice*. Dibbell's reporting gives us a good deal of clinical data.

The backdrop for the piece (which ought to be read in its entirety by any serious student of the topic) is that Dibbell is a newcomer to LambdaMOO, Pavel Curtis's object-oriented multiuser domain, which, since its public introduction via the Usenet newsgroup rec.games.mud in

January 1991, has been one of the most popular and active text-based user interfaces:

> A MUD is a software program that accepts "connections" from multiple users across some kind network (e.g., telephone lines or the Internet) and provides to each user access to a shared database of "rooms," "exits," and other objects. Each user browses and manipulates this database from "inside" one of those rooms, seeing only those objects that are in the same room and moving from room to room mostly via the exits that connect them. A MUD therefore, is a kind of virtual reality, an electronically-represented "place" that users can visit.
>
> MUDs are not, however, like the kinds of virtual realities that one usually hears about, with fancy graphics and special hardware to sense the position and orientation of the user's real-world body. A MUD user's interface to the database is entirely text-based; all commands are typed in by the users and all feedback is printed as unformatted text on their terminal. . . . A MUD is not goal oriented; it has no beginning or end, no "score," and no notion of "winning" or "success." In short even though users of MUDs are commonly called players, a MUD isn't really a game at all. . . . A MUD is extensible from within; a user can add new objects to the database such as rooms, exits, "things," and notes. Certain MUDS [such as LambdaMOO] even support an embedded programming language in which a user can describe whole new kinds of behavior for the objects they create. . . . A MUD generally has more than one user connected at a time. All of the connected users are browsing and manipulating the same database and can encounter the new objects created by others. The multiple users on a MUD can communicate with each other in real time. [Curtis 1996, pp. 347–348]

Calling himself Dr. Bombay, and not entirely comfortable with his new virtual surroundings, Dibbell happens upon an unusually crowded room (about thirty players) who are involved in a heated debate about the fate of one of the players, a certain Mr. Bungle, "a fat, oleaginous, Bisquickfaced clown dressed in cum-stained harlequin garb and girdled with a mistletoe-and-hemlock belt whose buckle bore the quaint inscription 'KISS ME UNDER THIS, BITCH!'" It seems that on a Monday night in March at about 10 P.M. PST (in "real" time) Mr. Bungle used a voodoo doll to perpetrate a number of acts that the assembled characters in the room upon which Dibbell stumbled two days later considered, by and large, to be heinous. These acts included forcing legba, a Haitian trickster spirit of indeterminate gender, to have sex with him and to eat legba's own pubic hair and to have "a rather pointedly nondescript female character" named Starsinger forced into unwanted sexual engagements with a number of other characters, as well as "jab a steak knife up her ass."

As a newcomer who appears most prominently to experience the awkward self-consciousness of virtuality, Dibbell is instantly intrigued by the apparent seriousness with which the characters gathered in evangeline's living room are taking these matters. Of course, it is this intrigue, and the ways in which Dibbell comes to understand and engage with it, that makes the article so relevant for the study of Internet relatedness. If, to quote Dibbell, "It's one thing to grasp the notion intellectually and quite another to feel it coursing through your veins amid the virtual stream of hot netnookie" (1996, p. 381), he, at that point, "was still the rankest of newbies then, my MOO legs still too unsteady to make the leaps of faith, logic, and empathy required to meet the spectacle on its own terms. I was fascinated by the concept of virtual rape, but I couldn't take it seriously" (pp. 386–387). The article, in large part, is about how, and to what extent, Dibbell comes to take seriously not only virtual rape, but the entire experience of virtuality. More precisely—and this is part of what makes the article so illuminating—Dibbell explores from within the MUD environment the tension between taking it seriously and rejecting it as absurd. As such, it becomes a piece about the tension between virtuality and reality that highlights much of interpersonal relatedness.

The central issue about which the group was stewing dealt with whether or not to "toad" Mr. Bungle, but the debate about toading included other issues, any number of which hinged upon issues of reality versus virtuality. Toading itself illustrates a few of these issues. At the simplest level, toading might be taken as the virtual equivalent of capital punishment. The earliest MUDs, such as MUD1 and Scepter of Goth, emerged from the role-playing adventure game Dungeons and Dragons, and were originally conceived of as multiuser dungeons. In such an environment, toading a character merely transforms a character's description and attributes into those of a toad, much like the fairy-tale transformations of princes. As such, there is always the tantalizing possibility, under the appropriate circumstances, of countertransformation, in the form of restitution as the original character. However, in a MUD such as LambdaMOO, to be toaded is quite different. Here, once toaded, not only does the character suffer the loss of its description and attributes, but there is no residual toad left to tantalize. In fact, it is not only the character that is erased from the process, it is the player as well, whose account is revoked. In Dibbell's words, "the annihilation of the character, thus, is total" (p. 383).

The compelling question for our purposes is the extent to which the analogy holds between virtual toading and corporeal capital punishment. This question becomes so compelling in the way in which it reflects upon our understanding of Internet relatedness, primarily because a central issue here is the complex relationship of the character being played to the player of the character, and thus, in turn, the relationships, or lack of such, among the various players whose characters are interacting. The matter requires analysis from at least two points of view—that of the object of the punishment and that of witnesses to the punishment. In this way we retain the relational significance, by attempting to come to terms with the interactions between the personal and the interpersonal, at least to the extent that they may be entertained as isolatable phenomena.

In capital punishment, the person awaiting execution may, and presumably does, have a complex psychological constitution with any number of aspects, presentations, and representations, both public and private. However, short of the religious, Cartesian mind/body dualisms seem, in many ways, resolved by irrelevance once the lethal action is taken. However we may have understood mind and body to collaborate with each other in the living relationship between essential subject and that subject's outwardly and inwardly presented characters, all have become collapsed into organic matter, which, from the outside, we may label formerly living. From the now nonexistent subjective point of view of its object, the object of capital punishment is no longer a subject, and the organic matter in question can no longer be labeled, not as self, not as part of self, nor as character, aspect of being, body, or former body.

From the point of view of the witnesses, the matter seems instantly more complex. Of course, no one is ever simply a witness. In witnessing we are always, in part, both the executioners and the executed, at least to the extent that we understand and live our experience through processes of identification. The phrase "dead men walking" and the movie that adopted that phrase as its title, assume part of their bone-chilling elegance from the understanding and symbolic representation of these experiential identifications. So from the point of view of the witnesses, Cartesian mind/body dualisms seem every bit as alive and well as the formerly living organic matter seems dead and departed. We witnesses have become the annihilated, just as we have become the annihilators. If we are, as Jack Abbott and Norman Mailer (Abbott 1981) suggest, in the belly of the beast, it is also we who have eaten ourselves. We perpetuate the object of the capital punishment, not only in our re-creations, revisions, fantasies, and elaborations of our former relations to it, but in our continuing identifications with the destroyer and the destroyed that are now embodied in that formerly living organic matter. These spectral "shadows of the object" are the processes at which Freud (1917) hinted in *Mourning and Melancholia* and which Melanie Klein (e.g., 1946) elaborated in her descriptions of depressive phenomena.

But what about Mr. Bungle? How does all of this play itself out in virtuality? And, since our subject is primarily the investigation of Internet relatedness, how does this playing out relate to phenomena such as the one I described in Chapter 2 when a man's "perfect love" vanished completely? Dibbell sets the stage for us once again:

> Every set of facts in virtual reality (or VR, as the locals abbreviate it) is shadowed by a second, complicating set: the "real-life" facts. And while a certain tension invariably buzzes in the gap between the hard, prosaic RL facts and their more fluid dreamy VR counterparts, the dissonance in the Bungle case is striking. No hideous clowns or trickster spirits appear in the RL version of the incident, no voodoo dolls or wizard guns, indeed no rape at all as any RL court of law has yet defined it. The actors in the drama were university students for the most part, and they sat rather undramatically before computer screens the entire time, their only actions a spidery flitting of fingers across standard QWERTY keyboards. No bodies touched. Whatever physical interaction occurred consisted of a mingling of electronic signals sent from sides spread out between New York City and Sydney, Australia. Those signals met in LambdaMOO, certainly, just as the hideous clown and the living room party did, but what was LambdaMOO after all? Not an enchanted mansion or anything of the sort— just a middling complex database, maintained for experimental purposes inside a Xerox Corporation research computer in Palo Alto and open to public access via the Internet. [p. 378]

Given this QWERTY and quirky context, what would the decision to toad Mr. Bungle mean? Who, or perhaps what, would be making that decision and upon whom, or what, would the decision be levied? Even to begin to address these questions, we squarely face the player/character issue and the Cartesian dualisms that that issue evokes. For example, as we read on in the Dibbell piece, we discover that "the puppeteer behind Bungle, as it happened, was a young man logging in to the MOO from a New York University computer" (p. 379).

Let us imagine for a moment that the characters gathered in evangeline's room agreed to toad Mr. Bungle (which they did not) and that such toading was more or less automatic once they reached such an agreement (which it is not). We know that once toading is carried out, Mr. Bungle will cease to exist as a character in LambdaMOO, in the sense that if one were to run the @who command (which normally tells you the status of any character in the system) on Mr. Bungle, you would receive a message saying, "Mr. Bungle is not the name of any player."

The syntax here is worth noting. In reporting that Mr. Bungle is not *the name* of any player, the LambdaMOO message scrupulously avoids implication about the player. Of Gary Gilmore, the convicted murderer who received a death sentence and who Mailer wrote about in *The Executioner's Song*, we would be most likely to report that "Gary Gilmore is dead," or "Gary Gilmore has been executed," and we would be quite unlikely to issue a report that said much of anything about Gary Gilmore's name. In point of fact, there are presumably many Gary Gilmores who remained "players" long after the particular Gary Gilmore was executed. Computer environments follow a naming protocol that is more like the Social Security system than the naming system, in that it is driven to assure uniqueness. Within a given system, once a name is taken, no one else may take that particular name. Thus, no one has the privilege, should they aspire to it, of emulating George Foreman by giving all of their virtual offspring the name George Foreman. The paradox is a familiar one. Within the Social Security system, to use just one illustration, the representation of each person by a unique number, the very arrangement that assures our unequivocal identifiability, is often used to symbolize consummate annihilation of individual identity by transforming us into numbers. Not surprisingly this MUDdying captures a significant, and apparently irresolvable, ambiguity in Internet relationships. Is this a "locale" in which we present ourselves uniquely, and have a unique opportunity to achieve such presentations? Or, alternatively, is this a system in which the essence of being human is annihilated by the process of reduction to ciphered representation?

Returning to the Bungle matter, once toaded, the LambdaMOO system tells us something about the relationship between Mr. Bungle and the set of players in LambdaMOO, namely that Mr. Bungle is the name, within LambdaMOO, of none of them. This is a fairly limited communication, at least in contrast to "Gary Gilmore is dead." Certainly, it tells us almost nothing about the players themselves. In fact, we have no idea whether or not the player who logged in to the NYU computer had died, although that seems both improbable and, even if true, highly coincidental. In truth, the communication tells us relatively little about Mr. Bungle, the character. Quite frequently, players will take the same character in more than one MUD. Even though he may have been toaded in LambdaMOO, Mr. Bungle may have continued to lead an active virtuality in, for example, FurryMUCK.

Superficially, at least, once a player's character has been toaded, that player is removed from the system. In fact, the closest approximation to capital punishment may be that, paradoxically, the system now punishes the player by refusing to accept the player's capital via the mechanism of eradicating their account. Thus, the account, usually banked by credit card, is truly subjected to capital punishment. But does this have any meaningful impact on the player? Most of us have more than one credit card, and, again in stark contrast to Gary Gilmore, it is a relatively trivial matter to log on again, using alternative resources, and once again to become a player in the system.

In the case of Mr. Bungle, this is precisely what happened:

> This truth was rather dramatically borne out, not too many days after Bungle departed, by the arrival of a strange new character named Dr. Jest. There was a forceful eccentricity to the newcomer's manner, but the oddest thing about his style was its striking yet unnameable familiarity. And when he developed the annoying habit of stuffing fellow players into a jar containing a tiny simulacrum of a certain deceased rapist, the source of this familiarity became obvious: Mr. Bungle had risen from the grave. [Dibbell 1996, p. 392]

So, Mr. Bungle's toading appears to have a rather limited effect on both the NYU player and on the character itself, at least to the extent that the player can carry on unhindered with the same character within other environments and with a fresh account and freshly named version of the same character within the same MUD environment. To the extent that there has been capital punishment at all, it is precisely as the LambdaMOO message expresses it: "Mr. Bungle is not the name of any player." The only thing that is dead, *in reality*, is the name Mr. Bungle and, even then, only within LambdaMOO.

If any punishment has been meted out, it seems more psychological than otherwise, and thus we could speculate about the intrapsychic effect on the NYU player of having had his character toaded. Dibbell appears to have carried out RL interviews with a number of the players, including the ones connected to the virtual victims, legba and Starsinger, but apparently he either had no opportunity to interview or did not seek out the NYU player. However, he does make a number of interesting observations:

> What *was* surprising, however, was that Mr. Bungle/Dr. Jest seemed to have taken the symbolism to heart. Dark themes still obsessed him—the objects he created gave off wafts of Nazi imagery and medical torture—but he no longer radiated the aggressively antisocial vibes he had before. He was a lot less unpleasant to look at (the outrageously seedy clown description had been replaced by that of a mildly creepy but actually rather natty young man, with "blue eyes . . . suggestive of conspiracy, untamed eroticism and perhaps a sense of understanding of the future"), and aside from the occasional jar-stuffing incident, also a lot less dangerous to be around. *It was obvious he'd undergone some sort of personal transformation in the days since I'd first glimpsed him in evangeline's crowded room—nothing radical maybe, but powerful nonetheless,* and resonant enough with my own experience, I felt, that it might be more than professionally interesting to talk with him, and perhaps compare notes. [pp. 392–393, italics added]

It seems noteworthy that in this passage in which he is alluding to psychological impact, Dibbell, no longer such a newcomer, begins to allow the conflation of character and player. Taken in context, he seems to be implying that it is the character pair that has made a "personal transformation" and that Dibbell would have a "professional interest to talk with" Dr. Jest/Mr. Bungle. Of course, this conflation is the central theme of Dibbell's article, which ends, "Increasingly, the complex magic of the MOO interests me more as a way to live the present than to understand the future. And it's usually not long before I . . . head back to the mansion, to see some friends" (p. 395).

We find similar conflations in most discussions of MUD experiences. Thus, in talking about a virtual wedding, Pavel Curtis (1996), the archwizard and creator of LambdaMOO, states,

> I do not know and cannot even speculate about whether or not the main participants in such ceremonies are usually serious or not, whether or not the MUD ceremony usually (or even ever) mirrors another ceremony in the real world, or even whether the bride and groom have ever met outside of virtual reality. . . . The very idea, however, brings up interesting and potentially important questions about the legal standing of commitments made only in virtual reality. Suppose, for example, that two people make a contract in virtual reality. Is that contract binding? [pp. 364–365]

Even more striking are Reid's (1996) comments: "Cyborgs are born out of virtual sex. At the moment of the virtual orgasm the line between player and character is the most clouded and the most transparent. Who it is that is communicating becomes unclear, and whether passion is being simulated on or transmitted through the MUD becomes truly problematic" (p. 341).

In the conflation between character and player, it seems apparent that something is happening. The toading process captures this perfectly. At the pure-player or pure-character level, it seems that little has happened. Mr. Bungle remains free to practice virtual sadism, either with the same name in other MUDs or with another name in the same MUD, and the NYU player is free to play in much the same way he has played, either in other MUDs or with another account in the same MUD. And yet, in the combined conflations of Mr. Bungle/NYU/Dr. Jest and Julian Dibbell/ Dr. Bombay, processes of transformation have occurred. Dibbell notes,

> I too was undergoing a transformation in the aftermath of that night in evangeline's, and I'm still not entirely sure what to make of it. As I pursued my runaway fascination with the discussion I had heard there, as I pored over the social debate and got to know legba and some of the other victims and witnesses, I could feel my newbie consciousness falling away from me. Where before I'd found it hard to take virtual rape seriously, I now was finding it difficult to remember how I could ever *not* have taken it seriously. I was proud to have arrived at this perspective—it felt like an exotic sort of achievement, and it definitely made my ongoing experience of the MOO a richer one. [p. 393]

As much as the processes of transformation are captured by toading, they are also apparent in the apprehension of the "rape in cyberspace." Dibbell states he has moved from a stance in which he "found it hard to take virtual rape seriously" to "finding it difficult to remember how I could ever *not* have taken it seriously." I will return to this statement momentarily, because in it I find one of the few, but most salient, weaknesses in Dibbell's presentation. First, however, since it leads us in an interesting direction, let me follow his argument a bit further. As Dibbell begins to take seriously cyber rape, he simultaneously begins to question other of his worldly views:

> Sometimes, for instance, it was hard for me to understand why RL society classifies RL rape alongside crimes against person or property. Since rape can occur without any physical pain or damage, I found myself reasoning, then it must be classified as a crime against the mind—more intimately and deeply hurtful, to be sure, than cross burnings, wolf whistles, and virtual rape, but undeniably located on the same conceptual continuum. I did not, however, conclude as a result that rapists were protected in any fashion by the First Amendment. Quite the opposite, in fact: the more seriously I took

the notion of virtual rape, the less seriously I was able to take the notion of freedom of speech, with its tidy division of the world into the symbolic and the real. [p. 393]

Paul Dowling (1996) makes a very similar point in his paper "Baudrillard 1–Piaget 0: Cyberspace, Subjectivity and the Ascension," extending the argument into a general condemnation of intellectual practices that simulate rationality and knowledge by producing simulacra (of which "the rape" is one) that have the function of concealing the absence of knowledge and rationality:

> Intellectual practices associated with the production of the mass media (management, engineering, journalism, etc.) and with the governance (the law, statistics) facilitate the codification and dissemination of illicit behavior. Thus a violent assault on a woman by a stranger is sublimated from a unique event within a community to an instance of a practice which is thereby reified. The intellectual extends the effectivity of patriarchy by establishing a fear of rape. In the UK, at least, it is men who are overwhelmingly the victims as well as the perpetrators of violent assault by strangers, yet it is women who are deterred from going out at night unless accompanied by a man. The rape is a unique event. Its codifications do not so much represent it as simulate a crime. [p. 12]

I find it of great interest that Dowling also enlists Matte-Blanco's notions of symmetry, asymmetry, and the fundamental antinomy between them in order to approach an understanding of some of the issues that confront us with cyberspace. In his work, however, Matte-Blanco facilitates the understanding of a use of cyberspace to develop something that Dowling labels a social unconscious through the ascension of subjectivity:

> The ultimate binary code of cybernetic practice corresponds to the good/ bad polarization of the unconscious. Being both binary states of single potentials, they both resolve to singularities: the individual unconscious being and the social unconscious being. Between these two extremes of

unconscious reside the various levels of individual/social subjectivity . . . within consciousness. This subjectivity is now antinomical to both poles of individual and social being. . . . Once subjectivity has been established, the antinomy can be resolved only by the constitution of the social unconscious. . . . We are now all caught in a global construction programme in the ascension to the technological social unconscious. [pp.16–17]

For both Dowling and Dibbell, the hard and fast distinction between rape and cyber rape become blurred in an analysis that dedifferentiates the symbolic or the virtual, and the real or the rational. How do we differentiate the cyber rape of legba or Starsinger from the hypothetical rape without pain or damage that Dibbell invokes as a highly implausible possibility? How do we understand the extension to cyberspace of the patriarchal codifications that, according to Dowling, deter woman, in resonance with the simulacrum, even though in England it may be men who are the more frequent victims?

Surprisingly, to me it is Dibbell rather than Dowling who produces the line of thought that is more in line with Matte-Blanco and transformational theory, even though Dowling's argument explicitly invokes Matte-Blanco. Dowling speaks of resolution of the antinomy as if this would be a goal, a favorable outcome, or even a nonpathological possibility. In fact, for Matte-Blanco, to be human is to exist within the fundamental irresolvability between experience that is organized at varying levels of symmetry and experience that is organized asymmetrically. The triadic nature of our being implies that the transformational work needed to relate these two disparate modes of experiencing must always be occurring in a fluid and flexible manner.

Dibbell captures this point brilliantly. If at times he wavers in his application of his own brilliant understanding, it may stand as testimony to the suasive, cult-like power of the Internet. Months after the virtual event, Dibbell interviews one of the players whose character was victimized by Mr. Bungle on the fateful night. It is important, for my discursive purposes, to note that elsewhere in the article Dibbell informs us that by this time he has become a devoted player himself. His experience, as Dibbell interviewing the "woman in Seattle," coexists and communicates with his experience as Dr. Bombay interacting with legba. He finds rich and textured ways of transforming these formidably different and variably organized ways of experiencing into each other. Of course, neither experience can exist, as it is experienced, on the other's terms, which is to say in keeping with the other's rules of experiential organization. Without transformational work, his experience as Dr. Bombay talking to legba in evangeline's room would be without sane meaning to Dibbell interviewing the woman in Seattle. Similarly, without transformation into something much more symmetrical, the sane meaning of the latter experience would create an artificial constriction in the nearly infinite plasticity of the MUDly world.

> Where virtual reality and its conventions would have us believe that legba and Starsinger were brutally raped in their own living room, here was the victim legba scolding Mr. Bungle for a breach of "civility." Where real life, on the other hand, insists that the incident was only an episode in a free-form version of Dungeons and Dragons, confined to the realm of the symbolic and at no point threatening any player's life, limb, or material well-being, here now was the player legba issuing aggrieved and heartfelt calls for Mr. Bungle's dismemberment. Ludicrously excessive by RL's lights, woefully understated by VR's. The tone of legba's response made sense *only in the buzzing, dissonant gap between them.*
>
> Which is to say it made the only kind of sense that *can* be made of MUDly phenomena. For while the *facts* attached to any event born of a MUD's strange, ethereal universe may march in straight, tandem lines separated neatly into the virtual and the real, *its meaning always lies in that gap.* [pp. 380–381, italics added]

I have quoted at length from Dibbell's article because, to my mind, it captures quite eloquently the power and the danger not only of MUDs but also of Internet relatedness in general. For those who develop the capacity to make meaning in that gap, the Internet has the capability of facilitating transformational processes in a manner that may, at least for the time, be stunted and thwarted in other venues because of the threats and exposure that may be felt in those venues. It is for those who can create meaning in the buzzing, dissonant gap that Sherry Turkle's (1995) romantic image of the MUD may hold: "On MUDs, the one can be many and the many can be one. . . . MUDs exemplify a phenomenon we shall meet often in these pages, that of computer-mediated experiences bringing philosophy down to earth" (p. 17).

For many of the people we have described and will describe, the Internet has facilitated experience in this gap between real life and virtual reality. They have found meaning in this experience between flesh and thought. When Dibbell states he has moved from a stance in which he "found it hard to take virtual rape seriously" to "finding it difficult to remember how I could ever *not* have taken it seriously," he aligns himself quite clearly with this group. My disagreement with Dibbell is not with him personally, for he is merely recounting his experience. I wish only to make it clear that his experience is not the only possible outcome. For many of the others we meet in these pages (and I might suspect that the NYU student/Mr. Bungle is one such person), the experience of Internet and email relationships fails to exist in this gap. For such people, being in an Internet relationship is not a matter of bringing philosophy down to earth; it is much more a matter of avoiding earth and avoiding any meaning of philosophy, whether that meaning be singular or multiple. As always, clinical data is helpful to amplify.

Clinical Example: The High-School Sweetheart—Version 1

Joel was raised from age 6 by his father and stepmother after having been abandoned by his mother at age 4½. Throughout his youth, he and his father maintained a limited, but generally satisfactory, relationship. Joel had always felt that his relationship with his father might have been much better were it not for the limitations imposed on it by the stepmother. Although she was not outwardly rejecting of him, Joel never felt comfortable with her, nor did she ever make an active attempt to become anything other than Joel's father's wife. However, Joel retained blurry, but rich, memories of his lost mother. In his most vivid memory, he sees her sitting with him on the front porch, playing jacks and in the memory (which he places, perhaps gratuitously, on the day of her departure) they are both laughing lovingly at their mutual ineptitude.

For a few years during his early adolescence, Joel probed his father for information about his mother and about her abandonment, but his father steadfastly refused to engage him on the subject and eventually Joel gave up. He was a strong student, reasonably skilled in sports, and attractive enough that as a teenager, despite his shyness, girls gravitated in his direction. After backing away from serious relationships with several of them, Joel became infatuated with a girl named Laurel who had pursued him relentlessly over a several-month period. At Laurel's insistence, they teamed up to try to locate his mother. They checked newspaper records, the Department of Vital Statistics, phone books from several major cities in the area— all to no avail. At one point, as their relationship approached a sexual crescendo, they even ran away for a day, ostensibly in search of a private investigator. That day proved catastrophic to the relationship. Laurel's father, an Englishman who had always been hesitant about raising his daughter in the States, seized on the opportunity to force the family's hasty return to their family home in northern England. For a brief time, Laurel and Joel corresponded, but he felt the heartbreak of distance and the limitations of correspondence too keenly, and soon, in the frenzy of preparations for college, he forgot about her, and about the search for his mother, almost entirely.

Soon after college, while in his first year of business school, Joel met the woman who would become his wife. Although their relationship was never a passionate one, Joel felt that he loved his wife and that, by and large, his marriage had been a happy one for the sixteen years they had been together. They had three children, a nice suburban lifestyle, a bit of economic security from his job as an investment banker, and a reasonably fulfilling sex life. As his father grew older and increasingly infirm, Joel's relationship with him grew even more distant, but his neutral feelings toward the stepmother had grown warmer as he witnessed her devotion to his father throughout a long and painful illness.

It was, in fact, his father's death that occasioned an unexpected email from Laurel, some 20 years subsequent to their last contact with each other. Unbeknownst to Joel, his father and Laurel's father, who had conducted business together many years earlier, had maintained much better contact with each other than their children had. When Laurel heard about Joel's father's death from her father, she sent him a fairly innocuous email to express her condolences. Joel responded civilly, asking her in return a few perfunctory questions about her life. A few weeks later, Laurel—who was also married with three children—responded, still casually, with a few inquiries about Joel's life. Joel responded the next morning and received her response that same day. The subsequent relationship grew more fervent, even passionate, at a rapid pace. Joel's business equipped him with earphones and a speaker wire for his telephone contacts, so that his hands were almost always free at his keyboard to be in contact with Laurel. As their on-line love life grew more intense, Joel found himself coming into the office earlier and earlier, so that he could take full advantage of the time difference to chat on-line with Laurel while her husband was safely away at work. For some time he succeeded in convincing his wife that his early rising was a necessary part of his business, but as his on-line involvement with Laurel grew more compelling, his increasing distance from the family grew sufficiently more pronounced that eventually his wife grew suspicious. When she confronted him with her doubts, he confessed to the on-line relationship.

When Joel and his wife entered couples therapy with a colleague of mine, Joel was quite clear that although he felt that he loved his wife and family, he had no intention or desire to end his on-line relationship with Laurel. Even if its existence threatened to undo the marriage, he found himself compelled to continue it. With the couples therapy at a complete impasse, Joel was referred for individual treatment.

In individual therapy it became clear to Joel quite quickly that his on-line relationship with Laurel constituted a replacement of his lost relationship with the flesh-and-blood Laurel of his adolescence. Even more profoundly, he understood this substitution to be for the mother who had played jacks with him on the stoop, whose loss he had never truly been able to mourn. It also became clear that not only did Joel have no desire to end the on-line relationship, but, like Miranda in the previous chapter, Joel had no desire to consummate it in real life. In every moment of every encounter on-line Joel simultaneously undid and redid his earlier losses. As a bright, psychologically insightful man, Joel brought these understandings to his own attention as he talked on in therapy. But for all the talking, he found himself no closer to a solution. He didn't want to leave the on-line relationship and he didn't want to leave the marriage. In fact, it was only when he came to realize that he didn't want to leave the therapy either, that Joel began to understand the way in which he was *avoiding meaning* no matter where he was living. Joel's case seems not to fit into Dibble's notion of living in the gap between real life and virtual reality. For Joel, virtual reality was ubiquitous; he could find it on-line, in a superficial marriage, at work, even in the superficial insight of a pseudo-therapy. Actually to be involved would be to suffer loss of a magnitude that he feared more greatly than he had even begun to imagine.

Clinical Example: The High-School Sweetheart—Version 2

Unlike Joel, Rex was keenly aware of his dissatisfaction with his marriage, and with the rest of his life, when he was contacted by his high-school girlfriend. With his life eroded by addictions to drugs and alcohol, Rex had sought drug treatment in a community mental health center at a point when the substances, which he had pursued as his only source of relief, had begun to attack him as relentlessly as he felt attacked in every other aspect of living.

Rex was raised in a middle-class, West Coast suburban neighborhood as the youngest child by five years in a family of eight. His father owned a small, local store, putting in sixteen-hour days and earning just enough to support the overflowing household, and his mother drank away any excess there might have been. At age 7, Rex was sexually abused one night by his chronically drunk eldest brother. Beginning two years later he had an ongoing sexual relationship with a 16-year-old neighbor girl who took care of him after school, by which time of day his mother was generally too drunk to manage. Recalling those encounters, which lasted for at least a year, Rex reported to his therapist that he had felt excited and afraid, that he felt put upon and forced into something he was unsure he wanted at the same time that he looked forward to the encounters and hated days when something prevented them from getting together. When the girl went away to college, Rex had felt both relief and a very familiar emptiness.

Rex began to drink and smoke pot daily while still in middle school. He joined ranks with a small group of teenagers, many of whom were similarly neglected. They went to school as little as they could get away with and stayed out at night almost every night, wandering the streets or lingering in one or another basement apartment or garage to smoke and drink. When Rex was 15, Nancy wandered into this loosely knit group and for the next two years they hung out together. Since they had sex with each other, usually after taking large amounts of quaaludes, they called themselves boyfriend and girlfriend, and Rex recalled feeling as much comfort in that as he did in being part of the group; both affiliations were better than nothing, but so little better that they felt as depriving as they did satisfying. At 17, Rex dropped out of school and moved away to live and work with the brother who had abused him years earlier, who now owned an auto-body shop in another state. Rex had never given Nancy another thought.

After learning the trade from his brother and saving up enough money to go out on his own, Rex moved East for no reason other than to get away. He got a reasonably high-paying job as a lead mechanic and for a few years he managed to stay away from drugs. During that time, he saved up enough to form a partnership with one of the other mechanics at work and together they opened their own shop. His partner also introduced Rex to the partner's sister, and within a year Rex was married, and had a successful business, and his wife was pregnant. In retrospect, through his reports to his therapist, Rex knew from the very beginning that he was in trouble. If he felt good for a moment about the partner's friendship and trust, about his wife's expressions of love, or about the idea of having a child, he felt trapped, dishonest, and threatened in the very next moment. The night Rex's wife went into labor, he went out on a binge. His son was 2 weeks old before he saw him for the first time.

Rex's substance abuse continued for the next several years. For whatever their own reasons may have been, both his wife and his brother-in-law clung to their conviction that Rex would be able to turn the corner and straighten himself out again. For his part, Rex had no such faith. As much as he may have hated himself for doing drugs and for drinking, he found his only solace in the solitude of intoxication. He told his therapist that he might have continued that way forever. However, one night he may have indulged himself too much, or else the years of abuse caught up with him. He recalls sitting at the kitchen table one minute and then waking up on a table in the emergency room with his wife and brother-in-law peering over him. He remained unsure whether it was brought about by the seizure or by the threats from his family, but after that night Rex sought sobriety and therapy.

Against a backdrop of depressed resignation, not knowing whether it was something he wanted to do or something he was being forced into, Rex had been struggling through eight months of relative progress, punctuated by a few brief slips, when he received an unsolicited email from his old girlfriend Nancy. In fact, it was Rex's wife who read the message first, since Rex rarely used the Internet himself. In therapy, he reported the event in a brief aside and then didn't speak of it again for several months. But in the meantime, the on-line relationship flourished. During the nighttime hours that Rex had previously spent in intoxication, he was now glued to the screen of the VDT. He would log on as soon as his wife went to bed and then stay on-line for hours. Rex had never read nor written as much in his life, but the feeling he had was a familiar one nonetheless. Typically, Nancy would start a subject—and progressively the subject became them and their relationship—and Rex would respond. The feeling of the connection itself, in the darkness illuminated only by the screen, was compelling, but he never felt connected to the content of the exchanged text. He would find himself incredibly aroused as Nancy communicated to him her aroused need for him, but when he reached orgasm it felt as autoerotic as any other masturbatory act. When he did, finally, bring the subject up in therapy, he recalled that the quaalude-blurred sex of years before had the same eery lonely quality at the point of climax. Just as he had tried to drown out the fear of his wife's awakening when he was drugging, he tried now to cloak himself in the intensity of his experience with Nancy to mask all other thought, and, seasoned as he was at this sort of indulgent avoidance, he always felt himself hinged between exposure and suffocation. As time went on, he found her pressuring him to be on-line more, to make phone contact, to plan a trip for them to meet. The day he broached the subject to his therapist came just after the first night that he had bought drugs before going on-line.

In the Internet return of his teenage relationship, Rex had found himself in an all-too-familiar confusion between attention and abuse, between salvation and condemnation, and, most frighteningly, between self-indulgence and self-destruction. Unlike the subjects of the Carnegie-Mellon report, he was neither more depressed nor more isolated than he had been before. But unlike Turkle's or Dibbell's MUDders he had not brought philosophy down to earth, nor had he found meaning in the gap between real life and virtual reality. Like Joel, Rex had merely discovered in the Internet a technology that facilitated a new way of repeating an old pattern of experience.

Discussion

In very different ways, both Joel and Rex had developed ways of living that were built around isolative structures. For Joel, these structures included the very elements of life that seemed, superficially, to have been endowing his life with meaning—his work, his wife, his children, his social circle. For Rex, alcohol and drugs brought him the isolation he appeared to need. Although their ways of isolating themselves were so different, Rex and Joel resembled each other to the extent that each was living within an isolating cell that was, itself, constructed within the perimeter of an outwardly related way of being. To live out the interpersonally related portions of their lives, which they both needed as a kind of moat around the fortress that protected them, both Joel and Rex used aspects of their personalities as emissaries.

D. W. Winnicott (1960) introduced the concept of the *false self* to describe how we establish ways of being to protect us against the sense of disappointment, rejection, shame, and, in more severe cases, retaliation that we fear would greet us were we to be more truly spontaneous.[20] For Winnicott, if we are raised in good-enough circumstance, that is, in a situation in which our spontaneous gestures are recognized and responded to favorably often enough, the false self will be a less significant part of way of our being than it will in circumstances in which our spontaneity is thwarted, unrecognized, or retaliated against. He writes, in particular, about a situation in which the mother—for Winnicott the mother is always the relevant environment—cannot emotionally survive the child's more destructive actions and thoughts (Winnicott 1971).[21] In these cases the person may learn ways in which to be with people, but never really learn to make use of them in any meaningful way. In such cases, people are constricted to such a limited role that they can be little more than projections of what the false self needs them to be in order to protect the unexpressed spontaneous self from being destroyed. In such constricted roles, people can never emerge, in relation to the false self, as "others" with their own subjective experiences and beings. In circumstances such as these, the purpose to which other people are put is the maintaining of a safe but insular status quo. The object of the false self can never be a transitional object. But long before they ever logged online, Joel and Rex had both crafted well-fashioned ways of engaging the world of others in what Winnicott calls false-self organizations. Given that constricted way of relating, an Internet relationship had no more hope of becoming transitional than any other relationship in which they might engage.

In the bi-logic vernacular of Matte-Blanco, to maintain rich relationships with other people requires the simultaneous experience of the symmetry of empathic identification (in terms both of what we put out and what we take in) and the asymmetry of individual, subjective difference. Joel had learned to insulate himself from repetitions of unendurable loss by adopting a totally different, and much more restrictive, strategy. Like the people at the other end of his earphones and speaker wire at work, all others—his wife and children included, perhaps even foremost—were symmetrically identical with each other. As potential abandoners, Joel needed to be in contact with everyone without touching them or letting them touch him. As such, the technology of the Internet proved an ideal vehicle, but he had done quite well at the task before the Internet. Similarly, Rex had learned to protect himself from abuse and misuse by relegating all external others to the same, symmetrical, drug- and alcohol-induced blur. He could, in fact he had to, remain in contact with others only by superimposing in front of them the sepia haze of substances that rendered their individual features indistinguishable from each other. Once again, the video display of the Internet connection facilitated a way of making contact, while not exposing himself to the risk of being touched, but this was a way of being with others that he had learned long before the Internet entered his life.

We remain closely linked to Winnicott, but closer to the experience of Dibbell and Turkle, when we look at a different form of false self etiology. In his essay on risk and solitude, Adam Phillips (1993) follows Winnicott's discussion of the therapist who makes early interpretations and the mother who insinuates herself on the infant so perniciously that the infant is unable to enter the magical world of omnipotent creation of the other from which emotional growth proceeds. Phillips relates the story of a patient, a 16-year-old boy, who portrays himself as a loner and a risk merchant, but who had been terrified of the water until age 10. The boy reports, "I knew I was safer out of my depth because even though I couldn't stand, there was more water to hold me up." Phillips concludes, "One of the central paradoxes for the adolescent is his discovery that only the object beyond his control can be found to be reliable" (p. 30). In treating his body as one of these objects, the adolescent takes risks in order to find the reliability of this object that he has never known. "In the usual risks of adolescence—that stage of legitimate criminality and illicit solitude—the adolescent survives danger *in a kind of virtual or 'as if'* absence of maternal care" (p. 32, italics added). However, if the adolescent (following the infant's lead) is too concerned about the reactions of the actual mother (or her surrogates of which his corporeal existence is seen to be one), he cannot enter into this developmentally necessary phase of risk taking. For fear of bringing about irreparable damage to the object (his body in one case, his mother in another), the adolescent must remain in a constricted state of self-expression that permits neither risk nor solitude. One of the possibilities in a case like this is that a falsely compliant, timid way of being comes to predominate over any more spontaneous and truly self-expressive existence.

In the following case, a teenager who was overwhelmed by "maternal care" uses Internet relationships to find the "virtual absence" of such care.

Clinical Example: A Teenage Escape

Lydia was the only child of a well-to-do couple who had married late and suffered a number of lost pregnancies prior to her, quite difficult, birth. In the fifth month of the pregnancy Lydia's mother, Grace, took a leave from her successful career as a corporate attorney and never returned to work, devoting herself instead to her daughter's well-being. In a community in which live-in child care was the sine qua non of parenting, Grace refused outside help of any sort. Lydia was 7 years old before she had her first baby-sitter, and then it was only because her mother had to undergo a surgical procedure that left her unable to care for her daughter herself. Lydia's father, Stewart, was also devoted to his daughter and, anxious by nature, he welcomed his wife's decision and supported it fully.

Although they could have afforded almost anything, Stewart and Grace were careful not to lavish material goods on their daughter; the toys Grace bought her were almost always educational games that they could play together. Similarly, Lydia's social calendar was typically a full one, but the activities almost invariably were ones in which Grace, or occasionally Stewart, could play a guiding and watchful role. Grace was a perpetual classmother throughout early school years, a scout leader, an assistant at dance class, and present at every birthday party and class trip, and Stewart was the coach of Lydia's softball and soccer teams. The family never went skiing or sledding and Lydia was never permitted to do skating, horseback riding, gymnastics, or any other activity that the parents perceived as being potentially dangerous. The issue of sleep-overs or sleep-away camp never emerged, because Lydia never voiced any desire to spend time apart from her parents.

Lydia was a bright, energetic child with abundant talents. Through elementary and middle school, she did well in her classes and in those athletic activities that she was allowed to pursue. She made friends easily and was generally perceived by those friends' parents and by her teachers as the ideal child. The first signs of trouble began to reveal themselves when Lydia was 14, when she began to stay home from school an inordinate amount because of illness. At first Grace was worried about her child's medical condition, but rounds of visits to physicians of all sorts ruled out a sufficient underlying medical condition to explain all the illnesses. Eventually, Lydia was referred for psychotherapy and, very reluctantly, Grace brought her to treatment with a woman she, herself, had visited many years earlier after one of the lost pregnancies.

For the first few sessions Grace insisted on staying in the room with her daughter, and even then it took a good deal of firmness on the therapist's part to get some time alone with the child. During those first few sessions, Lydia barely spoke other than to confirm her mother's statements in a soft, depressive voice. For her part, Grace offered little insight into her daughter's illnesses; the only unusual behavior she had noticed was that Lydia was spending a great deal of time on the computer, playing video games and doing research for school papers.

Much to her therapist's surprise, Lydia began to talk in a manner that seemed quite open as soon as her mother left the room. She complained about her parents' overprotectiveness, about her lack of a social life, about her mother's "breathing every breath" for her; but, for all of her talking, Lydia did little to explain to her therapist why, if she wanted more freedom, she chose to avoid school, which was the one place where her mother wasn't. They met for several months, and in occasional meetings with the parents, the therapist pressed for them to extend the girl a bit more freedom. Reluctantly, the parents acceded to the request, but although Lydia seemed a bit more cheerful, her symptoms continued unchecked.

A few months into the treatment, after Lydia had begun to trust her therapist a bit more, the therapist had occasion, in response to something Lydia said in passing, to recall Grace's comments about computer games. Lydia gave the therapist a sly grin and admitted that she did like computer games (the gorier the better) but that she rarely played them anymore. In fact, Lydia revealed that Grace knew nothing at all about computers, to the point of phobia about them. Most of the time that she was supposedly playing games or doing research, Lydia spent surfing the Net, right under her mother's nose. Her life on-line was one place where Grace left her entirely alone.

Little by little, usually with a good deal of embarrassment, Lydia opened up to her therapist about her private world. As Lydia began to talk, her therapist, who was not especially conversant with computers either, worried that Lydia was reporting dissociative behavior as the girl talked about the different personalities she assumed on-line—a daredevil female sky diver, a macho ski bum from Vale, a sadistic lesbian who loved chains, a gay male transvestite who was considering a sex change operation, a poker-playing former heroin addict who bred pit bull terriers. It took Lydia's teenage insistence that "everybody does it," along with the girl's broad grin and spontaneous vitality as she spoke of her chat room worlds, to make it clear to her therapist that these rooms were Lydia's playground.

Initially the therapist found herself recalling newspaper stories about girls being lured into apartments and raped after on-line encounters. She felt, but resisted, an overwhelming need to tell Lydia to be cautious about her behavior, understanding instinctively the dangers of repeating Grace's suffocating overprotectiveness. Instead, in a moment of inspiration, the therapist said to Lydia, "So . . . let's chat." For the next fifteen minutes Lydia helped her therapist with the unfamiliar activity of playing out different personae in an "on-line" world that they created by turning their chairs so that they sat back-to-back, writing notes and passing them over their heads to each other.

After the session Lydia asked her mother if she could increase her sessions to twice weekly and for the next two months Lydia and her therapist developed and embellished their "on-line relationships." After a month, Grace reported in a collateral visit that Lydia had missed only two days of school and by the end of the second month of "on-line" therapy play, the symptoms had vanished completely. As Lydia began to take advantage of the increases in freedom that her parents had granted her, the therapy began to shift back from "on-line play" to earnest, typically teen-age, discussions about her concerns, fantasies, and adventures with sex, drinking, smoking cigarettes, doing drugs, and taking risks.

Discussion

Expanding on Winnicott's view of the adolescent as an isolate, Phillips (1993) theorizes as follows:

> The infant depends on the mother and her care to prevent him from being out of his depth; in adolescence, as we know, this protection is both wished for and defied. Risks are taken as part of the mastery of noncompliance. One way the adolescent differentiates himself, discovers his capacity for soli-tude—for self-reliance that is not merely a triumph over his needs for the object—is by taking and making risks. He needs, unconsciously, to endan-ger his body, *to experiment with representations of it.* [p. 31]

Turkle (1995) observed,

> The Internet is another element of the computer culture that has contrib-uted to thinking about identity as multiplicity. On it, people are able to build a self by cycling through many selves. . . . The Internet has become a sig-nificant social laboratory for experimenting with the constructions and reconstructions of self that characterize postmodern life. In its virtual re-ality, we self-fashion and self-create. [pp. 178, 180]

Prevented by parental omnipresence from risk-taking in the flesh, Lydia happened upon the Internet as a realm in which she could try, as Phillips suggests, "to survive danger *in a kind of virtual or 'as if'* absence of mater-nal care." By creating and re-creating versions of herself and cycling through them, Lydia made use of the Internet to try on different ways of being until the world could provide her a more direct vehicle for alterations in self-expression. She could not find a way to take risks in the flesh, but in the Internet worlds that she forged between flesh and thought she found for herself a place to grow.

Rex and Joel lived in experiential states of paranoid withdrawal that simulated, but were not, intimately related to the world of others. For each of them, the Internet, and the relationships that they maintained through it, offered little more than a technologically altered version of the only way of being which they could tolerate. For people whose lives are confined in such paranoiac withdrawal, experience becomes dimensionally constricted. All experience, no matter what the backdrop—marriage, parenting, business, real-life affairs, or Internet relationships—will inevitably be transformed into the identical dimensional confines. For people like Joel and Rex, it takes much more than passive exposure to alter the experiential fortress in which they find themselves confined. Even psychotherapy will devolve into a similar simulation unless the therapist can find a way to bring about a radically different transformation of the experience.

Fortunately for Lydia, the constriction in which she found herself was more circumscribed, more open to change. As suffocating as her parents may have been, their overprotectiveness was not the psychotoxic (Spitz 1965) equivalent of the abandonment or the drunken abuse of Joel's or Rex's mother. Lydia's internal world allowed for the possibility of alternative transformations of experience, given the proper circumstances in her surrounding environment. For Lydia, the Internet proved to be just such a facilitating environment[22] in which transitional, and transformational, processes could take root. In many ways, the work that Lydia continued in her psychotherapy began, and flourished, on-line.

Lydia's case illustrates a transitional and potentially transformational experience of relating on the Internet, while the cases of Joel and Rex exemplify an Internet of repetition and fixity. The following case is more problematic, because it remains unclear whether the Internet is facilitating, debilitating, or irrelevant.

Clinical Example: The Virtual Volley

Tonja requested, through a friend, to be interviewed about her on-line experience. She is a strikingly attractive, light-skinned African-American woman in her mid-forties, married with four children to a Filipino-born, Hawaiian-raised man who is twenty years her senior. Tonja and Santos, who were both trained as architects, met on her first job after college. She was on the rebound from a three-year relationship with a man she had been sure she would marry as soon as she graduated and found work, but who had, instead, told her that he was breaking off the relationship because his family would never accept an interracial marriage. Santos had been her boss's boss, a man universally recognized to have such extraordinary talent and creativity that he was on his way to greatness. When Santos began to pay attention to her, Tonja flew into his embrace with boundless relief and with the expectation that she would be taken care of, and loved, forever.

Tonja was the middle of three daughters. Her parents, both of whom were raised in urban ghettos, lived on the border between suburbia and the city. Theirs was a predominantly white, middle-class neighborhood where they struggled, not just to make ends meet, but to keep up with the signs of material success of any neighbors, almost all of whom were better off than they. She considers her mother the primary agent of this futile keeping-up-with-the-Joneses quest. The mother was a beautiful, dark-skinned, chronically depressed, helpless woman, who disapproved of Tonya more than Tonya's sisters not only because Tonja was, by far, the most accomplished, but also because she was, by far, the lightest.

At age 14, Tonja lost her elder sister in a car accident, and her mother slid into a reclusive state from which she never emerged. Tonja also felt that she lost her father at the same time. Although he remained vital and committed to both work and his family, Tonja felt that the spark that had always been there between the two of them was doused, especially as he spent more and more of his time attending to her mother's depression. As the oldest remaining child, the household upkeep became her responsibility. In fact, it was only because she was such a gifted student, and athlete, that she was able to escape, on a full scholarship to an excellent college. Even then, she had felt guilty for abandoning her father, but once she was away at school on the opposite side of the country, she dreaded her trips back.

Soon after Tonya and Santos married, they moved to Hawaii, where Santos opened his own firm. For some time, Tonja worked with him, even after the birth of her first two children. During that time, the company thrived, as his creative genius and her ability to keep the operation organized and efficient coalesced into a perfect business synergy. At home, however, there was never such successful synergy. As soon as they were married, and even more after the children began to come, Tonja felt Santos withdraw from her into his work, into the material objects with which he surrounded himself, and into a brooding, pervasive depression that Tonja recognized all too well.

With Tonja no longer providing organization at their company, Santos's inattention to details began to take a toll. Where previously the money had flowed in like water, it soon became a struggle to cover expenses. As the debts increased, Santos's mood became even more acutely dysphoric and, despite the financial woes, he spent even more on material possessions, which Tonja came to see as compensatory to his depression. Their relationship, which had languished previously, became stormier as conditions worsened. A real-estate slowdown proved to be the telling blow. So far in debt that they could barely avoid bankruptcy, the couple sold what was left of their business, their house, and as many possessions as they needed to, and returned to the mainland. Santos took a high-paying job in a big firm, not far from where Tonja had grown up and she went back to school part time with the hopes of returning to architecture, on her own, once the children were out of the house.

With the economic catastrophe behind them, Tonja and Santos tried to repair some of the damage that had threatened their marriage. For some time, Tonja experienced a dramatic improvement. They spent more time together and with the children, and took some pleasure in planning their lives together. As Santos grew more miserable in his work—he hated being an employee—he began to slip, once again, into depression and into the material objects that he tried to use as a manic defense against the experience of that depression. Still, Tonja felt much more comfortable in the relationship; she found herself able to talk to Santos, as she never had been able to earlier, about their troubles, and these talks frequently proved rewarding. At the same time, Tonja was moving closer to a level at which she could get a decent job herself and, with two of her children in college and the remaining two very self-sufficient, she felt that this was the direction she should take.

Like Tonja, her next to the youngest daughter, Sheri, was a highly gifted athlete whose sport of choice was tennis. As a ninth-grader, the girl was already the best player on her high-school team and, with talk of a possible professional career, Santos scraped together the money to send her to a top-level, summer-long training camp. The parents were invited to spend the first weekend to help the children move in and to get to know the facility, but, since Santos had important meetings, Tonja took her daughter up alone. Herself an excellent player, who had almost always won the club tournaments when they lived in Hawaii, Tonja was beating Sheri for the first time in two years when she noticed that they were being watched by an exceptionally handsome young man. After the match was over—Tonja had played even better under scrutiny, but lost nonetheless—the young man came over and introduced himself as one of the leaders of the group that Sheri would be in.

From the moment she met him, Tonja was infatuated with Jens. Tall and blond, like her college boyfriend, he spoke with the slightest hint of a Scandinavian accent, and with his strong, broad shoulders and his sturdy stance he looked to her like he could carry the weight of the world. As they stood in the sun and chatted about the camp, Tonja guessed his age to be about 25, but the difference in their ages didn't stop her from responding to his overtly flirtatious gestures with her own, somewhat clumsy seductiveness. When they parted Sheri reprimanded her mother sternly for embarrassing her. But Tonja was so excited and aroused that she barely noticed her daughter's complaints, and that afternoon she basked in the afterglow of the encounter the entire drive home, her mind overflowing with sexual fantasies.

When she got home she looked through the paperwork to find out everything she could about Jens. At first she was taken aback to learn that he was only 22, but after a minute's reflection she decided that there was no difference between 22 and 25. The only other information about him was that he had grown up in Denmark until he was 12, that he had just graduated from college and that he was looking forward to a career as a tennis pro. She also noticed that each of the instructors had an email address. Tonja had become a bit familiar with the Internet through her schoolwork and had been keeping in touch with a few of her friends back in Hawaii via email.

That night Tonja felt as though she was assaulting Santos in bed, and in the middle of having sex she began to fantasize that he might have a heart attack. This was a fear she often had, given his high blood pressure and the fact that he always seemed under stress, but when she thought about the fantasy afterward she smiled, guiltily, with the realization that this time she was less afraid of his death than she was eager for it.

For a couple of days Tonja toyed with the idea of sending Jens an email, and on the third day, seeing that it would be three weeks until she would visit Sheri, she screwed up her courage, sat down at the keyboard and typed: "Hi, Jens . . . just thought I would check on how Sheri is doing. I bet you can teach the grown-ups a thing or two too." She stared at the text on the screen, pressed Delete and Undelete several times, then moved the mouse arrow over and clicked on Send. For a moment she sat horrified by what she had done, then searched desperately for the Unsend button, but realized to her dismay that her new browser didn't allow her to Unsend a message.

For the next day Tonja kept returning to her email account to see if Jens had replied. By the day after, she had decided that she would either ignore him completely when she went up to visit Sheri, or she would try to cover up her faux pas by offering to pay him for a private lesson. Two days later, having decided that she would just ignore him, she found an email from Jens waiting when she logged on: "Hi Tonja . . . Sorry I didn't answer you but I didn't even know I had this email address until today. Sheri is doing great, the best in her group! She must have learned from her mother. . . . You know your name sounds Danish, but I guess it can't be (LOL). Keep in touch. Jens."

Tonja read and reread the email, savoring every nuance of meaning that she could twist into a hint that Jens was interested in her. Encouraged by the wealth of these nuances, Tonja sent back a reply, this time without hesitation or afterthought: "Thanks for the good news about Sheri. I'm interested to learn more about the man in charge of my daughter. . . . Is tennis the only game you play?"

Just as her sexual appetite had been aroused a few days earlier, the stimulation of the email exchange seemed to infuse Tonja's entire being with a zest for life that she hadn't felt in years. Over the next two days, periodically thinking about Jens in fantasies about what might come to be, Tonja poured herself into the final tasks that remained for her to complete her masters in architecture. Always a competent housekeeper, she whipped the house into an order it had never had since the day the family moved in. She began to make social dates that she had been avoiding out of fear of exposing Santos's (and to some extent her own) depression. Not surprisingly, she made a date with her local tennis pro to begin intensive lessons.

In the eye of the hurricane of Tonja's activity was the screen of her computer. As she bustled about, her mind brimming, she returned with increasing frequency to the screen, to see if Jens had responded. By the end of the second day without a response, her burst of energy began to flag and she felt herself succumbing to a depression that was all that much stronger than it had been, because now she felt additionally depleted by the energy she had just expended. Just as she was on the verge of plunging into abject hopelessness, Tonja found a long message from Jens in her incoming mailbox. The message began with an apology for having taken so long to respond but explained the delay by saying that he had been so stimulated by her question that he didn't want to send the reply until he had answered it. The answer was a short autobiography. He wrote to her about his childhood, his parents, his dating history, what he had studied in college, and about his ambitions. Although Tonja knew at some level that she *should* find the email sophomoric, she found it nonetheless intoxicating. In his plaintive neediness she felt him reaching out for her, and she didn't care to scrutinize if that reach was for a mother or a lover.

In the letter, Jens had spoken about his dreams to start a tennis camp of his own with some ideas that he thought would make it both unusual and successful. In her response, Tonja focused on this dream, rather than on anything that might reflect her interest in a relationship. Encouraging him to move forward on his dream, she found even more energy for herself and her own efforts. As soon as she was through with the email, she opened up her word processor and revised her résumé. That evening, when she informed Santos she was ready to go back to work, she was surprised and delighted to hear him not only approve but also offer to ask around to find out where there might be suitable openings.

For the next two weeks, Tonja's life was a blur of activity. Santos had quickly found a number of possible positions and Tonja was delighted to learn that the doors seemed to be open everywhere for a talented, well-qualified woman of color. Every day brought either a new interview or a call-back for an old one. By the time Tonja was due to go to visit Sheri again, she already had two offers on the table—from companies that were willing to give her time to finish her degree—and it seemed that two higher paying and more prestigious offers were likely to follow any minute. Throughout these two weeks, the email exchanges occurred, at the very least, daily, and the tenor of the postings remained largely that of two friends pushing each other to pursue their ambitions. Occasionally Tonja included a comment that could be read between the lines to have a sexual, or at least a relational, innuendo, but these remarks seems to fall on the Internet equivalent of deaf ears. Aside from his encouraging words to her, and his daily feedback on Sheri's progress at the camp, Jens seemed most concerned with how he might go about raising the money he was going to need to begin his own operation. So it was at that level that Tonja answered most of the time. As the scheduled visit grew closer, Tonja's anticipatory anxiety made her feel as though her skin was going to explode. Having hoped beyond hope that Santos would, once again, find an excuse to avoid the trip, Tonja felt both angry and disappointed when he announced that he had booked a room for them in a top-of-the-line resort in the next town over and was going to drive up with her and stay for the weekend. She was clearly unable to conceal her reactions completely, because with surprise and anger of his own, Santos remarked, accurately enough, that she seemed disappointed that he had done the very thing she was always asking him to do.

The weekend proved to be an emotional disaster for Tonja, although she was careful to keep all of her emotions very well concealed. Sheri and Santos both complained to her that she was remote and uninvolved, and although she apologized and explained that she was preoccupied about the new job possibilities, the best Tonja could do was to remain distant. Inwardly she felt destroyed. All her hopes for the relationship with Jens seemed to vanish. He was polite and appropriate with her, as he might have been with any of the other mothers, but, if anything, he seemed to prefer Santos's company to her own. He had even given Santos, whose tennis was pathetic in comparison to her own, a free private lesson. During the entire weekend he uttered not a single word that she could remotely construe as personal. On the drive home, Santos made matters even worse, not only by complaining once again about her disengagement, but by mentioning Jens several times. He told her about the young man's ideas for starting up a new camp and said, to Tonja's bafflement, that the idea was the sort of thing he, himself, had always wanted to do.

When they got home and Tonja went to her computer there was an email from Jens waiting for her: "Hi T . . . seems we didn't get much chance to chat over the w/e. I guess on-line is easier sometimes. Santos is great and he had some wonderful ideas. He is such a lucky guy. Some people get everything. Hope to hear from you soon. J" Tonja stared at the email for some time. It felt so impersonal and rejecting, even though she could tell it was intended to flatter her. She had the urge, which she resisted, to show it to Santos or to print it out and tear it up. Instead she shut off her computer and, atypically for her, got up and poured herself a drink.

For two days she resisted writing, but after she got a job offer for twenty-thousand dollars more than she had even dreamed of, from one of the metropolitan area's most prestigious firms, she couldn't refrain any longer. She told Jens about her offer, inquired after her daughter, and ended by saying, "It seems that you value Santos more than you value me. Is that a Danish thing?"

Jens's immediate reply was enthusiastic about her new job and, for the first time, it made no mention of her daughter. It ended: "I had been wondering what had happened to you the past couple of days. I guess saying nice things about your husband isn't the way to your heart. Is that a black thing?"

Thrilled at the response, and immediately catapulted out of her depression, Tonja responded with her most direct reply to date: "Don't you know you don't need to find a way to my heart?" But in his next message, Jens ignored the remark completely. His attention had turned, once again, to how he was going to raise the money to start his camp. Still feeling captivated by the remark that she interpreted as his desire to have her heart, Tonja jumped on the bandwagon and offered her help to raise money for him. He accepted her offer enthusiastically.

For the next few weeks Tonja prepared for her new job, which would start the day after they brought Sheri home from camp, and she pulled out the stops in putting her organizational skills together to try to help Jens. Realizing that there was no way she was going to do this without Santos knowing, she enlisted his help, relying on the enthusiasm for the project that he had expressed. She even suggested to Jens that he make Santos a partner in the scheme. In those weeks her energy levels again felt boundless. She was excited about the new job and read up on all the things she felt she might need to know for it at the same time that she put the finishing touches on her masters thesis project. But even as she worked in all these different ways, Tonja's mind was constantly on the next, and last, visit to the camp. She felt desperate to advance the relationship. In lurid detail, she pictured the two of them in bed. She envisioned them running off together. With her desperation, her email messages grew increasingly bold, increasingly suggestive, and increasingly frequent. But Jens seemed to manage to fail to grasp every double entendre. His own emailings were jovial and playful, even occasionally interpretable as a bit flirtatious, but he steadfastly avoided any overt references to a relationship that they might have with each other and stuck to his single-minded focus—raising money. Jens's hesitance to respond on a more personal level bothered Tonja, but she attributed it to his reticence and became even more openly seductive in her own email postings.

Two days before she and Santos were scheduled to return to the camp to get Sheri, Santos came home from work with a mixture of outrage and sarcastic humor. Having to stop several times because he was laughing so hard, Santos told her that he had gotten a call at work from "that tennis guy of yours" who had the audacity to ask him to put up $250,000 for his cockamamie tennis camp. He had even told Santos that Tonja had told him to ask Santos for the money. Laughing hysterically, Santos told Tonja that Jens had seemed totally startled when Santos informed him that he and Tonja barely had a pot to piss in.

Listening, Tonja's first reaction was to be angry at Santos for his cold, humiliating tone. But she quickly realized that he had to be telling the truth, or at least mostly telling the truth, about the phone conversation with Jens. The doubt that had been gnawing at her, which up to that point she had repressed from conscious thought, sprang suddenly to the surface. Could it be that Jens had been using her to no other end than to get to the money that she didn't even have? Certainly they looked as though they had money, with Santos's fancy cars, Tonja's clothes and jewelry, and Sheri in the most expensive tennis camp in the area. Feeling more desperate than she had felt in the entire course of the relationship, Tonja sent off an email to Jens as soon as she could leave the room and get to her computer: "I've never been to Denmark and I have heard that Tivoli is beautiful and romantic. Want to show me the sights?"

Tonja could barely sleep that night so at five in the morning she got up and signed on. Jens had already answered: "Are you crazy? Even if you were close to my age, my parents and friends would disown me if I was with a black woman."

Tonja broke down in tears and shut off her computer. Humiliated and dejected, for the next hour she walked the neighborhood with thoughts of suicide. Buoyed only by thoughts of her children and the new job that she had on Monday, Tonja returned home and crawled back into bed. When Santos awoke, she told him that she didn't feel well enough to join him on the trip to pick up Sheri. Secretly she thought to herself that, in his absence, it would be a perfect time to kill herself. Alone in the house that day, the words *Are you crazy?* ran through her mind a hundred times. She felt he was right, that she was crazy for ever allowing herself to believe in her fantasies about a relationship with Jens. When Santos left for the weekend to pick up Sheri, Tonja took out all her pills and, in her typically organized way, laid them in a series of straight lines on the kitchen table. As she looked at the pills she imagined herself going to her computer and typing out a message to Jens telling him to fuck himself, but realizing that she didn't want to give him the satisfaction, she put the pills away and went back to bed. By the time Sheri and Santos returned, Tonja had talked herself into a somewhat better mood. On Monday she started her new job and soon was swept into a whirlwind of exciting new activity. For the first few weeks, she thought of Jens and of her humiliation almost constantly, but as time went along, she allowed her humiliation to wane. One night, she went into Sheri's trophy area and, seeing the first-prize cup her daughter had won at camp, Tonja realized she hadn't thought of Jens in some time. In telling her story in the interview, she said that she hoped she was finally putting the matter to rest.

Discussion

Tonja's Internet relationship, unlike those of others we have examined, began with a real-life encounter and shifted from there into a manner of communicating that took place almost exclusively in cyberspace. In the cases of Rex and Joel we were able to see quite clearly ways in which their experiences in on-line relationships represented little more than a further entrenchment in the cell-like experiential withdrawal that constituted so much of their lives, even before cyberspace played a role. In Lydia's situation, in contrast, she appears to have been able to make use of cyberspace experiences to carve out for herself new ways of being and relating which held out the promise of enriching her life.

In Chapters 2 and 3 I discussed the ways in which cyberspace relating may exist as one, perhaps one of many, ways of attempting to deal with a pervasive sense of exposure and vulnerability to attack. Since most people appear to need some amount of interpersonal relating in order to preserve a sense of being themselves in relation to the larger world around them, total withdrawal from potential vulnerability and threat is hard to achieve. To be with people, you have to be exposed to the threats that come along with being with other people. By using cyberspace relationships as a primary way of relating, people may be attempting to provide themselves with the sense of relating to others, while only exposing a portion of their being to a portion of the being of others.[23] However, after a lifetime of the experience of persecutory threats, the primary sense of vulnerability that most people retain does not necessarily emanate from without.

For many, the most relentless of the potential attackers reside within the depths of their own psyches. To rid themselves of the relentlessness and omnipresence of such internal attacks, they may experience them, at any given moment, as coming from something outside, and hence try to flee from it by retreat from the outside. But this form of retreat is entirely futile, since the attack is ultimately an internal one, with fairly limitless resources on which to draw in order to launch itself again. For people for whom this internalized experience of attack is sufficiently strong, the Internet may prove to be the best form of relating they can have, since the external correlates of the internal attacks are controllable; this is the case with Miranda in the previous chapter and Rex in this chapter. For others in this situation, Internet relating/pseudo-relating seems indistinguishable from any other form of relating/pseudo-relating in which they engage as a compromise between loneliness and annihilation or abandonment. Joel's case appears to be an example of this type of Internet experience. In either case— whether Internet relationships are better than, or the same as, non-Internet relationships—as long as the internalized attacker is sufficiently strong, relating to others over the Internet has little transitional potential.

If the experience of attack from within is strong, but not indomitable, Internet relationships may serve a transitional function, as we have seen in the case of Lydia. In such cases, the use of an Internet relationship may allow people to use the screen of the VDT as a screen for their projections and, in so doing, find that they are not quite so terrifying or threatening as they might have thought. Such people, and Lydia seems a good example, can use Internet relating as a transitional tool to enrich their ways of experiencing both themselves and others.[24] From within such a transitional experience, previous templates for experiencing self and others can be played out against a new backdrop, and contrasted with alternative ways of being. In the best of such experiences, new ways of being can be fashioned from the residue of experience that is, seemingly, similar to and of experience that is, seemingly, different from everything that has gone on before.

Tonja was already in a form of transition before her Internet experience began. She grew up in a world in which to be herself and to achieve was to be exposed to attack (from her mother and sisters). These attacks came not only for her abilities and accomplishments, but also, it seemed to Tonja, for the color of her skin, which, to them, and by proxy to her, left her suspended between white and black. When she found temporary refuge from these attacks, from her father, her boyfriend, or her husband, for example, she was inevitably disappointed. In these disappointments, the rescuers turned into attackers themselves. Her father became lost to her in the material world in which he needed to succeed in order to survive, himself, the attacks of the mother who appeared more powerful than he. As he grew more distant, Tonja experienced his remove as a deliberated criticism of her, a criticism from which she could escape only by taking leave of the situation. Her boyfriend abandoned her in a way that she experienced as an essential criticism of her; in devaluing her black skin as too black just as her sisters and mother simultaneously overvalued and devalued her skin for being too white, she experienced him repeating the essential criticism with which she was already familiar. As Santos withdrew his interest in her, in favor of an interest in the material world, he seemed at first an antidote to her experience with her father. But, as Santos's external world collapsed, and as he grew more depressed, she relived her paternal experience. Like her father, Santos was a false protector, and as such his abandonment of her became a repetition of her sense of being at risk in the world.

As before, Tonja's ultimate protection from the attacks and abandonments was her ability to draw on her own resources to push herself forward into the world. She had used her athletic and intellectual ability to remove herself from the household where she felt so threatened and undervalued. Again, after college, she had pulled herself together after her boyfriend's leave-taking, by relying on her talent to get a job. In her marriage, she had resurrected a sense of security by her ability to restructure her life in her new surroundings and to succeed in school. The transition that Tonja was making at the time that she met Jens was, in fact, one that she had needed to make at numerous points in her life.

For Joel, Rex, and Miranda, their Internet relationships—for better or for worse—recapitulated a way of being from which, for them, there seemed no escape. For Lydia, the Internet allowed her to make a transition to a richer and more fulfilling way of experiencing both herself and the others around her. For Tonja, her Internet relationship with Jens was certainly a recapitulation. Like her father and Santos, he appeared to favor a material world over her, and like her boyfriend from college he appeared to reflect an essential rejection of her place in the world. But, in all previous circumstances, Tonja had been able to rely ultimately on her own internalized sense of integrity to make a transition back into the world, and she was able to do that with Jens as well. The Internet relationship was neither transitional nor imprisoning; Tonja's entire life had played itself out on the battleground between resource and submission. There is little doubt that, on the verge of craving to go out on her own and once again prove her ability to thrive, she saw, in Jens, a rescuer from the attacks she anticipated. Similarly, there is little doubt that, in Jens, she reexperienced the failures, hence attacks, with which she was so familiar. But, as with Joel, it is unclear that Internet relating was unlike non-Internet relating. Unlike Joel, however, Tonja was ultimately able to use her experience to make transitions for herself as she had done in the past. Unlike Lydia, however, it doesn't seem that she made use of the Internet in any meaningful way to fashion this new and renewed transition.

Between Flesh and Thought

The subject of Shakespeare's Sonnet XLIV feels it as a death to be unable to *be* a thought. If he only had this ability to transcend the inflexible bounds between flesh and thought, to create and re-create himself and his beloved as his thought demands, he would be able once and for all to escape the prison cell of solitude and loss in which corporeal existence impounds him.

Four centuries hence, this barrier between the flesh and thought of subjectivity has, in the minds of many, eroded, and the relatedness of the Internet is, at the very least, a trope for this erosion. Searles (1960) has argued that the nonhuman environment forms one of the most compelling and significant aspects of the experience of every individual. He prepares us for our ambivalence about the role of the Internet by affirming his "conviction that there is within the human individual a sense, whether at a conscious or unconscious level, of *relatedness to his nonhuman environment,* that this relatedness is one of the transcendentally important facts of human living" (pp. 5–6). On the one hand, we live in relation to the nonhuman environment in a fundamental and resonant way, while, on the other hand, failure to differentiate between the human and nonhuman environments can lead to pathology and suffering.

Dibbell's brilliant exposition of the cyber world of the MUD has illuminated for us the complexity of this dilemma of subjectivity between flesh and thought in the age of the Internet. To what extent are virtual rapes and executions relationally signifiers of unconscious, and thus intrapsychically "real," rapes and executions, and to what extent do they represent a warped and pathological distortion through virtuality? Dibbell found himself moving from a stance in which he "found it hard to take virtual rape seriously" to "finding it difficult to remember how I could ever *not* have taken it seriously." By making this transition Dibbell aligns himself with those who have found in the Internet a way of bridging the gap between real life and virtual reality, or in the larger sphere, between flesh and thought. In this way, Dibbell is like Lydia, who discovered in the Internet a transitional, potentially transformational playground in which to locate a capacity for solitude, and for a form of self-reliance in which she had the capacity to try on and experiment with potential ways of being. This, in Turkle's (1995) lucid description is a way in which "the

Internet has become a significant social laboratory for experimenting with the constructions and reconstructions of self that characterize postmodern life. In its virtual reality, we self-fashion and self-create" (p. 180).

For others, such as people like Rex and Joel, however, the progression envisioned by Turkle and demonstrated by Dibbell and Lydia seems not to have been realized. Both of these men, and many like them, live in experiential states of paranoid withdrawal. For them, connection only simulates intimate relations in the world of emotional involvement with others. The relationships that they create and perpetuate through the Internet (or subsequently often in real life as a consequence of Internet involvement), constitute a technologically transfigured variation of the only way of being they have ever known.

For those Internet devotees who lead, and have always led, an existence within a cell of paranoid withdrawal, there is little possibility of transitional or transformational experience through the charisma of virtuality. Their experience remains dimensionally constricted, and it may even run the risk of becoming more so. For these Internet users, then, their experience in every setting, be it in real life or in Internet relationships, follows the selfsame inevitability of constriction into the "as if."

The case study of Tonja represents a different and significant group of Internet users. For Tonja, and those like her, the Internet is ultimately neither transitional nor imprisoning. These people, who have the capacity for resilience (even if through great subjective suffering), can, within reasonable limits, make transitional and potentiating use of the experience that the world serves up to them.

5 Being Between Two Lives: On the Vicissitudes of Cyberspace as Potential Space in Organizations

There are three conditions which often look alike
Yet differ completely, flourish in the same hedgerow:
Attachment to self and to things and to persons, detachment
From self and from things and from persons; and, growing
  Between them, indifference
Which resembles the others as death resembles life,
Being between two lives—unflowering, between
The live and the dead nettle . . .
  History may be servitude,
History may be freedom. See, now they vanish,
The faces and places, with the self which, as it could, loved
  Them
To become renewed, transfigured, in another pattern.
  "Little Gidding," T. S. Eliot (1942)

The proliferation of cyberspace has created, and is a trope for, profound conflicts that are as palpable and consequential in the contemporary workplace as they are in any other arena of human engagement. Lodged between symbol and cause, the nature of cyberspace within the workplace reflects the vicissitudes of cyberspace in society as a whole, involving conflicts between mastery and subordination, narcissistic extension and alien invasion, freedom and enslavement, autonomy and repression, relatedness and schizoid remove. How we come to view these conflicts depends both on our perspective and on the aspect of the conflict on which we focus. Viewed from the perspective of the individual in the workplace, these conflicts assume one shape, but often they appear quite different if viewed from the perspective of top management.

Smircich (1983) has developed a nosology of ways in which cultural analysis of organizations may proceed. Two of her categories are of particular interest to us here. She notes that organizational anthropologists review cultures as systems of shared symbols and meanings. Thus, they set out to investigate and interpret the themes of an organization "in order to explain the thematic systems of meaning underlying activity" (p. 350). To understand an organization, the investigator looks at the way in which experience becomes meaningful in the setting by examining the symbols that pertain to the setting. "The researcher is concerned with articulating the recurrent themes that represent the patterns in symbolic discourse and that specify the links among values, beliefs, and action in a setting" (p. 351). This type of study of links in symbolic modes of representation informs the theoretical approach here, especially in terms of the patterns of symbolic discourse and the specific linkages among values, beliefs, and actions, which arise in the context of cyber systems. But, in addition, Smircich notes, "Culture may also be regarded as the expression of unconscious psychological processes. . . . From this point of view, organizational forms and practices are understood as projections of unconscious processes and are analyzed with reference to the dynamic interplay between out-of-awareness processes and their conscious manifestation" (p. 351). This type of investigation, the elaboration of conscious and unconscious processes and the links among them, will reside at the very center of these inquiries.

The Individual Within the Organization

From the individual worker's perspective, the computer creates an opportunity for mastery at work, regardless of the type of work or the level of responsibility: research is faster and more comprehensive; letters are grammatically sound, perfectly spelled, and well formatted; inventories are planned, controlled, and maintained as never before; sales forecasting is vastly more sophisticated and accurate; and financial recording and accounting, scheduled maintenance, service and quality programs, and purchasing controls all reap the benefits of the age of the computer. In contrast, the personal touch, the pride in work as one's own, and the very sense of being master of one's mastery have become diluted, or at least shared by the machine, which is now a partner in every enterprise. In many cases, our sense of our own competency may be dwarfed by the monumental capabilities of the new machines. As workers, our productivity and range are vastly enhanced by the availability of the computer as a calculator, narcissistic extension, or even colleague, but we often find ourselves daunted, intimidated, overwhelmed, or even paralyzed by the complex, vast, mercurial, and alien phenomenal world that we enter when we engage with the machine.

The computer brings freedom to travel throughout the organization and throughout the world. Venturing into cyberspace, we may gather whatever information we might need. Our purpose may be immediate, for future reference, or simply to amuse and entertain ourselves. But once we have entered the world of the machine, we are controlled, at times even enslaved, by its architecture, governed by its protocols and rules, and assigned our given role. The computer and the systems associated with it have the potential to provide us with a newfound sense of autonomy, a freedom and ability to fashion our own environments, to devise and test hypotheses, to become creators of a self-ordained universe. But, from a more paranoid perspective, immersion in the world of the computer may also bring with it a form of slavery that exposes us to scrutiny, management control, monitoring, and measurement. The machine brings us closer with our colleagues, within the immediate workplace and throughout the world; with a few keystrokes we can be in touch with almost anyone, and yet we can no longer touch those with whom we are in touch, communicating instead with disembodied objects, represented in some fashion by a computer screen. As one writer has suggested, from the perspective of the individual embedded within the organization, it is becoming hard to tell if the electronic office is more a playpen or a prison (Winner 1996).

Top Management

Viewed from the perspective of top management, the ubiquity of cyber technology brings with it the promise of knowledge and the confusion between vast amounts of information and the fulfillment of that promise. It takes less effort than pushing a button to amass vital, dynamic, current information about an organization, even in its most remote and obscure venues, and to have that information organized, synthesized, correlated, contrasted, and artfully presented in compellingly graphic forms. But information, no matter how well it may be presented, is not the equivalent of knowledge.

Some ideas of the British psychoanalyst W. R. Bion serve to articulate this confusion between information and knowledge. Extrapolating from Bion's (1962b) integrations of Kant's philosophical and Klein's psychoanalytic theories into our current topic, what Bion calls beta elements might be likened to bytes of computer data. Extending Kant's thinking into the realm of Kleinian psychoanalysis, Bion defined beta elements as "things in themselves" (p. 6). These beta elements, like the huge quantities of unmetabolized information with which a manager may be confronted, can be stored only in the form of undigested facts and cannot be integrated in the form of thought, or even experienced as discretely digested phenomena (alpha elements). The transformation of sense impressions, via alpha functions, into forms of experience that are available for both consciousness and dreamwork, is a prerequisite for thought, and, hence, knowledge (in Bion's terms, K). However, such beta elements are transformable into actions without thought; this means that these beta elements are particularly suited for what many psychoanalysts have described as projective identification, or alternatively, they may be converted into action in the form of acting out.

Experienced as indigestible facts, these beta-element data may present themselves in such abundance, or in such complex, contradictory, or alien ways that they defy the capacities of the manager to integrate it into meaningful ideas. However well synthesized, well researched, or well organized the facts may have been, the result is simply too much to handle. Thus, information overloads may occur due to the nature of data, even before we take into consideration those aspects of the character structure of a given manager that might make certain types of information difficult to integrate. The information amassed from cybernetic technologies may provide the top managers with a quality of knowledge that provides a better basis for action than they had ever known in the past, or it may induce them into actions without thoughts.

Similarly, the promise of technology has always been the promise of productivity (Attewell 1996, Hirschhorn 1986). Computers, with their incredible capacities to extend human abilities to count and control, offer the seduction of vastly greater units of output per unit of input, and for the top manager this increase in productivity translates directly into improvements in the bottom line. But little is ever so simple, and in the introduction of new technology, along with the promise of improved productivity comes the invitation of enormous complication. To begin with there are the initial costs of the effort, both the obvious costs (the price of computers, of programmers, etc.) and the more hidden costs (e.g., learning entirely new ways of conducting business). Such costs may be amortized over time through increased productivity. But contemporary organizations exist in an environment in which a top executive is expected to beat expectations for current earnings generated by ever-hungrier and more egregious analysts. Given such demands, the length of time required for amortization may be a great deal longer than the average expectable corporate lifetime of the top executive who is accountable for the bottom line.

In addition, there is the distraction attendant to the introduction of new technologies that diverts management attention from other, equally pressing issues. The introduction of every new cyber system—from the "paperless office" to material requirement planning and Just-In-Time, to intranet-based work flow—has brought with it the appeal from every consultant and implementation team for top management support. But top management is rarely so idle that meaningful support in one area fails to undercut efforts in another area. Even when the efforts to improve productivity are reasonably successful, the consequences of success are not without their own complications, and some writers have suggested that this success is a relative rarity (see Attewell [1994, 1996] for a good summary of such arguments). If the new cyber systems in fact mean that each employee is able to produce more than before, and if supply does not succeed in creating its own demand at marginally satisfactory levels of return, then top management is faced with at least two dilemmas: encouraging workers to create their own obsolescence and downsizing. A decade ago, top economists estimated that the increase in productivity due to improved cyber systems could result in the displacement of 11 percent of the American workforce in slightly more than a decade (Leontief and Duchin 1986). While such forecasts have yet to be realized (Attewell 1996), the potential remains unless it is true, as Jacques Ellul (1964) suggested, that new technology creates needs that can be fulfilled only by more of that technology.

But the reluctance of top management to provide the types of support, both financial and attentional, requested by cyber-system implementation teams is not merely a function of scarce resources (time and money) being allocated to other tasks, or the fear of the organizational consequences of the implementations themselves. Top managers, too, face the sorts of characterological dilemmas I described when discussing the conflictual issues of embedded workers. If the cyber system represents a narcissistic extension for the individual worker, it often does so in far greater degree for the top managers, individuals who quite often have their own predispositions to narcissism (Kernberg 1979, Kets deVries 1984, Lasch 1979), or, at least, to egocentrism (Maccoby 1981). But, as with many narcissistic phenomena, if the would-be narcissistic extension (in this case the cyber system) emerges as something other than an aspect of the self, the reaction that may greet it may be quite the opposite of narcissistic gratification and pleasure. The result, in fact, may be paranoid rage. As many an implementation team leader has discovered, if the computer system fails to become a seamless extension of the narcissistic chief executive officer (CEO), it, and all who are attached to it, may well become perceived as persecutors or alien invaders.

Similarly, for the top executive the implementation of cyber systems holds the promise of enormous levels of control and power (Horowitz 1996, Marx 1996). The computer can keep track of inventory and productivity levels, sales volumes, manufacturing costs, purchasing costs, advertizing expenses, and a million other things. It can, in short, monitor whether people are doing their jobs. Beyond that, it can provide data on attendance; telephone, fax, and copying expenditures; expense reports; and hundreds of other items that monitor whether people are taking advantage of the organization in one or another form of stealing from the till. In this sense, the computer remains in what Turkle (1995) has called the "culture of calculation." But, in an age in which there is a PC at every workstation and in which intranet and Internet applications appear vital for the functioning of many organizations, the top executive faces other dilemmas. With the proliferation and sophistication of email, for example, in many work environments it becomes very difficult to determine what is work and what resembles work. Words, messages, and other forms of communication are easy to produce abundantly, often in such quantities that they may obscure efforts to gain access to information.

Quite some time ago, the American interpersonal psychoanalyst Harry Stack Sullivan (1954) noted the powerful ways in which language may be used to destroy meaning every bit as compellingly as it is used to create it. An organizational example involving use of cyber systems will help illustrate this.

Case Example: Mixed Messages

A university professor reported, with some considerable mixture of pleasure and shame, an experience from one of his first university positions, some time before email had reached anything like its contemporary level of sophistication. Although the episode had mattered little in his successful career, his actions continued to bother him. He had been, in his mind at least, harassed by a particularly zealous administrator to work more hours than he cared to work and on more projects than he cared to work on. The technologically sophisticated university had recently implemented a fairly good email system some time before most universities did so. The professor was quite comfortable with technological innovation and so, in the course of time, he discovered that this new system allowed him to give the appearance of doing a great deal more work than he actually was doing.

Using the standard email package, he found that he was able to create a macro program that would "write" messages. While in his office, he would make up a list of 10 or 12 sentences. The routine, which functioned as a precursor to a "bot," would then "compose" macro emails by picking a few sentences and adding a salutation. By having his "bot"-macro send out messages at all hours of the day and night, the professor gave the impression that he was burning the candles at both ends. He was quite aware that some of the messages had a bit of an autistic quality, but in academia that was rarely noticed. Of course, nowadays, such designs could be implemented much more effectively. Canned software can be used to create a much more effective "bot" (a cyber-being) that will even respond to incoming messages, for example by reflecting back key phrases or by asking for clarification on elements of the incoming message that are perceived to be key phrases.

The professor's own actions had served to generate words that were divorced from meaning, something quite akin to the conversion of words into beta elements. Taken a step further, his actions might be described as, in some measure, a complementary identification (Racker 1968) to some aspects of the unarticulated internal world of the zealous administrator, whose own unformulated meanings had taken the shape of the beta elements of his own prior communications, useful to him only as fuel for his own acting out. What I am suggesting by this is that the administrator may have had his own frustrations, his own feelings of being overwhelmed. He provided no conscious communication of such a state, but it may well be that his countless complaints to the professor about his dawdling contained an unspoken subtext of which he was unaware. That subtext, which may have been something like "I feel hatefully overwhelmed," was so disconnected from and alien to his experience of himself that he got rid of it by handing it off to the professor like a hot potato. This is what is meant by the transformation of information into action without thought.

Management's Dilemma

In a computer-driven world it seems that every workstation needs access to a computer simply to carry out the business of the day. But the manager's dilemma is that if every workstation has a PC, hence access to the Internet, every workstation has access to alternate worlds that may have little if anything to do with the work that the organization is demanding be done. How can the manager know what people are actually doing? PC users may be balancing their checkbooks, playing an endless array of video games, emailing around the globe, "chatting" about just about anything, immersing themselves in MUDs (multiuser domains), browsing mindlessly through the Web, or hundreds of other things unrelated to productivity. Entire companies and consulting organizations have emerged to combat and monitor such abuses, by restricting access or by tracking the time and locations accessed with log-analyses.

However, many organizations have had to come to terms with the stark reality that monitoring and restriction are fraught with difficulties of their own. To begin with, there is the vast amount of data and the addition of staff and protocols necessary to filter through and manage it. As one commentator has observed to companies who use these tracking protocols, "It probably didn't take long before you found yourself drowning in a sea of statistical reports relating to traffic patterns on your site" (Stout 1997, p. 147). Additionally, in an age when the ownership and control of the Internet and its access are so hotly contested (O'Reilly and Associates 1997) and the technologies are so rapidly shifting, such efforts are at best a cat and mouse game. If, in the vernacular of the cyberworld, the workplace is RL (real life), the top manager may face the dilemma that workers are wandering far away from RL while appearing to be engaged in their working routines. In this sense, Turkle (1995) may be understating matters when she observes that the computer has moved from a culture of calculation to a culture of simulation. The contemporary reality may be that via the computer we have progressed to a culture of dissimulation. In the verse quoted at the start of this chapter, in Eliot's hedgerow of the contemporary world, there are not only "attachment to self and to things and to persons," and "detachment from self and from things and from persons," but the ultimate dissimulation is that we find "growing between them, indifference which resembles the others as death resembles life." As we have seen throughout this book, much of the world of cyberspace exists in this hedgerow of the contemporary interface with conflicting and conflictual experience. The use of cyberspace within organizations brings with it no exception to this more general observation.

In addition to all that we have observed so far, the top executive faces a problem that is even more particular to computer systems, namely the exposure of the company's data to viruses, to hackers, and to other security problems (Kling et al. 1996, Platt 1996, Wallace and Mangan 1997). But, perhaps most importantly, the top executive faces, in even greater extreme, the dilemmas of mastery and competency that I described above for the embedded worker.

Few top executives have climbed their way up to the top because of their familiarity and comfort with computers. Just as the computer and the cyber systems create an opportunity for the top executive to master the work at hand in a way that is otherwise impossible, the executive is likely to be exposed to a world that is alien, daunting, and intimidating, and that appears out of the executive's capacity to control. Being confronted by an alien world beyond control is even more frightening since, as often as not, it is excellence in the trafficking of power and control that has led the executive to the top.

Central Themes and Their Relationship to Potential Space

Two themes shed light not only on the executive and worker, but on the interactions between them, the overall organization, and, at times, the larger society in which they reside. The first theme traces ways in which many of the problems of contemporary Internet and intranet-based cyber systems, as well as other computer systems, reflect the powerful capacities of a computer-based system to broadcast and amplify dissociated aspects of top executives' personalities. Having been broadcasted and amplified, these dissociated characterological phenomena reverberate through, and proliferate amidst, the personalities and characteristics of the rest of the organization. The second theme suggests ways in which, at times, in the corporate environment as in the rest of the social world, the Internet has come to facilitate a form of interaction that appears largely social and related, while remaining relatively isolated, asocial, or at best partially social, self-protective, and removed. This is a form of interaction that is characterized by partial relationships. It reflects confusion or ambiguity between what is happening and what is imagined, as well as confusion between what is occurring inside oneself and what is occurring outside, as manifested by the screen of a computer. This is a form of social interaction that, in these instances, creates ambiguity between knowing and making oneself known and hiding and making oneself less vulnerable. Most of all, this is a way of interacting in which we suspend, or even obliterate, the inherent tensions between our experience of ourselves and the world as structured and ordered and our experience of ourselves and of the world as disordered and chaotic.

I have subtitled this chapter "On the Vicissitudes of Cyberspace as Potential Space in Organizations." In earlier chapters, I outlined the development of the notion of potential space from Winnicott's revolutionary, but now seemingly obvious, observations about the psychological role of transitional objects and transitional processes. These objects and processes exist in irresolvable paradox. Such phenomena hover simultaneously and ambiguously inside oneself and outside oneself, and so hovering they remain phenomena that both belong to one, yet paradoxically are presented to one from outside. It was Winnicott's brilliant observation that it is primarily within such potential or transitional space that humans have the knack to develop psychologically. It is by the use of such transitional phenomena, be they teddy bears or abstract mathematical theories, that we humans manage to grow as we find ourselves thwarted, to integrate love and hate, and to create and re-create as we destroy, repair, and find ourselves repaired. Winnicott described how we live our lives in this paradoxical tension and ambiguity between that which is within our control and that which remains outside of our mastery. The relatively healthier of us often find ourselves able to make use of these paradoxical tensions to grow and develop. However, for the relatively less healthy of us, these paradoxes can be neither embraced nor used.

The issue in Chapter 2, further developed in Chapter 3, was the extent to which cyber systems, such as email and, more generally, the Internet, have the capacity to function as transitional objects. Some writers, most prominently Sherry Turkle (1984, 1995), have compellingly championed the cyber system as transitional object. I argue, more circumspectly, that while the cyber system may play a facilitative or transitional role for some people, such a system may thwart or arrest others, and for yet a third group of people the cyber system may have no particular valence or potentiating consequence one way or the other.

Both of the themes I am presenting in this chapter on organizational life reflect vicissitudes of potential space. But before proceeding with these themes, a couple of vignettes about transitional processes will serve to illustrate both Turkle's point and my own.

Clinical Example: The Use of a Computer System as a Transitional Phenomenon

Andrew was the third of five children born to first-generation Irish immigrants to the United States. From birth he bore the burden of his two elder siblings' manifest difficulties in many ways. His elder brother had such severe intellectual limitations that he never learned to speak and was committed to an institution when Andrew was 6. His elder sister was intellectually sound but so physically handicapped that she required special schooling. Andrew was a premature child who spent much of his first year of life in and out of hospitals. Perhaps because of their sadness about the elder siblings, or perhaps because of doubts about their own capacities as parents and as people, both of Andrew's parents regarded him as both physically and intellectually impaired. Both parents worked long hours and, confronted by another troublesome child, they gave up.

Lombardi (Rucker and Lombardi 1998) has cited an example introduced by Schepper-Hughes (1992) to refute our culture's essentialist notions of the maternal romance. Schepper-Hughes studied impoverished urban enclaves in Brazil in which babies are alternatively viewed as healthy and thriving "keepers" or as sickly and difficult "languishers" who are waiting to die. As Lombardi notes, these languishers "are deadened, both by their mothers' hardship and despair and by their mothers' difficulties supplying them, in both material and psychic senses, with resources that are too scarce to sacrifice" (p. 114).

Andrew might well be described as a stateside version of a languisher. In many ways his experience of living, at least in relation to the peers whose lives he came to know, was that he had been virtually left to die. Were it not for the cultural constraints of our society, which prevent such manifestly unnuturing parenting, he might have languished.

In retrospect, it seems clear that Andrew had talents that might have identified him, even to parents as disconsolate as his, as a child with the potential to thrive. But such talents went largely unrecognized by them. In his isolation, he learned no games, played no sports, and failed miserably in school. In general, he led the life of a loner, the sort of boy who was always bullied and rarely befriended. Had his parents attended more closely to his circumstances, they would have noted that the few friends he did acquire were among the most intellectually achieving in his neighborhood. More attuned parents might well have become confused that a child who was faring so poorly in school spent much of his spare time watching quiz shows and science programs rather than cartoons. They might have wondered how it could be possible that a boy with no record of achievement could spend countless hours picking out harmonies on the piano that his grandfather had built. But it was Andrew's unfortunate lot that his parents saw none of these details.

In the end, Andrew finished high school, barely squeaking by at the last moment because of a music teacher to whom he had ingratiated himself. While his friends went on to MIT and Harvard, Andrew moved on to a job as an assembly-line worker in an electronics company where he continued to languish for many years, increasingly friendless and increasingly isolated, barely managing to clear the monthly rent for his windowless, one-room apartment.

Andrew might, arguably, have continued to languish if he had not become the accidental victim of his own abilities. One day at work, a senior vice president came out onto the manufacturing floor, screaming for a spare part assembly for the company's most important customer. As it happened, the computer had broken down and no one could produce a pick list for the assembly. After listening to the vice president's voluble menacing of several layers of middle management for half an hour, Andrew screwed up his courage and intervened, meekly suggesting that if his immediate boss would allow him freedom in the stockroom, he would be able to pick the several hundred parts necessary for the job. Despite the scoffing of Andrew's boss and his boss's boss, the desperate VP escorted Andrew to the stock cage and watched as the young man picked out the parts effortlessly, even making appropriate substitutions where necessary parts were out of stock.

The VP was so delighted by Andrew's coming to his rescue and so impressed by the young man's memory, that he offered him a promotion to the computer room and an opportunity to learn programming and computer systems. Almost reluctantly Andrew accepted the new position. At first timidly, but then with increasing freedom and glee, Andrew began to play with computers. To him it was as if, for the first time, he had the capacity to express himself, both intellectually and physically. The computer quickly became the power that he had never been allowed to exhibit. He learned that he could make the computer order things to be done that he had always felt constrained to do himself, and that, lo and behold, the people in his surround would do those things. No one scoffed at him for these clandestine ventures into the world of potency; no one retaliated against him or ridiculed him. To the contrary, they responded.

He remained uncertain whether it was he or the computer that was responsible for it, but Andrew began to receive praise for the first time in his life. Having spent nine years dreading each new day at work, he now got to work early and stayed until fatigue forced him to leave; he played, created, and, most of all, accomplished. In the matter of a few months his entire experience of living began to change. After nine years of working at minimum wage, he suddenly received several unsolicited raises. With no small amount of trepidation, he moved out of his prison-like quarters into a much more pleasant apartment; he found a new circle of friends with whom, however awkwardly and hesitantly, he could go to lunch and talk about work; and he began to contemplate going to college to study computers and, most of all, to entertain his private fantasy of studying the music that had given his life meaning, even in his most isolated and depressive hours.

Within another year, he enrolled, part-time, and learned, again for the first time, that he could excel in school every bit as well as he could excel at work. Years later, Andrew's life had improved unrecognizably. He was earning close to a six-figure salary; he lived in a spacious, even luxurious apartment; he had completed his undergraduate education with honors and was well on his way to a doctorate in musicology; and not only did he have a circle of friends but, for the first time in his life, he had a girlfriend.

For Andrew, the computer had served a marvelously transitional function. Having lived a life in which his talents had been largely unrecognized, he had used the computer, however accidentally, to play with a realm of achievement that occupied an intermediate ground between being his and the computer's. At any point along the way, if someone had stopped to ask Andrew whether the successes he was achieving were his own or the computer's, he would not have known how to answer. With the computer and its output as his companion/extension, he was able to destroy the earlier, damaged and defective images of himself and his relation to the world and, even more, he was able to re-create new ones in their place. These new images facilitated his growth in ways of which he would never previously have been able to dream. For Andrew there seems little doubt that the computer, and the systems related to it, had been potentiating, or, to use Winnicott's language, transitional objects.

Clinical Example: The Use of a Computer System as a Thwarting Phenomenon

Andrew's girlfriend had a great deal more ambition for him than he might have had for himself. To some extent she kept these ambitions in check for quite some time, but after she and Andrew became engaged she began to push him with considerably more vigor. Andrew offered little resistance. In fact, to an outside observer it might have appeared that his fiancée was merely giving voice to ambitions that were originally his own. Encouraged by his successes at work and at school, he had privately nurtured a dream of advancing his musical training, for as much as he delighted in his success with computers and with people, the piano was his truest love. Addressing his own ambition and that of his fiancée simultaneously, he went on job interviews at the same time that he applied to Juilliard.

In keeping with his string of recent successes, Andrew obtained a fine new position that paid him far more than he had ever dreamed he might be earning. Within weeks of that, he was accepted into graduate school. By now quite used to hard work, Andrew accepted both the new job and graduate school, and put his nose to the grindstone. At first he continued to thrive. In school he was doing what he had always wanted to do and, no matter how demanding he found the tasks, he greeted the challenges with enthusiasm. He even experienced a feeling that felt foreign enough to him that he might have called it joy. At work, he had been hired to do much the same sort of thing he had been doing for some time. He found that he was in a position to make an immediate contribution to his new employer's computer systems and was gratified to be recognized for this contribution publicly and financially. With both of them basking in the glow of Andrew's triumphs, he and his fiancée set a marriage date a year in the future.

Soon after the wedding date was announced, the top executives in Andrew's company made a decision to install a new computer system and new client-server technology. Suddenly, Andrew was confronted with a type of system that he had neither encountered before nor studied, and, with the client-server system, he faced a type of technology that seemed extremely complex to him with a steep learning curve. Unfortunately for Andrew, these changes happened at the same time that his graduate training was beginning to propel him into areas that, for the first time, were both entirely unfamiliar and challenging.

Faced with two daunting situations, as well as what he experienced to be his fiancée's relentless and uncompromising demands on his time, and the need to plan the wedding, Andrew attempted to apportion his time as equally as he could. However, having tasted the pleasure of indulging himself in music, it proved increasingly hard for him to put that aside when it came time to devote extra time to learning the new computer systems. That difficulty and his anxieties grew in equal measure as the systems proved harder and harder for him to absorb. In fact, it seemed to Andrew that, if anything, he was falling further behind on the projects for which he was responsible, and it seemed to him that daily he had less of an idea of what he ought to be doing.

As he grew more uncomfortable at work, he found spending time there increasingly difficult. For the first time since his years on the assembly line, he had trouble dragging himself into work in the morning. Once there, he would turn on his computer and stare at the screen blankly, at a loss for his next step. He found himself taking long walks around the building, or just stepping outside, in order to avoid looking at the screen. He began to reacquire the once omnipresent image of himself as intellectually incompetent. In his relationship with his fiancée, he grew hostile and bitter, often blaming her and her ambitions for his frustrations with work. Soon the wedding date was postponed and as his troubles at work grew more severe, the engagement was broken off.

After a harsh warning from boss at work, who complained that Andrew was failing to meet his deadlines and observed that, if it were he, he would be putting in many more hours, Andrew "faced the music" by facing away from the music that had been his only true source of pleasure. Fearing an endless slide into the institutional life of his elder brother, he withdrew from school and surrendered himself to his job. With the computer staring him in the face every morning as a harsh reminder of his failures and his losses, Andrew grew increasingly morose and resigned to despair. Finally, in an act of sheer desperation, he called up his former employer and asked if they still had a position for him. At the moment that Andrew learned that his former employer would take him back, he felt, simultaneously, a flood of relief and a tidal wave of humiliation. Two weeks later, Andrew returned to the scene of his original triumphs, broken and nearly hopeless.

For Andrew, in the course of a few short years, computer systems had proved both transitional and, ultimately, thwarting. In the first instance he was able to make use of the computer systems to nurture aspects of his being that had gone unnurtured, to grow where his growth had been inhibited. In the second instance, the computer systems served to rekindle the self-doubt and denigration that had been his constant companions for the first thirty years of his life.

Andrew's unfortunate lot has provided us with an example of transitional process and of process that is thwarting. In both instances, organizational computer systems have played a significant, if not a central, role. Having used the case of Andrew to begin to explore some of the ways in which the computer can function as either a transitional or a regressive phenomenon for individuals within an organization, I now extend this exploration by turning to some related subjects. With the clinical illustrations and Winnicott's theories in the background, we will return our attention to the first of this chapter's two themes.

The Propagation of a Top Executive's Dissociated Experience

The first theme perpetuates the depiction of computer systems as thwarting, or regressive, phenomena. It deals with the use of cyberspace as both a symbol of and vehicle for the broadcasting and propagation of top executives' dissociated experience. An example from my own consulting experience will help illuminate some of these ideas at the same time that it provides a framework for the theoretical elaboration.

Clinical Example: The "Phantom" Meetings of the Minds

In the early 1980s I consulted for a foreign-based multinational corpora-tion that had decided to acquire a number of closely held U.S.-based high technology firms that offered the promise of synergy if grouped coopera-tively. My job was to assess the adequacy of the management at the vari-ous companies since my employer had no intention of introducing new management teams within the companies themselves.

One company, which functioned as a lynchpin for the master plan, had become the object of a great deal of concern for everyone on the evalua-tion team. The company's technology was at the cutting edge in its area, and as a result the company had enjoyed a prestigious position within its market niche for some time. However, recently it had begun to develop a bad reputation for failing to meet its manufacturing delivery promises. Management at the company attributed the order slippage to a recent, problematic installation of a new computer-based material requirements planning (MRP) system. MRP had been an interest of mine for some time, so I had been looking forward to this particular assignment. When I ar-rived at the scene, however, the picture that greeted me was quite different from anything I might have expected. The company had four locations within a fifteen mile radius, and employed about four hundred people. As I toured the various plants with the CEO/founder, it did, indeed, appear that engineering and marketing were tremendously busy; at the same time, manufacturing operations seemed at a virtual standstill, except for expe-diters rushing about with hands full of parts and assemblies. This picture seemed entirely consistent with the CEO's explanation of the company's recent problems.

However, sometime later he left me alone to wander around the plants and I began to meet with middle management. I found that everyone was in complete agreement that the MRP implementation had been a disas-ter, and that its failure lay at the root of their current problems. Still, their discussions with me were consistently punctuated by references to a different issue, introduced briefly in Chapter 1, that appeared to preoccupy them far more than the difficulties with the MRP system, even though each of them was quite apologetic about mentioning it.

As I spoke with people throughout the organization, I heard the same complaint: endless meetings were being called, disrupting people's work schedules. In itself, this was not an unusual complaint. But, in this case, what had people so frustrated and preoccupied was that, as often as not, unless they were able to figure out whom to contact to confirm the meeting, they never knew if the meeting was a genuine or fictitious one called by a character they had collectively labeled "the phantom." The problem had become so acute that a number of middle managers had taken simply to ignoring messages to appear at meetings at all, and this, naturally enough, was a situation that was causing practical and morale problems of its own. To combat the problem of the phantom, the company had recently taken corrective action by requiring that all meetings be established by phone contact with all involved. Although this directive eased the situation, it was proving an extraordinarily cumbersome procedure, especially in light of the crisis with ongoing production.

With my employer's blessing, I got approval to extend the scope of my work to include the phantom. To that end, I returned to the company a number of times and eventually managed to locate the most obvious source of the problem. The same computer system the company had installed to implement material requirements planning came with a comprehensive email network. One aspect of the forwarding procedure in this state-of-the-art program allowed someone working at workstation A to send outgoing messages that looked to the recipient like they were being sent from workstation B. The programs came with numerous security systems, but none of them was difficult to penetrate for anyone with a modicum of programming savvy. Since there was no meaningfully secure password system protecting the email system, this effectively meant that a person could quite easily appear to be someone else (or no one at all), and, in that camouflaged identity, send out messages that appeared to be emanating from somewhere and someone else. In addition, as is the case with most systems, it was possible to defer the sending of messages to a future time.

As luck had it, the deferred message component of the system was the key to solving the puzzle. The computer department was able to print out a log of all such deferred messages (which were considerable). In this case, the log recorded the *actual* workstation from which planned messages had been initiated. We were, in other words, in a position to intercept the phantom's planned messages before they were sent and track down the station from which they had been launched. Not surprisingly, it turned out that the employee who had most frequent access to that particular workstation was never singled out to attend any of the meetings that were being set up by the deferred messages.

The employee, Ralph, admitted almost immediately that he was the phantom, describing his actions as nothing more than an unfortunate practical joke. By all accounts, including his own, he was a loner. Having begun with the company after dropping out of college eleven years earlier, he had progressed through the ranks to his present position as assistant production manager. His main function was overseeing the manufacturing scheduling. In fact, he was in charge of all of the expediters whom I had witnessed rushing all around the company the first day I was there. Within the ranks of upper management, from his immediate superior to the CEO, everyone voiced astonishment that Ralph was the culprit. He had been highly valued as a loyal and devoted employee who frequently spent many unpaid hours sorting through production problems.

Ralph offered no direct explanation for his behavior, but after talking with him for an hour or so I recognized that he was disgruntled about the changes that were in progress, even though he voiced full support for them. In college he had planned to study computer science, but found the course of study uncomfortable and taxing, and he was a central figure in the manual systems that were being replaced by the current efforts at computerization. In addition to that, it appeared that he was quite bitter about having been left off the MRP implementation team. In counterpoint, the team leader reported that Ralph had been encouraged to participate several times, but had declined, saying he already had too much on his plate. In reference to the MRP implementation, Ralph used a number of similar metaphors during the course of our discussions: "forced down my throat," "fed up," "I've had it up to here" (raising his hand to just below his chin). It struck me as quite plausible that one function of invoking the phantom meetings was to retaliate for what he felt was being done to him.[25] Subsequently, Ralph was given a leave of absence and I went about my business evaluating the firm.

Some time later, when a deal between my employer and the company was about to be struck, I was asked to complete my evaluation of the CEO as part of due diligence. As soon as I renewed my focus on the CEO, I started to think about the phantom meetings once again. The CEO had founded the company twenty years earlier, basing early products on technology that he had insightfully, even presciently, understood to be underutilized in the marketplace. He was genuinely well liked and highly regarded by his employees, both as a man with a brilliant sense of how to guide the business and as a benevolent and concerned leader. Even so, he had few close connections within the company, and I came to suspect that he had even fewer close relationships outside of it. Nearing 60 at the time I met him, he had been married and divorced twice and had neither children nor current romantic interests. In fact, it appeared that his life revolved around the business, just as the business revolved around him. Although he was an electronic engineer by training, he had always worked in sales and marketing. Even so, it seemed as though his greatest pleasure while at work was to wander around the engineering areas. In fact, the engineering staff considered his presence there somewhat humorous, fondly joking that he would always ask interested questions and then turn glassy eyed and scurry off as they began to speak.

When we began to chat about the problems the company was having with the computer implementation, I quickly recognized what the staff had been describing. He knew all the buzz words and had, in fact, gone to a three-day conference on MRP for top management conducted by one of the most prestigious figures in the field. But as soon as I tried to steer the conversation into anything deeper than the familiar buzz words, he became noticeably uncomfortable and changed the subject to something with which he was much more conversant. I also noticed that neither he nor his secretary had one of the new computer terminals available. Given the extent to which computerized information transmission was featured at his company, the absence of computer access in his office seemed especially noteworthy.

It turned out that the CEO had an old-fashioned, highly nontechnological way of gathering information. In fact, it soon came to light that the CEO was really quite upset that Ralph had turned out to be the phantom, because it was Ralph and a handful of other old-timers whom the CEO always sought out when he wanted to find out what was really going on in his company. In an aside to me he chided, "Now I guess I'm really going to have to learn this damn new system, but I don't know when I'll ever find the time with so much on my plate already."

The Cyber System as Symbol and Vehicle for Dissociated Experience

I suggested above that contemporary cyber systems, including but not limited to those that are Internet-based, figure as especially powerful agents for the broadcasting and amplification of dissociated aspects of top executives' personalities. I believe that this vignette illustrates a fairly typical way in which a cyber system may become a symbol and vehicle for this type of broadcasting of the dissociated experience of a top executive throughout the entire hierarchy of an organization. When they are unconsciously used in this way, these systems enhance the capacity of such disavowed characterological phenomena to reverberate and propagate through the rest of the organization.

This view is based on a more general belief that organizations are particularly vulnerable to unacknowledged, unconscious influence. Quite often an unarticulated prerequisite for becoming a middle manager is the perception by upper management that the staff member has the capacity to internalize unspoken, often unconscious, attributes, characteristics, and belief systems of upper management (Civin 1987). Thus, middle managers are particularly well attuned to aspects of their boss's psychological makeup that may be uncomfortable or anxiety producing enough for the boss to have cast aside, or, in psychoanalytic terms, dissociated. In this way, the middle managers become fertile soil for the seeds of upper management's characterological issues. By paying close attention to the wishes of their superiors, even to the point of understanding and synthesizing wishes that have never been articulated formally, middle managers are doing their jobs and doing them well.

This middle management incorporation of the dissociated experience of top executives might be viewed as projective identification (see endnote 5). In such projective identifications, the unconscious elements of the internal world of one person result in the arousal of complementary unconscious reactions in other people. Using Racker's (1968) clinical model, we observed that one person, influenced by unconscious dissociative process of the type described in the case of the phantom, may treat another person not as that actual person, but rather as an aspect of their own internal world. And, in a manner that illustrates complementary identification, the second person is induced to behave in a way that corresponds to that dissociated aspect of the first person's internal world.

Organizational Illustration of Projective Identification

An example from the business world independent of cyberspace will help to illuminate this sometimes elusive, but, for our purposes, vitally important notion of projective identification. A large company that had long stood as a benevolent pillar of its community had fallen on such hard times that it had no alternative other than to merge with an even larger company, a former competitor that was located far away. Quickly the parent company began to "trim the fat," insisting that upper management at the daughter company review the ranks of middle management and downsize radically. After a few months of this I was called in as a consultant to help shed some light on issues of morale within the workplace. Before I had my second meeting, however, I found myself both furious and frustrated with my employers. After giving me the background of my assignment at some length, they rarely returned my phone calls, canceled meetings at the last moment, and, in general, treated me as if I had no value. I was able to recognize that my initial reaction of anger and frustration was induced by their behavior.[26] By viewing some part of my emotional response as induced by others, I am putting that reaction in the category of a complementary identification of the sort I described above. Notably, when I finally managed to secure additional meetings, I was able to use this understanding to help us all make some sense of what was happening within the organization.

Asked to make such deep cuts within the middle management structure, the upper level management felt in a terrible double bind. If they failed to make the cuts, their own jobs would be in jeopardy. But there was an unspoken consensus that once they made the cuts, there would be no reason to continue operations at their facilities and that the continuing profitable aspects of their organization would be moved. Once moved, there would be little or no need for the managers' services because the mother company was already overburdened with management. Without expressing it, or perhaps even without knowing it consciously, they were feeling just as I had felt, pushed around and of little value. In turn, they were telling their employees that, although there might be further cuts, all would turn out well in the end and that the operations would be continuing in the present locations. Lied to, misled, and abused, however unconsciously, the employees in turn had come to feel threatened, pushed around, and of little value within the organization.

More on Projective Identification and the Phantom

In the case of the phantom meetings, the cyber system figures significantly in the transmission throughout the organization of the dissociated experience of this particular CEO. Here was a man who had gained considerable personal wealth, power, and esteem within technology, and yet paradoxically it appeared that he lived with a good deal of intolerable anxiety about the details of technological matters. My general impression was that, unconsciously, he feared that he was intellectually unable to grasp the concepts and that his entire involvement in the business of technology formed a relatively adaptive manic defense[27] against his own sense of inadequacy. Characteristically, this technological discomfort created such anxiety that it proved difficult for him to remain aware of it. In fact, the notion of dissociation emerges from the idea that awareness of this type of anxiety would be intolerable, and thus in order to avoid awareness, the experience is relegated to the realm of the dissociated.

Despite his charm and salesman-like polish, the CEO suffered from a good deal of discomfort in almost any sort of relationships with others. He appeared to have, quite unconsciously, considerable feelings of being left out and interpersonally misfit. His failed marriages and apparently insular social existence outside of the sphere of his own business served as reasonable confirmation of these inferences. Even more strongly confirmatory, though, was his behavior within the company and with me. Just as he seemed uncomfortable with the details of any technology, he seemed subtly, but unmistakably, uncomfortable when a conversation lasted longer than a few minutes; when there was any break in the flow of topic-specific content, which might have left room for engagement of a more personal nature, he would fidget and begin to look for a way to exit. All the while, however, he gave every impression at the surface of being interpersonally engaged and at ease with himself.

The MRP system, and the insinuation of electronic communication within his organization, represented for the CEO an intrusion in the midst of his company of an alien system that he found himself unable either to embrace or to reject. As is the case for many people, digital technologies seemed to him to belong to another group of people, perhaps to a younger generation, perhaps to those with more technological comfort. Thus, the digital technology itself, the very technology that he overtly encouraged and promoted within his company, became an external symbol of the part of himself that he tried to keep so hidden, even from his own view, the part that was uncomfortable with technology and the part that felt left out and left behind as well. Given his close ties to Ralph and the similarity of some of their feelings about the technologies and about being left out, Ralph served as a conduit for these dissociated aspects of the CEO's psychological makeup.

The importance of the cyber system in the transmission of these dissociated phenomena does not end with its symbolic function. By far the most powerful point is that, in general, cyber systems and cyberspace serve both as symbol and as vehicle. Thus, in this example as in so many others, Ralph used the computer system not only as the symbolic representation of the CEO's dissociated experience, as metabolized and retransformed through his own psychological processes, but as the method of communication of these processes.

For the very reasons that the computer system is an extraordinary narcissistic extension of our capacities (to count, to research, to communicate, etc.), it functions as an extraordinary tool for the amplification and distribution of dissociated experience. Whatever the perceived human quality may be, the computer has the capacity to represent a symbolic amplification of that quality, *and* that symbolic representation is, quite concretely, able to be broadcast throughout an organization far more quickly and efficiently via the cyber system than in any other way. It was in such a manner that Ralph used the very cyber system by which he felt threatened, if not undone. In Ralph's complementary identification with the CEO, they unconsciously fused together in using the cyber system as a vehicle to induce others *into related states of being.* And, because of the power of the computer as a tool, they were able to do this quite effectively for some period of time. Now it was not just they who felt left out. Virtually everyone within the company came, at one time or another, to feel left out. It was not just they who felt uncomfortable with the new technology. The new technology, cloaked in the cyber disguise of the phantom, came to be public enemy number one within the organization.

Discussion of the Example of the Phantom

How may we come to understand this type of use of a cyber system? In the example I have given, the computer appears to be used as an agent that maintains, even fosters, dissociative states of being. In contrast to writers such as Turkle (1995), Stone (1995), and Faber (1984), I have argued that no object or process, the cyber system included, is essentially transitional. Within organizations as elsewhere, the computer or cyber system may be a transitional phenomenon, as in Andrew's initial experience of it in the example cited earlier in this chapter.

However, as we observed in Chapter 2, for parents and infants there is nothing essential in the nature of the teddy bear or blanket that assures the transitional nature of the object. As we know from Andrew's second experience of computers, the transitional nature of the potentially transitional object may become seriously undermined and even thwarted or turned into an object of fixity instead. Such is often the case within organizations when we come to consider the transitional, or potential, role of the cyber system. Within a relatively healthy company, a cyber system may be a transitional object in the way that Turkle and Faber depict. As our example of the phantom suggests, the less dissociated executive experience the system is endowed with, the more likely it is that this salutary effect of cyber systems will be the outcome.

In such happy circumstances the organization may enjoy an outcome that is facilitative and creative. People within the organization may be productively capable of harnessing the extensive power of digital phenomena, and therefore at ease in both a computational and, to recall Turkle's term, a simulational mode. In such favorable circumstances, the computer system will be far less likely to become an agent of dissimulation and dissociation. But there is little reason to suspect that in his second job Andrew was faced with such dissociated top executive experience. As I have cautioned, potentially transitional space faces vicissitudes of developmental use, whether we are talking about individuals in the privacy of their homes, in groups, or in organizations. When we invoke psychoanalytic metaphors in situations that are not purely analytic, it behooves us to be even more careful to avoid doing so in a partial or misleading manner. Thus, within organizations, we must note that even though cyber space may potentiate, it may also thwart and debilitate. The broadcasting and amplification of dissociated executive experience, as illustrated in the case of the phantom meetings, is one clear example of such a debilitating process at work. Andrew's second experience is another.

As we will see next, however, other outcomes are also possible.

The Organizational Application of a Cyber System as a Facilitator of Relatedness Within Paranoid-Schizoid Functioning

In Chapters 2 and 3 I developed the argument that cyber systems such as the Internet may facilitate the development of certain capacities for relatedness even though these capacities may still have qualities that reflect paranoid withdrawal. This is a type of relatedness that I refer to, following Melanie Klein (1946), as paranoid-schizoid, or part-object, functioning.

The second of this chapter's themes deals with the organizational application of this concept. In Chapters 2 and 3 we used Klein's notions of the paranoid-schizoid and depressive positions, persecutory and depressive anxieties, and part- and whole-object relating, to develop and illustrate the cyber space application of this concept of paranoid-schizoid relatedness.[28] Here I would like to extend these ideas to observations about organizational functioning.

Inside organizations, just as outside of them, many people crave more than partial relationships (or in Kleinian terms, part-object relations). In Chapter 2, I described people who strive to have more than partial relationships even though they may feel the need to isolate themselves as protection against real or fantasied others. This happens within organizations as much as it does outside of them. These people may feel the compelling need for relationships with the very same others from whom they are secured. Without these others, or at least the illusion of others, the fortress they have built for themselves within the organization may become a place where they will perish. A glimpse of this could be seen in the case, described above, of Andrew's second job.

In organizational cases, confinement in the cell of paranoid-schizoid withdrawal or regression is generally self-imposed, although it may become organizationally reinforced. In fact, these people have unconsciously elected to isolate themselves within an inviolable fortress for the very purpose of removing themselves from the organization of whole-objects that they experience, in fantasy or actuality, to threaten them with persecution. These persecutory fantasies may frequently take the form of dismissal from the organization, or at the very least demotion, but it is not uncommon to find that in employees' fantasies they fear that they will be publicly humiliated, even murdered, as retaliation for the damage they perceive themselves to have done (or unconsciously wish to do) to the organization.

As we noted above[29] in the review of Harlow's rhesus monkeys, the study of Internet relations leads us to the possible conclusion that people confined in cells away from connection with others may choose to seek *the best illusion* of something that seems like a whole-object, even when they, themselves, have volunteered for that confinement to seek protection from actual contact with whole others.

Persecutory Anxiety Within Organizations

Having already observed how widespread persecutory anxiety is within our culture, how startling can it be to hear the suggestion that in a company, a university, a hospital, or any other organization, a cyber system may foster, even exacerbate, such anxieties? Certainly for most of us who work within or consult to organizations, it may seem self-evident that cyber systems contribute to persecutory anxiety. This contribution becomes especially evident with cyber systems that are oriented toward communication, such as the Internet and most intranet networks. This conclusion has two interwoven strands: (1) Individuals within organizations are subject to a relatively high level of persecutory anxiety whether or not a computer is present; (2) When those anxieties are present, cyber systems may serve to exacerbate them greatly. Concerning the first strand, these persecutory anxieties exist in significant measure within organizations, but I am not suggesting that these anxieties are any greater now than in the past, nor that their existence is per se debilitating.

The easiest of these anxieties to identify are those that pervade in annihilatory form. Even in years when the unemployment level falls below the full employment threshold, few employees feel invulnerable to downsizing or reorganization. Many organizations, even those with long records of benevolently familial respect for their members, cannot assume their own "going-on-being" in any meaningfully static way in an era of mergers, acquisitions, hostile takeovers, and market-forced reversals in direction. Within many publicly held organizations, the pressures for ever-increasing earnings reverberate with immediacy throughout the entire network of management hierarchies; inevitably a sense of organization and personal peril accompanies this reverberation. Even in organizations, such as civil service or universities, where the security of lifelong employment often substituted historically for higher wages, recent decades have witnessed an erosion of certainty, with entire branches of civil service having been disbanded and with job security and university tenure under ever-increasing pressure.

Nor are organizations that appear more refractory to these annihilatory tendencies immune from their own versions of persecutory anxieties. I have already reviewed some of the ways in which computer systems reflect a number of fundamental conflicts within many organizations, for embedded workers and top managers alike. These conflicts extend into areas such as mastery or subordination, productivity or paralysis, freedom or enslavement, autonomy or scrutiny, intimacy or alienation, knowledge or bombardment, narcissistic extension or alien invasion. Gergen (1991) has suggested that these tendencies may be an outgrowth of postmodern attitudes, in which we, as participants in an organization, can no longer trust ourselves, or others, to know and guide. When "leaders lose their credibility as 'superior knowers,' and guiding rationales prove empty", when "the very possibility of a single individual, or small group, determining the actions of the whole is challenged" (p. 250), the entirety of the organization, leaders and followers alike, may feel catapulted into conflict. And when we wish for calmness, security, and guidance, conflict takes on the mantle of persecution. In his recent book *Reworking Authority: Leading and Following in the Post-Modern Organization*, Hirschhorn (1997) makes a similar point. He notes that the very notion of authority is undermined when we can no longer even define what it is that the organization is supposed to be doing. Do copier companies sell copiers, or do they manage information? Do hospitals provide medical care or do they attempt to satisfy the often whimsical guidelines of managed care? How can a worker find security and guidance when roles are so poorly defined and so multiply determined that no one is in a position to secure or to guide?

These are conflictual issues to which all organizations are vulnerable, whether or not the organization has a computer system, and any one of these areas of conflict retains a potentially persecutory dimension. For example, many workers (and managers) experience a feeling of persecution when their sense of mastery is transformed into a sense of subordination; this feeling of persecution may emerge whether or not that subordination has anything at all to do with a computer. Likewise, an employee may come to feel persecuted if his or her independence and autonomy falls under overly rigorous scrutiny. Or, as Hirschhorn and Gergen note, an employee or manager may feel persecuted merely because the guidance, or ability to guide, that feels so necessary is experienced as so absent.

Of course, we are most keenly interested here in communication-based cyber systems that exacerbate underlying persecutory anxieties. As I have noted repeatedly, there is nothing inherent in the computer that makes it a persecutory object, just as there is nothing inherent in the teddy bear or the blanket that make them transitional objects. Whether the context is the privacy of one's own home or the cubicle of a corporate office, the individual's subjective experience of the object is contextual. The context consists of both historical and psychological factors that are largely internal to a person's being, as well as factors that seem much more external and palpable than internal.

Within organizations, the historical and psychological factors vary for each individual. Organizations, however, tend to breed culturally syntonic persecutory metaphors of the sort we looked at when we talked about Big Brother, *2001*'s Hal, and the FBI. If anything, cyber systems have merely added a new wrinkle to age-old organizational images of Scrooge-like bosses exploiting and persecuting defenseless employees.

A similar picture emerges when we examine external or environmental factors that render the cyber system both a symbol and an agent of persecutory anxiety. If we narrow our focus from the broader culture to the immediate environment of the organization, we may observe a related set of metaphors. For individuals embedded within an organization with a cyber system, that system, symbolically if not in fact, may represent the aspect of the organization that looms larger than they; this, then, is an element of the organization that has more power, more knowledge, and more resources than the individual has, and that can threaten the individual's ability to go on being within the organization. But, to add teeth to the fantasy of annihilation, the cyber system is potentially invasive (via email for example); in this sense, if so used by an organization, the sanctuary of the once-private workspace of the individual may become increasingly public and vulnerable to scrutiny.[30] Because the management presence that underlies computer scrutiny is so disembodied and remote, it can easily appear that it is the computer itself that is doing the invading and broadcasting. In other words, the computer may come to symbolize the "persecutory others" who challenge an individual's autonomy and security.

The objects of these persecutory anxieties, the threatening "others," symbolized by the computer, do not even need to be a part of the organization itself. Mitroff (1983) has developed the notion of the stakeholder:

> Where organizational sociology in particular and political science and sociology in general treat stakeholders that are *external* to the skin of a given individual in society, psychoanalysis and depth psychology treat *internal* stakeholders—those that constitute the innermost core of the individual's psyche. . . . There is a constant interaction, overlap, and interplay between these two broad classes of stakeholders, internal and external to the individual, the organization, the institution, and the state. The concept of the stakeholders, suitably framed, provides a way of seeing the various social sciences in tandem, not in opposition to one another. [pp. 6–7]

The symbolized persecutory other may be any stakeholder in an individual's psychic realm, whether internal or external, or, most typically, some amalgamation or integration of overlapping influences.

Even when the computer is not the direct agent of persecution, it frequently becomes the focus of defensive reactions in societies dominated by the postmodern attitudes described by Gergen (1991) and Hirschhorn (1997). This computer-condemnatory tendency is observed even by some of cyber systems' staunchest supporters:

In government, business, and industry, there is much talk of distributed, parallel, and emergent organizations, whose architecture mirrors that of computer systems. This utopian discourse about decentralization has come into vogue at the same time that society has become increasingly fragmented. Many of the institutions that used to bring people together—a main street, a union hall, a town meeting—no longer work as before. Many people spend most of their day alone at the screen of a television or a computer. [Turkle 1995, pp. 177–178]

An organizational illustration will further develop some of these ideas about cyber systems as symbols and agents of persecutory anxiety that is already present in the environment, but becomes instantiated in the computer system.

Clinical Example: The Cyber System as Agent of Persecution Within a University

A university had been in considerable strife for some time, caught in the grip of irresolvable conflict. The administration was viewed by its foes as narcissistic, arbitrary, self-promoting, egregiously self-indulgent, and willing to sacrifice all to achieve its own self-interested ends. The faculty, in turn, was viewed by its foes as equally self-promoting, disrespectful, antiauthoritarian, adolescently rebellious, defensively protecting its own mediocrity, and willing to sacrifice all to achieve its own self-interested ends. To the extent that substantive issues emerged, these issues focused on the nature of the curriculum and hiring practices, matters of tenure, faculty participation in collective bargaining, and the propriety of the financial conduct of the administration and board of directors. However, most discourse revolved around personal attack on the character and integrity of focal individuals on both sides of the dispute. On the outside, panels had been convened to conduct investigations; criminal action was threatened and media coverage created a continuous stir. Internally, divisiveness and paranoia predominated, in areas that pertained to the conflict directly as well as in areas that were influenced only indirectly. Within the university, as the conflict reached a fever pitch and enrollment tumbled, an air of calamity fell over the entire institution to such an extent that no one seemed impervious to it. Departmental meetings, always either dull or petty, became contentiously fractious in photographic likeness of the conflicts within the university at large; in most departments similar splitting and divisiveness became the rule of thumb. Eventually, even within the classroom, students' discontent, and often unspoken blame, at the positions they were thrust into as a consequence of the overall conflict created another conflict. Yet more splitting and universal feelings of persecution resulted.

As I have noted above, many people respond to pervasive, experientially inescapable, persecutory anxiety by radical attempts to insulate themselves from threat and invasion. These attempts at self-protection may be extreme enough to be characterized clinically either as schizoid withdrawal or as paranoid regression. In each of these versions of the ascendence of the paranoid-schizoid position, people are merely trying to protect themselves from the experience of threat by creating their own impenetrable bulwark.

In the movies and television there is an old standby scene in which the bank robber, surrounded by the police, takes one of the hostages and uses that person's body as protective armor. In the case of the type of paranoid-schizoid behavior that I am describing, the felt experience is the same as in this familiar scene, viewed from the perspective of the robber. However, it is as if instead of using a hostage for protection, the person uses a split-off part of himself or herself in order to become invulnerable to persecutory attacks. Properly shielded, everything persecutory remains on the outside and everything inside remains pure and safe.

There are a couple of difficulties in this particular strategic defensive operation. The first is that it may prove quite difficult to isolate your own experience of parts of yourself to such an extent that you can absorb all the bullets, or experience all the anxiety of absorbing the bullets, without feeling it. Thus, as one shielding part of yourself comes to experience pain or anxiety and communicates this experience to the rest of you, you have to jettison that part and quickly find another. The second difficulty is even more problematic. Typically many of the experiences that we may apprehend as toxically invading us from the outside are, in fact, internal to begin with. This internal toxicity may be the recapitulation and reenactment of earlier life experiences and fantasies of profound frustration, even perhaps persecution, that have long since been woven into the fabric of our own beings. We experience this toxicity to come from the outside because we make every attempt to get rid of it internally. In psychodynamic terms, we project out the toxic experience and simultaneously introject the very same projected material. Thus, the bulwark we have constructed always seems too exposed and vulnerable, because it is always trying to protect us from attacks that originate from inside but are experienced as emanating from outside. So in this defensive stratagem, we are constantly trying to shift the part of ourselves that we use as armor and we are continuously shrinking the perimeter of the protective barrier.

Within the university, the concretization of this paranoid-schizoid defensive stratagem of withdrawal took the form of a retreat into small groups, and eventually into the total isolation of individual offices. However, as isolated as individuals became physically, it remained the case that almost all of the faculty offices were equipped with computer terminals and, naturally, the university had an email system.

The computer system initiation, or sign-on, sequence had been designed with a default condition that routed a user to email whenever the station was turned on or reactivated after a time delay. This meant that, unless the user was sophisticated enough to alter the default condition (which few were), the first screen the user would see was a listing of all incoming email messages; this was true even if a user wanted to get to word processing, library search, database manipulation, or the Internet.

At first, the email system reflected the surrounding conflicts in relatively tangential and innocuous ways, providing notice of meetings or reporting the results of faculty votes or administrative decisions. However, as the conflict grew more pervasive and as the various participants grew more astute in their use of communication tools, the email strings became increasingly long and assaultive. By the time the turmoil reached a fever pitch, to turn on the computer was to be pummeled by a barrage of messages alternatively citing or rebutting each and every media report, as well as any action or reaction by either faction, or by any outside agency.

Interviews with members of the faculty and administration revealed that initially their tendency had been to read, or at least scan, the messages. But as the number and fervor of messages increased, and as the desire to escape the invasive assault grew stronger, all sides began to delete the messages without reading them. According to one faculty member's description, "Deleting the messages was like swatting off black flies. I'd spend five minutes getting rid of them and just when I thought they were all gone, more would appear." In keeping with the metaphor of a narrowing of the walls, a number of people reported that eventually they *stopped turning on their computers* because the experience felt too distressing.

In this instance the information system ceased to provide information. Instead, the data that emanated from it were like Bion's beta particles: things-in-themselves, inescapable shrapnel-like missile fragments of facts that covered the terrain and ricocheted about so that it grew impossible to conclude if their source was internal or external. In Bion's (1929) words, it was "a situation in which the personality attacked its object with such violence that not only was the object deemed to become minutely fragmented, but the personality likewise" (p. 58). The computer system and its contents came increasingly to symbolize *and* to realize the persecutory experience *in both its externalized and its internalized forms.*

It is vital to remember that if circumstances at this university had been different, the email system might have been used primarily to facilitate scholarship or collegiality, perhaps even to promote the delivery of higher education to the students. Like the example of the phantom meetings, this vignette illustrates a use to which the system can be put and the ease with which this can be accomplished.

These examples have illustrated some of the many ways in which a cyber system can enhance the likelihood of paranoid-schizoid functioning within an organization. My central thesis, however, is not so one-sided. I am arguing that such irresolvable paranoid-schizoid functioning is not the only possible outcome. Rather, I would like to demonstrate that even in the face of such paranoid-schizoid organizational process, the cyber system can also be used to mobilize the close likenesses of whole-object relationships, which I am calling paranoid-schizoid relatedness.

Paranoid-Schizoid Relatedness

In previous chapters I developed the notion of paranoid-schizoid relatedness by adding to the mix of Melanie Klein's ideas that we have already used, her notion of scotomization, or the denial of psychic reality (Klein 1935), Matte-Blanco's notion of the fundamental antinomy between a symmetrical and symmetrical organizations of experience, and my own thoughts about transformational processes. In the first four chapters I have used these ideas to focus primarily on individuals' use of the Internet and email in more private aspects of their lives. Among the examples I used as illustration were the case of Patrick to illustrate transformational processes (Chapter 3), the case of the man who lost his "perfect love" (Chapter 2), the case of Miranda (Chapter 3), and the case of Tonja (Chapter 4) to illustrate different aspects of paranoid-schizoid relatedness.

These same processes are at work within our organizational lives as well. Thus, for many people the feeling of being in relationship to others is vitally important. For them, it is a vital part of their continuing to function well on their jobs that they develop the illusion of whole-object experience. This craving for the feeling of relatedness may remain present even within workplaces in which individuals consider themselves to be surrounded by persecutory motive and intent; in other words, people may still crave relatedness at the same time that they remain trapped in paranoid-schizoid withdrawal. The following case illustrates one such instance of paranoid-schizoid relatedness in an organizational environment.

Clinical Example: Intranet-Based Paranoid-Schizoid Relatedness in an Organization

A large domestic company with diversified holdings and decentralized operations made the decision to install common, but individually tailored, intranet-based, work-flow and work-analysis systems in each of its centers of management operations. Conceptually, the system was designed to allow each center to analyze its own work-flow patterns so that the corporation-wide consulting team could create a specific version of the software package to fit the needs of the individual company while remaining consistent with overall design parameters. As a whole, the system would facilitate for top management the sort of instantaneous view of overall operations that it felt it needed without unduly interfering with individual operations management.

As an intranet-based system, the company decided to harness the power of Internet communications, but to isolate and insulate that power so that a finite universe of users (its employee base) could have available all the information they might need at all times. So, to cite a few examples, if a salesperson needed to determine the status of a special manufacturing work order, that information was available in real time. Similarly, if management determined that prices should change, price sheets could be distributed over the intranet and management could determine which salespersons were selling at the revised prices. System statistics and log-analyses could be used to determine which employees actually received which intranet transferred documents, and when and how often they did so. Much of what had traditionally been paperwork was now scanned in and moved from location to location electronically, leaving a perfect audit trail, rendering current operations much more efficient and making work status determinations transparent.

In many ways the installation approached optimal levels. The implementation team was superior and well versed in overcoming employees' fears and trepidations about change. In most situations the changes were relatively straightforward and left little room for major design error. Since top management was wholeheartedly behind the changes, middle management throughout the majority of the operations facilitated the implementations and assisted the implementation teams in motivating employee compliance.

Technically, despite the requisite number of glitches and schedule slippages, implementation was encouragingly successful in most of the management centers. Typically, the more isolated a satellite operation was from corporate, the more difficult the implementation was, but even these operations eventually fell into line. Initial reports suggested that, even with the errors and misgivings that inevitably accompany the introduction of new technologies and new ways of doing old business, efficiency and productivity were indeed on the rise. Similarly, management was ecstatic with the availability of up-to-the-minute data on operations.

Soon, however, a curious phenomenon appeared to emerge from work analyses. Rather than continuing to demonstrate improving efficiency, or even reaching a plateau, efficiency and productivity appeared to be on the course of a rapid decline. After exhausting almost all other possibilities, management suspected a decline in morale, but, surprisingly, initial job satisfaction questionnaires revealed stable levels of job satisfaction. It was only when detailed, confidential, clinical interviews with company personnel were undertaken that it began to emerge that the picture was even more complicated than management had suspected and that the very topics we have been considering were playing a key role in what was happening.

From the points of view of workers embedded within the system, the installation of the new intranet-based systems had any number of consequences. In general, employees reported that they were able to do their jobs much more easily than before, that they felt increasingly comfortable with the technology, that they were visiting more intranet locations more frequently, and that they found these visits more useful. The first two of these reports were subsequently confirmed by site statistics and log-analyses. But these analyses also found that although people were staying on the wire longer during each visit, fewer bytes of data per minute were being transferred. Management's inference was that people were using the sites for other than their intended business.

This inference proved consistent with confidential clinical dialogues with individual employees. From the perspectives of a number of these employees, despite the technological improvements, and despite their satisfaction with their increased capacities to perform their jobs, they recently had begun to find the work environment increasingly hostile. Many of their perceptions fell into two global categories. On the one hand, workers perceived the management environment to be more invasive. Even if they could do their jobs better, their performance was more open to scrutiny. In fact, the interviews themselves were cited as an instance of this intrusion. Several employees, at various levels of responsibility, reported that their performance reviews had turned sharply harsher subsequent to the installation of the new systems and that they felt much more vulnerable, and, even more distressing to them, they were not always even certain about the nature of their vulnerability. They knew they were being monitored, but it was not always readily apparent what they were being monitored for.

Most condemning of the new systems, however, was a complaint that seemed to cut across all levels of the management hierarchy, even to the ranks of top management. In addition to the complaints about vulnerability, workers and managers alike reported that with the advent of the newer and most sophisticated technologies, much of what had been fun about their jobs had changed. There was less of a sense of community, less time for social interaction, less fun. The consensus was that with the improvement in work flow and data access, they had lost a great deal of something that had provided them with satisfaction in their jobs. Quite simply, people were missing the very sorts of inefficient, but enjoyable, interpersonal interactions that the new systems were designed to minimize.

Consistent with the findings of decreasing productivity and the log-analyses showing greater time per call with less data transferred per minute, it became evident that the intranet system was being used increasingly as a social instrument. In fact, a number of employees reported that the relationships they had developed within the company, often with co-workers in distant locations whom they never met in person, were relationships that they valued greatly. It became clear that many of the workers feared that among other more overtly fearful punishments, their intranet privileges would be taken away if the real truth were to emerge.

Sarah was typical of this group of employees. A highly sophisticated, well-educated woman, she had worked in technical marketing for five years before the implementation. Enthusiastic about technology in general, she had been among the torchbearers for the new systems, volunteering to use her work area as a beta test site for the marketing section of the system. As enthusiastic as she was, Sarah's adaptation to technology was, as Turkle (1995, p. 51) aptly puts it, "associative . . . a 'soft' style as opposed to a hard one." She loved to work from the bottom up, trying everything she could try to get the feel of it, making mistakes for the sake of learning experientially rather than through preplanned analysis. She was what Turkle, borrowing from Lévi-Strauss, calls a *bricoleur*, someone who thinks through situations by using the materials at hand and whose work was "marked by a desire to play" (p. 52) rather than to accomplish. Outside of work she was an artist who loved to experiment with different media but who ultimately preferred to work "with things that I can feel in my hands."

Sarah had always been reasonably confident and proud of her work, and felt that she had enjoyed a wide range of casual social relations within the company. Much to her dismay, her first performance review after the installation was resoundingly negative. For the first time in her recollection, her boss, who had always valued her work highly, confronted her with a set of data analyses that showed that her performance levels were substandard, that her planning efforts were not on a par with the rest of her department, and that she was out of sync with progress-reporting requirements.

For Sarah, her performance at her job had long been a cornerstone of her identity. She was crushed by the harshness of review, and as she sought comfort and reassurance in the wake of it, she also realized that she had become progressively isolated from co-workers with whom she might have shared her dismay and confusion. Some of her previous friends, people in her department who earlier had shared a common work area, were working on different technologies and had been moved to different floors. Sarah had found little opportunity to interact with the people in her immediate physical surround even though they were working on different dimensions of the same projects as she. Whenever she tried to initiate a conversation, she found that they didn't share her marketing interests and appeared to have little interest in getting to know her. Even when they needed reports and analyses that Sarah had, they got the information they needed from her off the intranet.

In the beginning, Sarah started chatting over the Net with her friends who had been moved to different locations, stretching to find valid marketing reasons to make the initial contacts and then using the opportunity to socialize. However, in the course of her wanderings through a business day on-line, she soon found new partners, several in different geographical locations altogether. These were people who, more than anything else, shared her experience of what was happening to them within the organization.

Sarah did not ignore her job. In fact, she had become haunted by a fear that a failure to perform would result in her losing her job. But, perhaps even more than systematic planners, *bricoleurs* such as she react poorly to pressure and anxiety. In the past Sarah had approached her work in a spirit of playful experimentation, but progressively she came to experience it as a random walk through a minefield. Whenever the pressure felt too great, or she feared that her next step would blast her into tiny bits, she found herself switching screens and relieving her anxiety by chatting on the intranet until she felt calm enough to resume her efforts. Refreshed and renewed, she approached her work again; but now Sarah had been forced into the much more unfamiliar role of the systematic planner than the *bricoleur*. For a while she would toil with as much regimentation as she could muster, until she once again felt overwhelmed and had to repeat the process anew.

Sarah's case study demonstrates one version of the use of a cyber system to facilitate paranoid-schizoid relatedness within an organizational environment. For Sarah, and for many of her co-workers, the corporate environment had become increasingly persecutory. As she tried to do her job, she experienced crescendos of anxiety, which reached levels that she found intolerable. Seeking refuge from her psychic reality, Sarah plunged into the intranet. She abandoned the processes of transformation that had always guided her through her playful work before and came to alternate between periods of timeless, goalless symmetrical experience, afloat in the intranet, and periods of asymmetrical experience, carefully inching her way through the minefield. Each of these experiences of living, when being lived, constituted the entirety of living. Concretely and completely, Sarah had divided her world at work in two, and this division remained unchallenged and total, with no transformations between these separate spheres and, in the spirit of concreteness, no anxiety.

For Sarah, the persecutory atmosphere of her working world had reached a level she no longer could tolerate. Splitting apart her experiences of symmetry and her experiences of asymmetry, and keeping these ways of organizing her sense of living as separate as they could be kept, allowed Sarah to continue living in a world that would have driven her crazy. Her paranoid-schizoid adaptation to the working environment shielded the aspects of her being that craved relating with people from the aspects of her being that knew with certainty that relating with people implied annihilation. Just as Miranda did within her world (see Chapter 3), Sarah created for herself within her workplace a potential space. In this facilitating environment, in which whole-object relating could be played at within the safety and security of a part-object, concretely symmetrical world, Sarah once again learned to take pleasure at, if not in, her work.

Sarah's case has served to illustrate one use of cyberspace as potential space within an organizational environment. Sarah was able to establish a form of relating that allowed her to go on functioning despite her constant anxiety about organizational annihilation. In the case of the university, in contrast, the cyber system became an extension of persecutory experience. In the case of the phantom, Ralph, the cyber system became a surrogated retaliatory vehicle, a separate world without creative potential in which he found himself unconsciously enacting dissociated elements of the CEO's behavior. In many other, more benign, cases a cyber system may function within an organization with neutral valence, neither fostering persecution nor abetting escape from persecutory anxieties.

Summary

Organizational life has been altered profoundly by computers and computer systems. Few organizations remain that have resisted dependence on computers to execute vital aspects of internal functioning. As Turkle (1995) has suggested, this reliance on the computer has moved far beyond its capacities as a calculator, and thus, to borrow her suggestive ideas, we live now as much in an age of simulation as we do in an age of calculation. However, from the first use of computers within military organizations to their present ubiquity, they have brought with them the specter of malfunction and misuse. From fears of inadvertent computer-generated nuclear attack to inventory miscounts, we arguably have lived in fear of computer mis-calculation as much as we may have benefited from the speed and accuracy of computer calculation. Similarly, our increased levels of organizational paranoia reflect ways in which we have learned to fear computational dis-simulation as much as we may have benefited from a capacity to simulate. These contradictions bring along with them profound anxieties and conflicts that extend to every worker and manager whose life is touched by these systems. In the current atmosphere of organizational life, few remain untouched. In this chapter, I have hinted at the complexity of these conflicts, describing a few of the ways in which computer systems serve both to enhance and to attack the sense of psychological well-being that exists within the organization, for both managers and workers.

I have attempted to trace some of the ways in which contemporary Internet and intranet-based cyber systems demonstrate a commanding power to broadcast and amplify dissociated facets of top executives' personalities, serving both as a symbol of the dissociation and as a vehicle to propagate these dissociated characterological phenomena through the functioning of the rest of the organization. I have used a number of psychoanalytic ideas to demonstrate some ways in which, in organizations just as elsewhere, the Internet facilitates a type of functioning that has a subjective feeling of sociability and relatedness, while remaining relatively isolated, asocial, or at best partially social, self-protective, and removed.

In his book *The Wired Neighborhood*, Stephen Doheny-Farina (1996) argues that computers have led us away from the geographical and physical communities around which our lives had been centered previously and that this movement toward a wired neighborhood has a tremendous personal cost. The same ideas may extend to organizational life as well. In Sarah's case we saw her reaction to the loss of the physical community that had meant so much to her within her workplace. To the extent that she replaced this physical community with a wired community she epitomizes both the loss, of which Doheny-Farina speaks, and the effort to recapture at least the illusion of the lost. It is this effort to recapture on which I focus ultimately. For many of us, despite the dramatic increase in cyber commuting, a great deal of our waking life is still spent in an organizational context. Even though computers may have made it possible to extend this context beyond the physical, we still rely on psychological strategies to make our organizational lives more tolerable.

Within organizations, as well as in our private lives, computers and their associated systems have enhanced our functioning and augmented our abilities to play and express ourselves. At the same time, they have fostered the wholesale organizational broadcasting of dissociated experience and engendered persecutory anxieties, based on both real and fantasied threats. This is the context of irresolvable conflict in which all of us now lead our organizational lives. In this chapter I have described ways in which some people have tried to adapt and go on functioning.

6 At the Still Point of the Turning World: Transformation and Potentiation or Constriction and Annihilation

At the still point of the turning world. Neither flesh nor fleshless;
Neither from nor towards; at the still point, there the dance is,
But neither arrest nor movement. And do not call it fixity,
Where past and future are gathered. Neither movement from nor towards,
Neither ascent nor decline. Except for the point, the still point,
There would be no dance, and there is only the dance.
I can only say, there we have been; *but I cannot say where.*
And I cannot say, how long, for that is to place it in time.
The inner freedom from the practical desire,
The release from action and suffering, release from the inner
And the outer compulsion, yet surrounded
By a grace of sense, a white light still and moving,
Erhebung *without motion, concentration*
without elimination, both a new world
And the old made explicit, understood
In the completion of its partial ecstacy,
The resolution of its partial horror.
Yet the enchainment of past and future
Woven in the weakness of the changing body,
Protects mankind from heaven and damnation
Which flesh cannot endure.

"Burnt Norton," T. S. Eliot (1935)

In the preceding chapters I have described ways in which a number of individuals have made use of computer-mediated communication. In many of these descriptions personal experiences of anxiety have played a considerable role. From these descriptions I am inferring a theoretical model regarding the technologies involved and the anxieties that fuel the use of these technologies in the context of a larger social picture.

I am suggesting that here at the millennial interface of Janus, many people experience the world as profoundly, unalterably, and unavoidably menacing. By "the world" I mean both the external environment—the invasive threats of violence, oppression, politics, economics, crime, pollution, and the like—and the internal environment—the retaliatory, potentially annihilatory menace occasioned by private frustrations and personal desires, by profoundly individual experiences of inadequacy, overwhelming and insatiable needs that may bring a person to fantasize destroying the very same objects they depend on and love the most.

I am borrowing from the psychoanalytic theory of object relations the concept that, in the face of profound persecutory anxiety, people strive to keep separate, and thus keep safe, aspects of experience that, if seen as a whole, would become wholly contaminated. However safe this splitting apart may feel, many people retain a simultaneous desire for wholeness that contradicts the desire for security. The use of technology facilitates this striving for separation and desire for wholeness in unique, remarkable, and profoundly ambiguous ways. Communication mediated through the computer-linked web of the Internet has the potential to be, to quote Eliot once again, "At the still point of the turning world. Neither flesh nor fleshless; Neither from nor towards; at the still point" where the dance is, where there is neither arrest nor movement. In its position between the flesh and fleshless, between substance and thought, the Internet may facilitate the experience of the partial as if it is the whole.

From Winnicott (1971) we have learned about the transitional object that exists in the middle ground between "me" and "not me" as well as between fantasy and reality and between that which is created and that which is found. We have learned from Winnicott that play is the archetypal process through which we mature psychologically. Like the Internet, which is neither flesh nor fleshless, neither substance nor thought, play "is in fact neither a matter of inner psychic reality nor a matter of external reality" (p. 96). For Winnicott, "cultural experience [which] is located in the *potential space* between the individual and the environment. . . begins with creative living first manifested in play" (p. 100).

These ideas have brought me to a formulation of one question that is at the center of this investigation. Given the ways in which the Internet may serve as a shield from persecutory anxiety by simulating whole experiences out of the substance and thought of partial ones, to what extent and under what conditions is communication mediated through the computer links of the Internet one form of the type of cultural life that constitutes playful transition?

As a simple corollary of this question, I have been led to ask related questions. Thus, I have asked: Is the valorization of playful transition a bias that does a disservice to the exigencies of living here at the millennial interface of Janus? Is life at the interstices between substance and thought, flesh and fleshless, in fact an optimal adaptation to the experiences of persecution and abandonment that, for some individuals, attend to alternative ways of being? Can experience at the still point in a turning world dis-enchain past and future, avoid the anxieties "woven in the weakness of the changing body," and still protect those people from the striving for heaven or the fleeing from damnation that "flesh cannot endure"? Is a preference for life on-line something we should not think of as fixity? Is it, for some people, a way of experience that locates otherwise missing meaning in being?

> And do not call it fixity,
>
> Where past and future are gathered. Neither movement from nor
> towards,
>
> Neither ascent nor decline. Except for the point, the still point,
>
> There would be no dance, and there is only the dance.
>
> I can only say, *there* we have been; but I cannot say where.
>
> And I cannot say, how long, for that is to place it in time."
>
> "Burnt Norton," T. S. Eliot (1935)

The ideas underlying the exploration of these questions begin with the theories of Harold Searles and of Melanie Klein. From Searles (1960) I borrow the notion that "there is within the human individual a sense, whether at a conscious or unconscious level, of *relatedness to his nonhuman environment*, that this relatedness is one of the transcendentally important facts of human living" (p. 6). Searles writes that the infant experiences himself to be as much in a state of relative undifferentiation from the nonhuman environment as from the balance of the human environment. Moreover, "The human being is engaged, throughout his life span, in an unceasing struggle to differentiate himself increasingly fully, not only from his human, but also from this nonhuman environment, while developing, in proportion as he succeeds in these differentiations, an increasingly meaningful relatedness with the latter environment as well as with his fellow human beings" (p. 30).

From Melanie Klein, I borrow a number of ideas, in particular her developmental theory in which the classically Freudian view of ratchet-like, stepwise psychosexual stages (oral, anal, etc.) is exchanged for nonsequential, overlapping "positions."

> I am now using the word "position" in relation to the child's early developmental psychotic anxieties and defenses. It seems to me easier to associate with this term than with the words "mechanisms" or "phases," the differences between the developmental psychotic anxieties of the child and the psychoses of the adult: e.g., the quick change-over that occurs from a per-

secution-anxiety or depressed feeling to a normal attitude—a change-over
that is so characteristic for the child. [Klein 1935, p. 276 n]

These psychological positions mirror the different ways that our experience is organized as a function of the specific form of anxiety that prevails within our experiential realm at a given moment in time. The developmentally earliest of these positions, characterized by the prevailing
experience of large amounts of persecutory anxiety, is termed the paranoid-schizoid position. Although the paranoid-schizoid organization of
experience typifies very early development, it reappears in continuous
oscillation with alternative positions throughout the life span; the paranoid-schizoid position is most felt whenever aspects of our experiential
world regain a prevalence of the persecutory. The hallmark of paranoid-
schizoid functioning is the defensive process of splitting. Splitting attempts
to isolate from experiences perceived as positive the experiences perceived
as negative that might contaminate and ruin them. In the presence of
abundant experience of persecutory anxiety, an individual might try to
use splitting to attempt to preserve loving experience from contamination by hateful experience, to preserve good experience from being
ruined by bad experience, to save love from the external environment from
contamination by internal foulness or vice versa.

Still following Klein, the theory dictates that in splitting, and in other
ways, we use various projective and introjective mechanisms to keep separate good and bad experiences. For example, when hate overwhelms the
possibility of feeling good, we try to project out the hate, even if we risk
accidentally losing the good feelings as well. The splitting and the projective and introjective mechanisms function to promote relationships
among parts of things rather than whole things; this includes, but is not
limited to, preferring partial, or part-object, relatedness to whole, or whole-
object, relatedness.

In contrast to the paranoid-schizoid position, the depressive position
features depressive anxieties. In this developmentally later way of experiencing, we relate to whole versions of others and whole versions of self.

The depressive anxiety emerges from the realization that the part objects of our hatred are identical to the part objects of our love. We can no longer keep a clean separation between the aspects of our being that we hate and the aspects that we love. In the depressive position we become forced to deal with feelings of guilt, to struggle to make amends for the hurt we have caused ourselves and others by our hatred. Quite naturally, most people manage to deal with depressive anxiety and remain, for the most part, in the world of whole objects. Nonetheless, whole-object relations are always vulnerable to excessive persecutory experience. Countless sagas of war and natural tragedy reveal extreme situations in which experience becomes so intolerably persecutory that splitting of one sort or another is the only way to survive. Even in the face of less dramatic or tragic events, we perpetually oscillate back to paranoid-schizoid organizations of experience when our experience becomes too menacing.

Life at the millennial interface of Janus confronts many individuals with such large measures of persecutory anxiety that they undergo, simultaneously, a *dedifferentiation* between human and nonhuman environments and a *reversion* to predominantly paranoid-schizoid organizations of experience. Thus, in a manner consistent with Klein's ideas, under the sway of this persecutory anxiety, people may attempt to create for themselves large areas of functioning that are split off, or at some remove and protected from the most overtly perceived sources of potential persecution. Simultaneously, in a manner consistent with Searles's ideas, people may experience a dedifferentiation, or a de-focusing, of the boundaries between nonhuman (machine) and human.

But, this is far from the whole picture. To apprehend the whole of Janus we must accept simultaneously the opposing poles of the cyberspace dialectic. This is a dialectic that finds at one pole a view of the individual in cyberspace as insular and disconnected from the influence of others; at the opposite pole that same individual is viewed as intensely involved in complex exchanges between aspects of self and aspects of others.

I have cited Turkle as an articulate and convincing proponent of the primacy of the latter pole. In her arguments, Turkle invokes Winnicott's

(1971) notions of transitional and potential space, those realms of nearly infinite fascination that are "neither inside the individual nor outside in the world of shared reality" (p. 110). As their designations imply, for Winnicott, hence for Turkle, these are realms of progress and growth; these "spaces" represent the capacity for human beings actually to be and to go on being. Turkle advances the French psychoanalytic notion of a de-centering of the ego in stressing the importance of the facilitation of multiplicity of being. To this end, she argues that computer-mediated communication serves a transitional or potentiating function, that cyber-space is, in fact, a potential space. Others, notably Haraway (1997), Stone (1995), and Faber (1984), advance similar views.

Within the dialectic of cyberspace, in the full face of Janus, each of these poles is wedded to the other. All use of the computer-mediated communication tools of the Internet is not in the service of paranoid-schizoid retreat to a realm of dedifferentiation between nonhuman and human; nor is all use of cyberspace necessarily transitional or potentiating. For some who have felt themselves compelled to seek retreat from most connection with actual others, the Internet may serve as a tool for engaging in something that can pass for a complete and satisfying relationship. Even among these people, we have found at least two groups: those who, wittingly or not, use this experience as a transitional process to facilitate the turn or return to more conventional relatedness and those who find it best to remain in the comforting security of their own, now nearly infinite, realm of control. For yet another group, these issues seem to cloud the picture. For these people, communication mediated by the computer has no particular relational valence, no greater signification than telephone contact, writing letters, or shaking hands at a party. For them, communicating via the Internet is merely another way of making contact without being completely in touch.

In developing a deeper theoretical argument for these distinctions, and the causes underlying them, I have made use of Matte-Blanco's concept of the fundamental antinomy between symmetrical and asymmetrical organizations of experience, as well as some of my own ideas about the transformations between these organizations of experience. Asymmetrical logic may be thought of as the logic of most conscious experience in which experience is always located with respect to the three dimensions of Euclidean space in the same way that it is uniquely oriented in time. In asymmetry, cause and effect prevail. The logic, or method of organization, of symmetrical experience is the logic of emotional experience, of dream life, and of fantasy. If somebody or something stands in a certain relation to another thing (or person), then that other thing (or person) stands in the equivalent relation to the first thing. In symmetrical logic, the converse of any relation is experienced as identical to the relation itself. Thus, nothing differs clearly from any other thing, nothing happens clearly and uniquely before anything else, and nothing is in clear and unique causal relation to anything else.

Since both symmetrical and asymmetrical organizations are aspects of all experience, they are in constant relation to one another. However, since they are so differently composed, the relation requires continuous psychological work; it is this work of connecting that I term the processes of transformation. In this book, I have traced ways in which the triadic model of symmetry, asymmetry, and transformation help explain the varying roles of computer-mediated communication using the Internet.

This way of framing experience helps to clarify different reactions to persecutory anxiety. This triadic model suggests any number of ways to minimize persecutory threats, many of which I have illustrated with examples drawn from Internet relationships. At the extremes, for example, people might try to minimize anxiety by eliminating one modality of experience or the other, or eliminating the transformational processes that connect the two. If the capacity to organize experience symmetrically is extinguished, people would lose contact with intuitive and impressionistic ways of being, as well as with the ability to generalize, symbolize, and create. This grossly obsessive style relegates experience to facts. Persecution is kept outside because inside no longer exists as a meaningful experience. Anxiety is just a word.

Persecutory anxiety also may be avoided by jettisoning reason and order, by eliminating the asymmetrical experience of logical thought, spatial/temporal orientation, intentionality, and causal relations. Without asymmetry to fashion meaningful distinctions, this grossly hysteric style leaves "meaning" without meaning. Persecutory anxiety cannot occur since anticipatory anxiety itself depends on a linear, forward-moving impression of time as well as causal relations.

Yet another way of avoiding excessive persecutory anxiety may occur by isolating our experience of order and causality from our experience of emotion and association. Under normal circumstances, symmetrical and asymmetrical experiences are linked via processes of transformation. However, if these processes of transformation are disconnected, so is the link between persecutor and persecuted. This grossly borderline style creates alterations between order and disorder, emotion and logic, chaos and structure, with no connections between the poles of experience. In this experience without transformation, meaning becomes so disarrayed and disjointed that it is meaningless. Persecution and anxiety lose signification in disconnection; if there is no link between them, there can be no meaningful meaning to the words *hunter* and *hunted, attacker* and *attacked, destroyer* and *destroyed.* For example, for there to be meaning, the hunter would have to be hunting the hunted and the hunted avoiding the hunter. Without these connections, the words remain only potentially meaningful.

These are a few of the mechanisms through which psychic reality may be denied. This concept of the denial of psychic reality, in the context of Matte-Blanco's conception of the antinomy of symmetrical and asymmetrical organizations of experience, as well as my own elaboration of the notion of transformational processes, has shed light on ways that computer-mediated communication can facilitate a number of forms of paranoid, or part-object, relatedness. In one form of paranoid relatedness, the links of the Internet function as ways of playing with aspects of being. In this version of paranoid relatedness, persecutory experience is obscured through the veil of part-object experience that simulates whole-object experience. The simulated experience of being a whole person (or a multiplicity of being), once again dealing with other whole (or multiply experienced) people, facilitates the restoration of triadic experience that includes symmetrical and asymmetrical organizations as well as an infinite array of transformational processes connecting the two. In this way, Internet links become transitional links from the cell of withdrawal to the world of interpersonal engagement. In another form of paranoid relatedness, however, life on-line emerges as substitutive for the qualities and characteristics of real-life relatedness. In this version, the anxiety of persecutory experience is also avoided, but the restoration of flexibly triadic experience is subordinated to the maintenance of fixed and isolative ways of linking symmetrical and asymmetrical forms of experience.

In this book I have relied heavily on case studies to formulate and illustrate these complex and unfamiliar theoretical ideas. These case studies have grown out of clinical and consultational contacts, out of conversations with colleagues and supervisees, and out of the rapidly growing literature about and on the Internet. Here, at the millennial borderline between substance and thought that I have called the interface of Janus, it is easy enough to find our own still point in a turning world; these theories can be tested out by any reader as easily as the computer is booted up and the Internet is accessed.

In a recent discussion on one Internet newsgroup, one subscriber related his personal story of having been the victim of chat-room terrorism. His story was echoed, and commented on, by a number of other subscribers. As with Dibbell's "rape in cyberspace," through the interpenetration of the isolative and the attacking, much is revealed about persecutory anxieties and people's attempts to escape from them. Stories like these are available on-line for all to read and ponder. Nor is reading and pondering the only mode of study. From a vantage point in the midst of the millennial interface of the Internet, a reader may lurk over these messages at a safe distance, become intensely involved in dialogue, or, with a swift double-click, switch to participate safely in another activity—perhaps in heated discussions of the latest news on the impeachment of a president, the bombing of a nation halfway around the globe, or the co-creation of a dance at the still point of a world that never will have to turn.

Notes

1. There is a good deal of the oedipal in this historical anecdote. In the male version of the positive oedipal dynamic of classical psychoanalysis, the young man desires emancipation, to have for himself what the father has. While the most notable instantiation of this desire is the mother herself, in a larger sense it may be seen to encompass the whole range of powers and freedoms that the boy attributes to the father. To achieve this desire, the boy sees in his father an adversary against whom he must take up arms and triumph, however fearful he may be of the retaliation that may ensue. In the proto-story of the Luddites, Ludlam smashes his father's knitting loom in the process of emancipation, and the Luddites themselves take up arms against their powerful mechanistic oppressors. In a favorable outcome to the oedipal struggle, the boy achieves his emancipation by resolving the conflict with the father through internalization and subsequently identification with the powerful image of the father. In this sense, the mythical General Ned Ludd himself becomes the internal oedipal imago, meant to foster a sense of personal powerfulness in the would-be emancipation of the followers. Clearly, not every oedipal outcome is favorable.

2. The Turing game can be described in terms of a game that we call the "imitation game." It is played with three people, a man (A), a woman (B), and an interrogator (C), who may be of either sex. The interrogator stays in a room apart from the other two. The object of the game for the interrogator is to determine which of the other two is the man and which is the woman. He knows them by the labels X and Y, and at the end of the game he says either "X is A and Y is B" or "X is B and Y is A." The interrogator is allowed to put questions to A and B thus:

Will X please tell me the length of his or her hair? Now suppose X is actually A, then A must answer. It is A's object in the game to try to cause C to make the wrong indication. His answer might therefore be

"My hair is shingled, and the longest strands are about nine inches long."

In order that tones of voice may not help the interrogator, the answers should be written or typewritten. The ideal arrangement is to have a teleprinter communication between the two rooms. Alternatively, the questions and answers can be repeated by an intermediary. The object of the game for the third player (B) is to help the interrogator. The best strategy for her is probably to give truthful answers, but it will avail nothing as the man can make similar remarks.

We now ask the question, "What will happen when a machine takes the part of A in this game?" Will the interrogator decide wrongly as often when the game is played like this as he does when the game is played between a man and a woman? These questions replace our original, "Can machines think?"

3. These are the theoretical and expository problems with which psychoanalytic thought has struggled from its beginning. From the preconscious (Freud 1900) and the complemental series (Freud 1905) to potential space (Winnicott 1971) and bi-logic (Matte-Blanco 1975), psychoanalytic theory has concerned itself with the infinitely dimensioned intersections of people's lives in relation to their internal experiences and their social surround.

4. Winnicott speculates that earlier in infancy, prior to these transitional experiences, the infant lives in a world in which its "primary love" for the caregiving figure intersects to a large extent with the caregiver's "primary maternal preoccupation" for taking care of the child. In such an environment, what befalls the infant lies either within its realm of omnipotent control (whether that control is initiated by the caregiver or the infant) or outside of that omnipotent control. Quite naturally, most "good" experience lies within (and is, therefore, "me") and most "bad" experience lies without (and is therefore "not me"), but there is no ambiguity between these two experiences. As the infant matures physically and emotionally within a "good enough" caregiving environment, the teddy bears or blankets emerge in a new, ambiguous middle ground. They are always with the child, and therefore a part of it and within its omnipotent control, and yet, simultaneously and irresolvably, they remain outside the physical envelop. Thus, for example, if tossed over the edge of the crib, they may be seen but not retrieved. Winnicott suggests that it is in this paradoxical tension and ambiguity between that which is within our control and that which remains outside of us that we live for the rest of our lives. In relative health, we find ourselves able to use the paradoxical tension to make transitions, to grow and develop, and, thus, the term *transitional*, or *potential*, *space*. However, in the absence of relative health, the paradox can neither be embraced nor used.

The use of the word *space* in both *cyberspace* and *potential space* has become a convention. I believe that we are dealing not with spatial constructs, but rather with aspects of process.

5. The broadcasting and amplification of dissociated experience via projective identification is one clear example of such a debilitating process at work. Within many Kleinian and post-Kleinian psychoanalytic views, dissociated issues, which remain unformulated consciously and are thus unavailable for symbolic (e.g., linguistic) communication, are communicated via what are known as projective and introjective identificatory pathways. Differing views of such projective identificatory processes are

far too numerous to summarize here (see, e.g., Kernberg 1975, Ogden 1982), but the manner in which I am using projective identification here is closely related to Racker's (1968) concept of complementary identifications and Searles's (1979) concept of pathological symbioses. Within both of these theories, dissociated or unconscious and hence unavailable aspects of the internal world of one person mobilize unconscious complementary reactions in other people. Following Racker, influenced by such unconscious dissociative process, one person may treat another not as that actual person, but rather as an aspect of their own internal world and, in a complementary identification, the other person is induced to behave in a way that corresponds to that aspect of the first person's internal world.

To illustrate, imagine a woman who, for whatever reasons in her own personal history, comes unconsciously to expect of intimate others that they will not attend to her or be genuinely interested in her. In one or another way, through her overt behavior or more subtle ways of being, perhaps by hiding her true desires, perhaps by attacking the intimate other, she manages to induce in that person, at an unconscious level, the very lack of interest or lack of genuine concern that she had anticipated. The projective identification then functions as the self-fulfillment of a prophecy that has never been given conscious voice. In this way, the use of an object for projective identification is the opposite of the use of a person as an element of transitional space.

The issue here is the extent to which cyber systems, and email in particular, serve as particularly convenient vehicles for projective identification. In an example from the world of organizations, in Chapter 5 I show how the email system is used to broadcast and amplify dissociated aspects of the personality of a CEO through the ranks of an entire organization, creating mayhem in the process. I provide a number of other examples in which the computer appears to be used as an agent that maintains, even fosters, dissociative states of being. Such use stands in considerable contrast to the ways in which some writers, notably Turkle and Faber, have portrayed the potential of cyberspace.

6. The way in which I discuss relatedness and disconnection may be thought of in terms of the Kleinian concepts of positions. The psychoanalyst Melanie Klein redirected psychoanalytic thought in many ways. Of particular moment here is her replacement of the Freudian concept of stepwise psychosexual stages (oral, anal, etc.) with nonsequential, overlapping "positions." "I am now using the word 'position' in relation to the child's early developmental psychotic anxieties and defenses. It seems to me easier to associate with this term than with the words 'mechanisms' or 'phases,' the differences between the developmental psychotic anxieties of the child and the psychoses of the adult: e.g., *the quick change-over that occurs* from a persecution-anxiety or depressed feeling to a normal attitude—a *change-over* that is so characteristic for the child" (Klein 1935, p. 276n, italics mine). As Hinshelwood (1991) has elucidated, by the choice of this term, Klein "wanted to convey, with the idea of position, a much more flexible to-and-fro process" (p. 394). These positions reflect differing ways in which we come to organize our experience according to the prevalence of differing forms of anxiety within our experiential realm. One such position, characterized by the experience of abundant persecutory anxiety, is termed the paranoid-schizoid position. This paranoid-schizoid organization of experience typifies very early development, but is seen to recur and coexist in ever-shifting ways later in life, whenever aspects of our experiential world regain a prevalence of the persecutory. Paranoid-schizoid functioning is characterized by splitting, or the keeping separate of experiences that might be described along a number of different dimensions. Thus, within such a persecutory world, we try, for example, to keep hateful experience from contaminating loving experience, bad experience from contaminating good experience, internal experience from contaminating external experience, the experience of self from contaminating the experience of other. Hand in hand with splitting, in the service of keeping separate these competing organizations of experience, comes the use of various projective and introjective mechanisms. For example, if we feel we are being invaded by hateful experience, we may try to project it out,

even at the risk of evacuating loving experience as well. Similarly, if we feel that loving or good experiences reside outside ourselves, we may try to devour them, even at the risk of introjecting potentially bad or hateful experience accidentally. Since our basic mode of being is to keep aspects of experience separated from each other, it is quite clear why functioning in such a way would serve to promote relationships among parts of things rather than whole things. Adopting the psychoanalytic convention, derived from Freud, of calling people objects (for Freud, somewhat schematically, they are the objects of drives), it is easy enough to envision why the paranoid-schizoid world is the world of part-object relatedness rather than whole-object relatedness. Within the realm of paranoid-schizoid experience, everything is separated and in pieces, including relationships among things. In contrast, the depressive position is an organization of experience characterized by depressive anxieties. In this way of experiencing, we put the parts of objects together into whole visions of others and whole visions of self. As a result, we have to deal with the realization that the part objects of our hatred are either one and the same as, or intimately attached to, the part objects of our love. Similarly, within the depressive position, as much as we might like to, we cannot manage to disentangle the aspects of our being that we abhor from the aspects that we esteem. Such depressive anxieties force us to contend with guilt and to struggle to repair the damage we have done to ourselves and to others by hating that which we love, and loving that which we hate.

While most of us may strive for relatedness that emerges out of relatively whole integrations of both self and other, such relatedness is always under the pressure of aspects of our experience that feel intolerably persecutory. Hence, we perpetually oscillate between depressive and paranoid-schizoid organizations. The concept of whole object and whole self should not be confused with notions of centralized ego, or with static concepts of self and of other. Such static views would be more consistent with ego-psychological views of human functioning. Indeed, as we will see below in discussing Matte-Blanco, within whole-object and whole-self formulations, there is an inherent tension between that which is characterized by fixity and structure and that which is characterized by fluidity and lack of structure. Although it may be debatable how clearly articulated the point is within the writings of Klein herself, it seems logical enough that increasingly strong doses of persecutory immersion will lead to increasingly strong tendencies to function in ways characteristic of paranoid-schizoid organizations of experience.

7. In Kleinian terms, this cell is a version of the paranoid-schizoid position and the complete others are whole-object representations. The limited and partial connections are typical of the types of relatedness that Kleinian psychoanalysts have called part-object relations.

8. An illustration of this emerges from reflection on Harlow's famous research (see, e.g., Harlow and Woolsey 1958). Harlow performed experiments with rhesus monkeys that required housing them for a considerable length of time. Having these lab animals die prior to conducting the experiments was an expensive and troublesome business. Harlow presumed that if he wanted to decrease the mortality rates among the newborn monkeys, he stood the best chance by optimizing their care, rather than leaving it to the caged, perhaps less than perfectly motherly, mothers. Consistent with the thinking of his era, Harlow decided on a procedure of scientific bottle-feeding, separating the baby monkeys from their mothers and isolating them in wire cages. Alarmingly, however, the baby monkeys began to perish at high rates. By chance, some of the monkeys were placed in cages that had been equipped with protective cloth padding. Surprisingly, these monkeys evidenced a greater likelihood of surviving than the monkeys in the bare cages. In fact, they had great resistance to being detached from the padding. Even these monkeys fared poorly, and this led Harlow to conduct his famous experiments. Bowlby (1969, p. 214) notes, "In one experiment eight infant monkeys were raised with the choice of a cloth model and a wire model. Four infants were fed (on demand) from the cloth model and four from the wire model and the time the infants spent on each model was measured. The results showed

... the infants came rapidly to spend most of their time on the cloth model." Even when the wire monkey-mother model was equipped in a manner that could feed the babies and the soft terry-cloth monkey-mother model could not feed, the babies favored the terry-cloth mothers, except for the actual times when they were in the process of nursing. As Allport (1997, p. 167, italics mine) has noted, "Clearly they were very attached *to these seemingly poor maternal substitutes.*"

Harlow, Bowlby, Allport, and countless others have made appropriate use of these studies to advance attachment theories of development and behavior for both offspring and parents. My use of these research observations, while related, has a different focus. One inference we might arrive at from Harlow's studies is that living creatures in the confinement of a cell will seek the best illusion of something that seems like a whole-object.

9. In Kleinian theory the view is that these threats are experienced as coming from without as that which is within is being evacuated, projected outward to be gotten rid of, and subsequently reconsumed.

10. One definition of "flame" is provided by J. C. Herz (1995): "1. (Verb) To publicly post a vituperative ad hominem attack. Because there are no physical cues or verbal inflection on the Net, small misunderstandings often escalate into bouts of serial flamage: flame wars. Flaming is the Net analog of 'talking trash' on the basketball court, or the high-flown vitriol of Slavic curse. 2. (Noun) An instance of flaming" (p. 314).

11. This activity might be explained, in Kleinian psychoanalytic terms, as a sort of mania. In her classic study of manic-depressive states, Melanie Klein (1935) introduced the notion of scotomization, or the denial of psychic reality. In this study, Klein focused particular interest on manic denial. Normally, the mechanisms of denial originate in the paranoid position and are conceived of as ways of keeping separated the good and bad, the inside and outside, and so on. But in Klein's use here, unlike the denial of the paranoid position, "which leads to withdrawal and apragmatism, manic denial is accompanied by hyperactivity and the maintenance

of relations with objects and the external world. The psychic reality against which it is directed is more developed than that of the paranoid position; it is in fact that of the depressive position" (Petot 1991, p. 24). The essence of this form of denial is the attempt by the ego to extricate itself from its objects without giving them up by, on the one hand, denying the importance of the goodness of good objects as well as the dangers of the attacks of bad objects, while, on the other hand acknowledging that "it endeavors ceaselessly to *master and control* all of its objects" (Klein 1935, p. 277).

The concept that I am developing here is, like the one described above, a form of manic denial of psychic reality. However, here the mania and the psychic denial operate from within the paranoid-schizoid position, rather than from within the depressive position and serve to impart a sense of whole-object relatedness while dealing with part-object experience. The mechanism is one of denial because the partial nature of the experience is kept out of awareness. The mania becomes clear in the context of Ingber's (1981) descriptions of computer addiction cited in the main text. Yet, unarguably the overall experience belongs more to paranoid-schizoid organizations of experience than to depressive ones because the undenied psychic reality is in fact one of splitting and part-object relations.

12. This paranoid relatedness is a version of a Kleinian paranoid-schizoid part-object relatedness. This effort keeps "the good apart from the bad, and the real from the phantastic objects. The result is a conception of extremely bad and extremely perfect objects" (Klein 1935, p. 268). The experience of the object as a fragmentation, as "the bits to which the love object has been reduced" is too devastating and "thus, the effort to undo the state of disintegration to which it has been reduced presupposes the necessity to make it beautiful and 'perfect'" (p. 270).

13. Freud's model is based on a theory of human psychological functioning in which drives (aggressive and sexual) are primary. Klein's theory of psychic functioning is a complex one in which the language of drive discharge predominates, at the same time that she appears to be describ-

ing a model of human psychological functioning in which the fantasies and actualities of relatedness predominate. For Matte-Blanco, the drive-theory aspects of the Freudian model are irrelevant.

14. As noted, in many ways we can associate the logic of asymmetry with conscious experience. As conscious experience, it is organized in a manner consistent with the four dimensions of space and time that we share as a species. This organization follows, for the most part, the laws of causality and temporal spatial reasoning that form the cognitive-affective continuum with our fellow humans. This would be consistent with the Kantian theorem, as invoked by Freud (1920), that time and space are necessary forms of thought.

What we are considering here is environmental experience, an inherently subjective phenomenology, not the actual properties of an objectifiable transcendent external surround. The subjectivity of conscious, or environmental, experience is an important point. To be sure, we may both be aware of many other things, and our awarenesses may be impinged upon and filtered through these other conscious phenomena. But each of us is, nonetheless, conscious of our experience. To take this a step further, each of our experiences of consciousness is an entirely subjective experience.

In an argument aimed at deflating various approaches to the mind-body question, J. R. Searle (1992) makes a compelling and convincing case that all consciousness is not only subjective, but ineliminably and irreducibly subjective. Thus, following Searle, consciousness cannot, for example, be equated with neurophysiological material process, even though it is still being conceived of as a higher order biological process. As Matte-Blanco (1975) states, "Space is a way in which the mind translates certain objective relations (i.e., relations of the external world). It is, in summary, an indication or hint of the external world which has been passed through the network of our mind: a hint of a . . . correspondence between something of our thinking and something of the external world" (p. 400).

15. It seems quite obvious that in this contrast between asymmetrical experience and symmetrical experience, we are looking at two very dif-

ferent ways of living in the world. As I implied above, such symmetrical experience may be considered in a manner consistent with Freud's (e.g., 1900, 1915) view of the unconscious to be without anchor in either time or space. It is, in other words, dimensionless and impervious to the logical laws of causality and temporal-spatial organization. I have suggested elsewhere (Civin and Lombardi 1990) that we might view internal experience to consist of an infinite number of dimensions (an *n*-dimensional space), in which each dimension represents something akin to the mnemonic trace of a sedimentation of experience. Although the notion of a sedimentation has an unfortunately concrete rootedness in the four-dimensional time-space continuum, we might envision some of these sedimentary dimensions as relativistic swirling vortices, black holes, multidimensional Mobius strips, antisedimentations, and what have you. In keeping with the quote from T. S. Eliot, such traces may have had their origins as earlier, simultaneous, or perhaps even subsequent internal experiences or as environmental experiences transformed into internal experiences. Quite clearly, the organizational principles of the time-space continuum and the categories of secondary process reasoning do not govern the organization of our experience in this domain.

16. Since the time of James (1890) and Titchener (1898), psychology has struggled with ideas of structuralism and transformationism. Within this struggle, a central question is whether we can characterize psychological phenomena by fixed inner and outer properties (structuralism) or by sets of transformations both within and outside the organism (transformationism).

The transformational model we are developing here represents an amalgam of these two views. In some sense, the theory relies on structure in that each modality of experiential organization represents, at any isolated moment in time, a structure. However, because the theory is preeminently transformational, no structure can exist in static equilibrium. What I mean by preeminently transformational is that the transformations, which are perpetual, continually act upon the structures to change them. In this sense, then, the structural nature is more a theoretical phenomenon than an actual, observable one. In fact, I began by noting that these structures exist at any isolated moment in time, but we can never truly isolate a moment in time.

Transformational theory (Civin 1998, Civin and Lombardi 1990), which emerges from the triadic view of experience in Matte-Blanco's theories, relies on a vision of human psychology in which the embeddedness of modes of human experience is more central to our understanding than are notions of primary psychological motivation and structure. In this model, modes of experience that are organized and governed by the vastly different rules and logic of symmetry and asymmetry are continuously being transformed or mapped from one experiential modality into the other. To be human, according to this view, is to maintain and, in one way or another, communicate between these differing modes of experiential organization that stand in antinomy to each other.

The concept of transformation has been used in far too many ways within psychology to permit a comprehensive survey here, but a few of these ways are relevant. As noted above, within nonpsychoanalytic psychology, transformation has been opposed to structure (see, e.g., Chomsky 1965, Chomsky and Halle 1968, Riegel and Rosenwald 1975). Pertinent to our application is Bion's (1965) use of the term *transformation* to describe the relationship between the *realization*, or following Kant, the thing-in-itself, and the *representation*, or the phenomenon, corresponding to the thing-in-itself, as it exists in the mind, in order to discuss the group of elements that comprise the total analytical experience. In some ways Bion's use of transformation corresponds with Matte-Blanco's if we substitute asymmetry for realization and symmetry for representation.

Brakel (1994) reviews the epistemology of geometry and space (Kantian and post-Kantian) in order to discuss the knowability of the unconscious, and, even more, the knowability of the rules of organization that govern unconscious operations. In so doing, Brakel advances our theory, elucidating the nature of transformations by contrasting them with translations. If systems have similar rules of organization, we may create maps between one system and the other by means of translation. In translation from one system to another, like the translation of the words and phrases of one language to the words and phrases of another language, there is only a trivial conveyance of information. This is the type of process that I am calling isomorphic or a null transformation. However, if the systems are built upon rules of organization that are different fundamentally, such as Euclidean and non-Euclidean universes, or, for our purposes, symmetrical and asymmetrical modes of experiential organization, the mapping from one system to the other requires the conveyance of nontrivial information. It is such a conveyance of information that Brakel terms a transformation.

Cornell (1993) uses transformation to imply the simultaneity of a dynamically transformable subject-self and an actual empirical self, embedded in a social system that is rendered transformable through gradual slippages in meaning over time. The subject-self has the quality of a symmetrical formulation, and the actual empirical self has the quality of an asymmetrical formulation. This use of transformation will assist us to integrate the transformational model we are developing with the social surround in a way that will prove central to the thread of the argument.

As I am using it, the concept of transformation incorporates aspects of each of these views while adding its own unique emphasis. To summarize, transformation involves the processes of mapping between systems organized with radically differing rules and dimensionalities. Because these systems are organized so differently, neither the contents nor the rules of organization of either system may be translated between systems in a trivial manner. There is no one-to-one correspondence, isomorphism, or null transformation. And, because the transformations, like the processes of projection and introjection, are continuous, dynamic, and nontrivial, each system will be changed profoundly and continually over time by the processes of transformation themselves. Thus, in concert with the physics of quantum theory, we lack any simultaneous capacity to describe and locate the structures. Finally, these dynamically transformable modes of experiential organization exist in a social surround that is itself transformable through gradual slippages in meaning over time.

The scientist Hölder (1901) demonstrated that as the complexity of the rules of internal organization increases, the complexity of transformations that can be imposed upon the system decreases. Thus, since the rules of intrasystemic organization of symmetrical experience are relatively few, it is possible to impose a relatively large number of transformations on that organization of experience. At least the number of transformations seems large in comparison to the relatively small number of transformations that can be imposed on environmental experience, an organization governed by a far greater number of intrasystemic rules. This observation appears consistent with Freud's (1900) discussions of associational pathways. It is also consistent with Kant's notion of antinomy as applied by Matte-Blanco, where to be human requires us to employ simultaneously modes of organization of experience that are fundamentally alien and antithetical to each other. From advances in infant research (e.g., Stern 1985), it seems at least reasonable to speculate that from the earliest moments, if not in utero (Piontelli 1992), the infant is faced with the transformation of these simultaneous modalities of organizing experience as a psychological concomitant to existing.

Within this theoretical framework, we are able to conceptualize certain basic aspects of human psychological functioning in a manner that decentralizes notions such as structure (whether that structure be the sequelae of vicissitudes of drive or conflicts around relating) and motivation (again, drive or relational primacy). In a similar manner, we may understand developmental norms and psychopathology in terms of transformations and not structures. Many forms of problems that mental health workers encounter in clinical practice and that organizational consultants encounter within the workplace, problems that typically we consider to be manifestations of psychopathology or dysfunction, may be understood in terms of constrictions (or, at the extremes, obliteration of the functions) of processes of transformation between the modalities of experiential organization.

17. Psychoanalytically we would refer to this as a form of splitting characterized as either paranoid regression or schizoid withdrawal.

18. In an earlier paper (Civin and Lombardi 1990) we compared Winnicott's potential space with the preconscious of Freud's tripartite model and offered the conclusion that within each triadic model (reality–fantasy– the space in-between for Winnicott; conscious–unconscious–preconscious for Freud) the middle organization might be thought of as a theoretical precursor of the processes of transformation. If this is so, then it seems paradoxical to claim that this strategy of using computer systems to facilitate paranoid-schizoid relatedness is a use of cyberspace as potential space. The paradox arises because paranoid-schizoid relatedness, as I have described it, is a process in which, for the sake of the semblance of whole-object relations within a part-object universe, the very processes of transformation that we have linked to potential space are abandoned. But for those who have read much of Winnicott, it will probably come as no surprise that paradox emerges from the application of one of his principles. Paradox remains at the center of a great deal of Winnicott's work— objects that are not things, perfect mothering that is not good enough, silence that is communication, hate that is love. In fact, as Deri (1978) states, "Winnicott's paradox . . . must be accepted and *not* resolved. Once resolved, the fatal Cartesian split between inside and outside will take place, and reality, even though 'dealt with' adaptively, will never feel fully enjoyable" (p. 51).

19. The Carnegie-Mellon report has been widely criticized, both on- and off-line. For example, a *New York Times* article reports, "Critics assert that the study has fatal flaws that neutralize its findings and that they are appalled at the authors' far-reaching conclusions about the impact the findings might have on Internet policy and technological development"

(September 19, 1998, p. C5). The article cites a Vanderbilt University professor, Donna Hoffman, as finding the research close to meaningless because of the lack of a control group and the lack of random selection of subjects.

20. Winnicott (1960) classifies such false-self organizations as matters of degree. At one extreme the false self sets itself up as real, and outside observers tend to think of that false self as the real person. At the other extreme, in relative health, the false self is little more than the polite, well-mannered social attitude that obeys convention. In between these two extremes are ways of being in which (1) the false self defends the true self, which maintains a private being; (2) the false self searches for conditions in which the true self might emerge; and (3) the false self is built on identifications.

21. In one of Winnicott's most important papers, "The Use of an Object and Relating Through Identifications" (1969), he distinguishes object relating from object use. In object relating, the object remains an object that is subjectively created because it is known, in large part, through projective and introjective mechanisms. It is only after the subject has destroyed the object countless times, and the object has managed to outlast destruction, that the subject can recognize that the object has its own, objective, presence. Furthermore, only an objective object can really be made use of as a part of the external world (Winnicott 1971).

22. Winnicott's groundbreaking book, *The Maturational Processes and the Facilitating Environment* (1965), articulated this notion of a facilitating environment and the relationship of that environment to transitional objects. These ideas were elaborated in his later book, *Playing and Reality* (1971).

23. This idea relates, once again, to the idea of using part-object experience to simulate whole-object relatedness, or, in other words, to operate from a primarily paranoid-schizoid position while maintaining a semblance of depressive experience. By analyzing the dominant forms of anxiety, these semblances almost always become transparent; even though

the experiences resemble depressive ones, the primary anxiety remains persecutory.

24. It might be argued that inherent in this line of thought is an over-valuation of real-life experience and an undervaluation of virtual reality. To some extent, I must confess that this is true. It *is* conceivable that a person could use computer-mediated communication as a transitional modality and still decide that Internet relating is preferable to any other type of relating. As a general rule, however, I would expect that the alternative with the most transformational potential would be one in which Internet relating, while not ruled out, is seen as one choice among many.

25. In psychoanalytic terms we might say that Ralph was trying to expel, or project out, material he felt was being forced into him and attacking him from within.

26. The psychoanalytic notion of induced countertransference, of which this may be seen as an example, has been viewed as a significant clinical tool by many analysts for decades (e.g., Heimann 1950, Joseph 1987, Searles 1979, Segal 1981).

27. See endnote 11.

28. See endnotes 5, 6, and 11.

29. See endnote 8.

30. Workers have always been vulnerable to outside scrutiny. However, much of this scrutiny has historically been institutionalized into reporting systems. Even in "spot inspections" and other things of that ilk, the worker has generally known when and under what auspices the inspections are being conducted. In a cyber system, all these rules change.

References

Abbott, J. H. (1981). *In the Belly of the Beast.* New York: Random House.

Abram, D. (1996). *The Spell of the Sensuous: Perception and Language in a More-Than-Human World.* New York: Pantheon.

Adamse, M., and Motta, S. (1996). *Online Friendship, Chat-Room Romance and Cybersex: Your Guide to Affairs of the Net.* Deerfield Beach, FL: Health Communications.

Allport, S. (1997). *A Natural History of Parenting.* New York: Harmony.

Attewell, P. (1994). Information technology and the productivity paradox. In *Organizational Linkages: Understanding the Productivity Paradox*, ed. D. Harris, P. Goodman, and D. S. Sink. Washington, DC: National Academy of Sciences Press.

———— (1996). Information technology and the productivity challenge. In *Computerization and Controversy: Value Conflicts and Social Choices*, ed. R. Kling, 2nd ed., pp. 227–238. New York: Academic Press.

Bernstein, N. (1997). On frontier of cyberspace, data is money, and a threat. *The New York Times*, June 12, p. 1.

Bion, W. R. (1962a). *Learning from Experience.* London: Maresfield Library, 1991.

——— (1962b). *Second Thoughts: Selected Papers on Psycho-Analysis.* New York: Jason Aronson, 1984.

——— (1965). *Transformations.* New York: Jason Aronson, 1983.

——— (1979). *Elements of Psycho-Analysis.* New York: Jason Aronson, 1983.

Birkerts, S. (1994). *The Gutenberg Elegies: The Fate of Reading in an Electronic Age.* New York: Fawcett Columbine.

——— (1996). *Tolstoy's Dictaphone: Technology and the Muse.* St. Paul, MN: Graywolf.

Blake, W. (ca. 1790–1793). The marriage of heaven and hell. In *Blake: Complete Writings*, ed. G. Keynes, pp. 148–158. London: Oxford University Press, 1969.

——— (1793). The tyger. In *Blake: Complete Writings*, ed. G. Keynes. London: Oxford University Press, 1969.

Bowlby, J. (1969). *Attachment.* New York: Basic Books.

Brakel, L. A. (1994). On knowing the unconscious: lessons from the epistemology of geometry and space. *International Journal of Psycho-Analysis* 75: 39–49.

Breuer, J., and Freud, S. (1895). Studies on hysteria. *Standard Edition* 2.

Bruckman, A. (1992). Identity workshop: emergent social and psychological phenomena in text-based virtual reality. Unpublished manuscript, available via anonymous ftp://media.mit.edu/pub/asb/papers/identity-workshop.

Bruner, J. S., Goodnow, J., and Austin, G. A. (1956). *A Study of Thinking.* New York: Wiley.

Chomsky, N. (1965). *Aspects of the Theory of Syntax.* Cambridge, MA: MIT Press, 1969.

Chomsky, N., and Halle, M. (1968). *The Sound Pattern of English.* New York: Harper & Row.

Civin, M. A. (1987). Object relatedness and empathy in a simulated management environment: a study of the relationship among levels of object relatedness, empathy and accurate prediction of decision making behavior within simulated manager-subordinate dyads. Unpublished doctoral dissertation, Adelphi University, Garden City, NY.

———— (1998). Therapeutic symbiosis, concordance and analytic transformation. *Free Associations* 7(42): 260–268.

Civin, M. A., and Lombardi, K. L. (1990). The pre-conscious and potential space. *Psychoanalytic Review*, 77(4): 573–585.

Cornell, D. (1993). *Transformations: Recollective Imagination and Sexual Difference*. New York: Routledge.

Curtis, P. (1996). Mudding: social phenomena in text-based virtual realities. In *High Noon on the Electronic Frontier: Conceptual Issues in Cyberspace*, Peter Ludlow, pp. 347–374. Cambridge, MA: MIT Press. Also available via anonymous ftp://parcftp.xerox.com/pub/MOO/papers/DIAC92.

Custance, J. (1952). *Wisdom, Madness and Folly—The Philosophy of a Lunatic*. New York: Pellegrini & Cudahy.

DeAngelis, T. (1997). Do online support groups help for eating disorders? *APA Monitor* 28(3): 43.

Deri, S. (1978). Transitional phenomena: vicissitudes of symbolization and creativity. In *Between Reality and Fantasy*, ed. S. A. Grolnick and L. Barkin. New York: Jason Aronson.

Derrida, J. (1977). Signature event context, glyph 1. *Johns Hopkins Textual Studies*.

———— (1996). *Archive Fever: A Freudian Impression*. Chicago: University of Chicago Press.

Dibbell, J. (1996). A rape in cyberspace; or how an evil clown, a Haitian trickster spirit, two wizards, and a cast of dozens turned a database into a society. In *High Noon on the Electronic Frontier: Conceptual Issues in Cyberspace*, Peter Ludlow, pp. 375–396. Cambridge, MA: MIT Press.

Doheny-Farina, S. (1996). *The Wired Neighborhood*. New Haven, CT: Yale University Press.

Dowling, P. (1996). *Baudrillard 1–Piaget 0: Cyberspace, Subjectivity and the Ascension*. Available via http://www.ioe.ac.uk/ccs/ccsroot/ccs/dowling/1996.html#anchor74319.

Dreyfus, H. L. (1992). *What Computers Still Can't Do.* Cambridge, MA: MIT Press.

Dreyfus, H. L., and Dreyfus, S. E. (1989). Making a mind versus modeling the brain: artificial intelligence back at a branchpoint. In *The Artificial Intelligence Debate: False Starts, Real Foundations,* ed. S. R. Graubard, pp. 15–43. Cambridge, MA: MIT Press.

Eliot, T. S. (1925). The hollow men. In *Collected Poems, 1909–1962.* New York: Harcourt, Brace, & World, 1963.

———— (1935). Burnt Norton. In *Collected Poems, 1909–1962.* New York: Harcourt, Brace, & World, 1963.

———— (1941). The dry salvages. In *Collected Poems, 1909–1962.* New York: Harcourt, Brace, & World, 1963.

———— (1942). Little Gidding. In *Collected Poems, 1909–1962.* New York: Harcourt, Brace, & World, 1963.

Ellul, J. (1964). *The Technological Society.* New York: Knopf.

Faber, M. D. (1984). The computer, the technological order, and psychoanalysis: preliminary remarks. *Psychoanalytic Review* 71(2): 263–277.

Foner, L. N. (1993). Agents Memo 93–01. Available via ftp://ftp.media.mit.edu...Agent-Anyway--Julia.mss.

Freud, S. (1900). The interpretation of dreams. *Standard Edition* 4/5:1–626. London:

———— (1905). Three essays on the theory sexuality. *Standard Edition* 7:125–244.

———— (1905a). Fragment of an analysis of a case of hysteria. *Standard Edition* 7:1–122.

———— (1909). Analysis of a phobia in a five-year-old-boy. *Standard Edition* 10:1–147.

———— (1909a). Notes upon a case of obsessional neurosis. *Standard Edition* 10:151–250.

———— (1910). Leonardo Da Vinci and a memory of his childhood. *Standard Edition* 11:59–138.

———— (1915). The unconscious. *Standard Edition* 14:159–215.

———— (1917). Mourning and melancholia. *Standard Edition* 14:237–258.

———— (1920). Beyond the pleasure principle. *Standard Edition* 18:7–64.

———— (1925). A note upon the "mystic writing pad." *Standard Edition* 19:227–232.

———— (1925a). An autobiographical study. *Standard Edition* 20:1–74.

———— (1939). Moses and monotheism. *Standard Edition* 23:1–138.

Gergen, K. J. (1991). *The Saturated Self: Dilemmas of Identity in Contemporary Life.* New York: Basic Books.

Grolnick, S. A., and Barkin, L. (1978). *Between Reality and Fantasy: Transitional Objects and Phenomena.* New York: Jason Aronson.

Haraway, D. J. (1991). *Simians, Cyborgs and Women: The Reinvention of Nature.* New York: Routledge.

———— (1997). *Modest_Witness@Second_Millennium.Female-Man©Meets_OncoMouse™.* New York: Routledge.

Harlow, H. F., and Woolsey, C. (1958). *Biological and Biochemical Bases of Behavior.* Madison, WI: University of Wisconsin Press.

Heim, M. (1993). *The Metaphysics of Virtual Reality.* New York: Oxford University Press.

Heimann, P. (1950). On countertransference. *International Journal of Psycho-Analysis* 31:81–84.

Herz, J. C. (1995). *Surfing on the Internet.* New York: Little, Brown.

Hinshelwood, R. D. (1991). *A Dictionary of Kleinian Thought.* London: Free Association.

Hirschhorn, L. (1986). *Beyond Mechanization.* Cambridge, MA: MIT Press.

———— (1997). *Reworking Authority: Leading and Following in the Post-Modern Organization.* Cambridge, MA: MIT Press.

Hölder, O. (1901). Die axiome der quantität und die lehre vom mass. *Berichte der Sachsischen Gesellschaft der Wissenschaften, Leipzig, Mathematische—Physikalische Klasse* 53:1–64.

Holub, M. (1980). On the origin of the contrary. In *The Vintage Book of Contemporary World Poetry*, ed. J. D. McClatchy. New York: Vintage, 1996.

Horowitz, T. (1996). Mr. Edens profits from watching his workers' every move. In *Computerization and Controversy: Value Conflicts and Social Choices*, ed. R. Kling, 2nd ed. New York: Academic Press.

Ingber, D. (1981). Computer addicts. *Science Digest.* July.

James, W. (1890). *The Principles of Psychology.* New York: Holt.

Joseph, B. (1987). Projective identification: some clinical aspects. In *Melanie Klein Today: Development in Theory and Practice, Volume 1: Mainly Theory*, ed. E. B. Spillius. New York: Routledge, 1988.

Kant, I. (1781). *Critique of Pure Reason.* New York: St. Martin's Press, 1965.

Keller, E. F. (1994). The body of a new machine: situating the organism between telegraphs and computers. *Perspectives on Science* 2(3):302–323.

Kernberg, O. F. (1975). *Borderline Conditions and Pathological Narcissism.* New York: Jason Aronson.

——— (1979). Regression in organizational leadership. In *The Irrational Executive: Psychoanalytic Studies in Management*, ed. M. F. R. Kets deVries. New York: International Universities Press.

Kets deVries, M. F. R. (1984). *The Irrational Executive: Psychoanalytic Studies in Management.* New York: International Universities Press.

Klein, M. (1935). A contribution to the psychogenesis of manic-depressive states. In *Contributions to Psychoanalysis, 1921–1945.* New York: McGraw-Hill, 1964.

——— (1946). Notes on some schizoid mechanisms. In *Envy and Gratitude and Other Works, 1946–1963.* New York: Delacorte, 1975.

Kling, R. (1996). *Computerization and Controversy: Value Conflicts and Social Choices*, 2nd ed. New York: Academic Press.

Kling, R., Ackerman, M. S., and Allen, J. P. (1996). Information entrepreneurialism, information technologies, and the continuing vulnerability of privacy. In *Computerization and Controversy: Value Conflicts and Social Choices*, ed. R. Kling. 2nd ed. New York: Academic Press.

Kraut, R., Patterson, M., Lundmark, V., et al. (1998). Internet paradox: a social technology that reduces social involvement and psychological well-being? *American Psychologist* 53(9):1017–1031.

Landow, G. P. (1992). *Hypertext: The Convergence of Contemporary Critical Theory and Technology*. Baltimore, MD: Johns Hopkins University Press.

Lasch, C. (1979). *The Culture of Narcissism: American Life in an Age of Diminishing Expectations*. New York: Norton.

Lea, M., & Spears, R. (1995). Love at first byte? Building personal relationships over computer networks. In *Under-Studied Relationships: Off the Beaten Track*, ed. J. T. Wood and S. Duck, pp. 197–233. Thousand Oaks, CA: Sage.

Leontief, W., and Duchin, F. (1986). *The Future Impact of Automation on Workers*. New York: Oxford University Press.

Ludlow, P. (1996). *High Noon on the Electronic Frontier: Conceptual Issues in Cyberspace*. Cambridge, MA: MIT Press.

Maccoby, M. (1981). *The Leader*. New York: Simon and Schuster.

Mahler, M. S., Pine, F., and Bergman, A. (1975). *The Psychological Birth of the Human Infant*. New York: Basic Books.

Marx, G. T. (1996). The case of the omniscient organization. In *Computerization and Controversy: Value Conflicts and Social Choices*, ed. R. Kling. 2nd ed. New York: Academic Press.

Matte-Blanco, I. (1975). *The Unconscious as Infinite Sets: An Essay in Bi-Logic*. London: Duckworth.

——— (1988). *Thinking, Feeling, and Being: Clinical Reflections on the Fundamental Antinomy of Human Beings and World*. New York: Routledge.

Mazlish, B. (1993). *The Fourth Discontinuity: The Co-evolution of Humans and Machines*. New Haven, CT: Yale University Press.

Mitroff, I. I. (1983). *Stakeholders of the Organizational Mind*. San Francisco, CA: Jossey-Bass.

Negroponte, N. (1995). *Being Digital*. New York: Vintage.

Offe, C. (1978). Political authority and class structure. In *Critical Sociology*, ed. P. Connerton. London: Penguin.

Ogden, T. H. (1982). *Projective Identification and Psychotherapeutic Technique*. New York: Jason Aronson.

O'Reilly and Associates. (1997). *Who Owns the Internet? The Harvard Conference on the Internet and Society*. Cambridge, MA: Harvard University Press.

Orwell, G. (1949). *1984*. New York: Signet, 1961.

Petot, J.-M. (1991). *Melanie Klein, Volume II: The Ego and the Good Object 1932–1960*. Madison, CT: International Universities Press.

Phillips, A. (1993). On risk and solitude. In *On Kissing, Tickling, and Being Bored: Psychoanalytic Essays on the Unexamined Life*. Cambridge, MA: Harvard University Press.

Piontelli, A. (1992). *From Fetus to Child: An Observational and Psychoanalytic Study*. New York: Routledge.

Platt, C. (1996). *Anarchy Online*. New York: Harper Prism.

Provenzo, Jr., E. F. (1991). *Video Kids: Making Sense of Nintendo*. Cambridge, MA: Harvard University Press.

Racker, H. (1968). *Transference and Countertransference*. Madison, CT: International Universities Press.

Rayner, E. (1995). *Unconscious Logic: An Introduction to Matte-Blanco's Bilogic and its Uses*. New York: Routledge.

Reid, E. (1995). Virtual worlds: culture and imagination. In *Cybersociety: Computer-Mediated Communication and Community*, ed. S. G. Jones, pp. 164–183. Thousand Oaks, CA: Sage.

——— (1996). Text-based virtual realities: identity and the cyborg body. In *High Noon on the Electronic Frontier: Conceptual Issues in Cyberspace*, P. Ludlow, pp. 327–344. Cambrige, MA: MIT Press.

Rice, E. (1923). *The Adding Machine*. New York: Doubleday Page.

Riegel, K. F., and Rosenwald, G. C. (1975). *Structure and Transformation: Developmental and Historical Aspects*. New York: Wiley.

Roheim, G. (1971). *The Origin and Function of Culture*. New York: Anchor.

Roszak, T. (1986). *The Cult of Information: A Neo-Luddite Treatise on High Tech, Artificial Intelligence, and the True Art of Thinking.* Berkeley, CA: University of California Press, 1994.

Rucker, N., and Lombardi, K. L. (1998). *Subject Relations: Unconscious Experience and Psychoanalysis.* New York: Routledge.

Schepper-Hughes, N. (1992). *Death Without Weeping: The Violence of Everyday Life in Brazil.* Berkeley, CA: University of California Press.

Searle, J. R. (1992). *The Rediscovery of the Mind.* Cambridge, MA: MIT Press, 1994.

Searles, H. F. (1960). *The Nonhuman Environment: In Normal Development and in Schizophrenia.* New York: International Universities Press, 1979.

——— (1979). *Countertransference and Related Subjects.* New York: International Universities Press.

Segal, H. (1981). *The Work of Hanna Segal: A Kleinian Approach to Clinical Practice.* London: Jason Aronson.

Shakespeare, W. (1609). Sonnet XLIV. In *The Love Poems and Sonnets of William Shakespeare.* Garden City, NY: Hanover House, 1957.

Sleek, S. (1998). Isolation increases with internet use. *APA Monitor,* September, *29*(9), pp. 1, 30.

Smircich, L. (1983). Concepts of culture and organizational analysis. *Administrative Science Quarterly* 28:339–358.

Spillius, E. B. (1988a). *Melanie Klein Today: Developments in Theory and Practice, Volume 1: Mainly Theory.* New York: Routledge.

——— (1988b). *Melanie Klein Today: Developments in Theory and Practice, Volume 2: Mainly Practice.* New York: Routledge.

Spitz, R. A. (1965). *The First Year of Life: A Psychoanalytic Study of Normal and Deviant Development of Object Relations.* New York: International Universities Press.

Stern, D. N. (1985). *The Interpersonal World of the Infant.* New York: Basic Books.

Stoll, C. (1995). *Silicon Snake Oil: Second Thoughts on the Information Highway.* New York: Anchor.

Stone, A. R. (1995). *The War of Desire and Technology at the Close of the Mechanical Age.* Cambridge, MA: MIT Press.

Stout, R. (1997). Website traffic reports: a simple analysis. *Net Guide,* March 18, p. 147.

Sullivan, H. S. (1954). *The Psychiatric Interview.* New York: Norton, 1970.

Tennyson, A. (1833). The two voices. In *Poems of Tennyson,* ed. J. H. Buckley, pp. 70–84. Boston: Houghton Mifflin, 1958.

Titchener, E. (1898). *An Outline of Psychology.* New York: Macmillan.

Turing, A. (1950). Computing machinery and intelligence. *Mind,* 59:434–460.

Turkle, S. (1982). The subjective computer: a study in the psychology of personal computation. *Social Studies of Science* 12:173–205.

——— (1984). *The Second Self: Computers and the Human Spirit.* New York: Simon & Schuster.

——— (1992). Epistemological pluralism and the revaluation of the concrete. *Journal of Mathematical Behavior* 11:3–33.

——— (1995). *Life on the Screen: Identity in the Age of the Internet.* New York: Simon & Schuster.

Wallace, J., and Mangan, M. (1997). *Sex, Laws, and Cyberspace: Freedom and Censorship on the Frontiers of the Online Revolution.* New York: Owl.

Winner, L. (1996). Electronic office: playpen or prison. *In Computerization and Controversy: Value Conflicts and Social Choices,* ed. R. Kling. 2nd ed. New York: Academic Press.

Winnicott, D. W. (1958). The capacity to be alone. In *The Maturational Processes and the Facilitating Environment.* New York: International Universities Press, 1965.

——— (1960). Ego distortion in terms of true and false self. In *The Maturational Processes and the Facilitating Environment.* New York: International Universities Press, 1965.

——— (1965). *The Maturational Processes and the Facilitating Environment.* New York: International Universities Press.

——— (1971). *Playing and Reality.* London: Tavistock.

Index

Abbott, J., 97
Abram, D., 20–22, 86, 91
Adamse, M., 87–90
Adding Machine, The (Rice), 4
Allport, S., 210n.8
Anticipatory anxiety, 200
Antinomy, 33, 60, 62–63, 79, 180,
    216n.16
    between symmetrical and
        asymmetrical logic, 104–
        105, 198–201
Anxiety. *See also* Persecutory
    anxiety
    about technology, 163–164,
        167–169
    anticipatory, 200
    depressive, 196–197
    in developmental positions,
        196
Attewell, P., 145–146

Bernstein, N., 3–5
Bion, W. R., 144, 179, 214n.16
Birkerts, S., 6, 33, 86
Borderline personalities, 69–70,
    200
Brakel, L. A., 214n.16
Breuer, J., 87
Bruckman, A., 86
Bruner, J. S., 22–23

Capital punishment, toading
    compared to, 96–100
Carnegie-Mellon report, on
    Internet use, 83–86,
    217n.19
Case study method, 86–90
Chat rooms
    terrorism in, 201
    uses of, 45–47, 54, 74–75
Chomsky, N., 214n.16

Civin, M. A., 165, 213n.15, 217n.18

Communication, technological changes in, 31–33

Community(ies)
death of, 24–26
global, 31
substitution of computer-mediated for physical, 188–189

Competence, at work, 142–143, 174

Complementary identification, 148, 165–166, 168, 206n.5

Computer addiction, 211n.11
as insatiability for relationships, 52, 55
signs of, 92–93

Computer-mediated communications, 31, 94, 188, 219n.24
changing modes used, 65, 67
effects of, 9, 78, 83–86, 217n.19
examples of, 75–76
as partial experienced as whole, 193–194
and persecutory anxiety, 44–51
repeating old patterns in, 113–114, 121, 133–135
as transitional, 197–198
uses of, 34–35, 84–85, 119–121, 132–137
at work, 11, 141–189

Computer-mediated relationships, 10
extramarital, 109–110, 113, 126
isolation *vs.* richness of, 35–36

in MUDs, 93–107
perfectness of, 12, 16–17, 54, 70

Computers
increased competence through, 142–143
and persecutory anxiety, 44, 172

Conscious, asymmetrical logic of, 60–71, 199–201, 212n.14

Continuities, and discontinuities, 22–23

Cornell, D., 215n.16

Cult of Information, The (Roszak), 6

Culture, 42, 44, 142
of calculation, 147, 150
computers changing, 38–39

Curtis, P., 14, 93, 102

Custance, J., 52

Cyber systems, as transitional, 169–170

Cyberspace
characteristics of, 26–27
individuals in, 37, 40–56
poles of experience within, 197–198
as potential space, 76–77
as symbolic, 51, 168, 174–176, 179
symbolism in, 33
two-dimensionality of, 59–60
unconscious in, 104–105

Cyber-technology, protests against, 6

Defenses
against anxiety about technology, 167

from persecutory anxiety, 68–71, 177–179

splitting as, 78, 177, 186–187, 193, 196– 197

withdrawal as, 41–42

Dennis, B., 3–4

Depression

effects on family, 122–124, 126

increased through Internet use, 83–85

Depressive position, 196–197, 208n.6, 211n.11

Deri, S., 217n.18

Derrida, J., 59

Development, child, 205n.4, 216n.16

effects of lack of parenting, 153–154, 209n.8

need for separation in, 116–121

and nonhuman environment, 91–92

overlapping positions within, 195–197, 207n.6

in potential space, 37–38, 152

Dibbell, J., 93–107, 136

Dichotomy, of dimensional experience, 59–71

Discontinuities, and self-knowledge, 22–23

Dissociation, 170, 188, 205n.5

of management, 167–168

promoted by computer use, 78, 159–165

Doheny-Farina, S., 9, 25–26, 86, 188–189

Dowling, P., 86, 104–105

Drive theories, 36–37, 211n.13

Dual unity, of self, 39, 42

Duchin, F., 146

Ego, decentering, 198

Ego psychologies, 36

Eliot, T. S., 42–43, 62, 213n.15

Ellul, J., 146

Email systems, 31, 178, 205n.5. *See also* Computer-mediated communications

invasion by, 45–47

mindless production in, 147–149

misuse of, 161–164, 179–180

Embodiment, of cyber relationships, 13–14, 17, 35, 85

avoidance of, 54, 75, 110

Empowerment, through computer "confinement," 52

Executioner's Song, The (Mailer), 99

Faber, M. D., 198

on computers as transitional, 39–40, 42, 169

on fears and fantasies about computers, 44

False self, 114–116, 218n.20

Families, effects of Internet use on, 83–85

Flaming, 50, 210n.10

Foner, L. N., 14–15

Freud, S., 60, 62, 97, 216n.16, 217n.18

on discontinuities, 22–23

drive theories, 211n.13

Freud, S. (*continued*)
  on individual psyche *vs.*
    relational self, 36–37
  use of case study method, 87

Gender, in computer-mediated
    communications, 9, 52,
    204n.2
Gergen, K., 9, 86, 173
  on postmodern attitudes, 175
  on technology and identity, 24–
    25
Global community, 31
Gutenberg Elegies, The (Birkerts), 6

Halle, M., 214n.16
Haraway, D., 8, 9, 86, 198
Harlow, H. F., 171, 209n.8
Heim, M., 33, 86
Herz, J. C., 86, 210n.10
Hinshelwood, R. D., 207n.6
Hirschhorn, L., 145, 173, 175
Hoffman, D., 217n.19
Hölder, O., 216n.16
"Hollow Men, The" (Eliot), 42–43
Holub, M., 27
Horowitz, 146
Hysteria, organization of reality
    in, 69

Idealization, in computer-
    mediated relationships, 12,
    16–17, 54–55
Identity, 13, 18, 26, 185
  in computer-mediated
    relationships, 35, 99

self as multiplicity of, 20, 22,
    120, 198
  and technology, 24–25
Impermanence, of computer-
    mediated relationships, 12,
    16, 98–99
Individuals
  in cyberspace, 40–56
  in work organizations, 142–143
Induced countertransference,
    219n.26
Information
  assault by, 179
  vs. knowledge, 144, 147
Ingber, D., 52, 210n.11
Internal experience, during
    Internet use, 34, 83–85
Internet. *See also* Computer-
    mediated communications
  effects on communities, 25–26
Intranet, 151, 172, 181–187
Introjection, 196, 207n.6
Invasion, 219n.30
  and persecutory anxiety, 44–47,
    219n.25
  via cyber systems, 175, 177, 179,
    183
Isolation, 114, 167, 176
  in computer-mediated
    relationships, 10–11, 15,
    41–56, 54
  as defense, 47, 51, 68, 177–179
  due to lack of parenting, 153–
    154
  and paranoid relatedness, 71–
    79, 171

James, W., 213n.16

Kant, I., 60, 144, 214n.16
Kernberg, O. F., 146
Kets de Vries, M. F. R., 146
Klein, M., 19, 97, 144, 205n.5
  on denial of psychic reality,
    180, 210n.11
  on developmental positions,
    195–196, 207n.6
  on individual psyche *vs.*
    relational self, 36–37
  on paranoid-schizoid
    relatedness, 170–171
  on psychic processes, 60,
    211n.13
Kling, R., 150
Knowledge, *vs.* information, 144,
  147
Kraut, R., 84–85

Lacan, J., 19
LambdaMOO, 93–107
Language, and meaning, 147–
  149
Lasch, C., 146
Lea, M., 55, 86
Leontief, W., 146
Life on the Screen (Turkle),
  37–40
Logic, 212n.14
  symmetrical and asymmetrical,
    60–71, 79, 104–105, 198–
    201, 212n.15
Lombardi, K. L., 153, 213n.15,
  217n.18

Loneliness. *See also* Isolation
  increased through Internet use,
    83–85
Lovers, email, 9–10, 15, 109–110,
  113, 126. *See also* Computer-
  mediated relationships
Ludd, General Ned, 6, 203n.1
Luddites, protests against
  technology, 5–6

Maccoby, M., 146
Machines. *See also* Computers;
  Technology
  vs. humans, 23
Mahler, M., 92
Mailer, N., 97, 99
Management, 162
  and computers at work, 143–
    147, 149–151
  dissociation of, 159–165, 167–168
  evaluation of, 160, 163–164
Mangan, M., 150
Manic denial, of psychic reality,
  210n.11
Marx, G. T., 146
Material requirements planning
  (MRP) system, 160–164,
  167–168
Matte-Blanco, I., 79, 104–105,
  198–201, 212n.13,
  214n.16
  on antinomy, 180, 214n.16
  on dualism, 60, 212n.14
*Maturational Processes and the
  Facilitating Environment, The*
  (Winnicott), 218n.21

Mauldin, M. L., 14
Mazlish, B., 22–23
Meaning, 110, 144, 200
    in analysis of organizations,
        141–142
    and organization of reality,
        68–70, 106–107
    relation to language, 147–149
MediaMOO, as replacement for
    communities, 26
Metromail, suit against, 3–4
Mind/body dualism, 97–98,
    212n.14
Mitroff, I. I., 175
Modest_WitnessSecond_Millenium.
    *Female-Man©Meets_*
    OncoMouse ™ (Haraway), 8
Morale, at work, 182–184
Mothers, need for separation
    from, 116–121
Motta, S., 87–90
MUDs, 14, 52–53, 93–107

Narcissism, 146, 168
Nature, human relationship with,
    21–22, 91
Negroponte, N., 86
1984 (Orwell), 5
Nonhuman environment, 195
    dedifferentiation of, 197–198
    role of, 90–92, 136

Object relations, 19, 78, 193,
    211n.12, 218n.21
    vs. drives, 36–37
    whole *vs.* part, 196–197, 200–
        201, 208n.6, 217n.18

Obsessives, organization of reality
    by, 68–69
Offe, C., 39
Online Friendship, Chat-Room
    Romance and Cybersex
    (Adamse and Motta), 87–90
O'Reilly and Associates, 9, 149–
    150
Organizations
    analysis of, 141–142
    paranoid-schizoid relatedness
        in, 170–187
    unconscious of, 164–165

Paranoia, 143
    and computer-mediated
        communications, 5, 34–35,
        89
    fragmentation caused by, 6, 75
    and insularity in cyberspace,
        41–56
    responses to, 7, 47–51, 84–85,
        132–134, 137
    from technology, 146, 188
    and withdrawal, 35, 78, 121
Paranoid relatedness, 71–79
Paranoid-schizoid processes, 196,
    207n.6, 211n.11
Paranoid-schizoid relatedness,
    170–187, 217n.18, 218n.23
Parenting
    isolation due to lack of, 153–154
    and need for separation, 116–
        121
Part-object relations. *See also*
    Object relations
    within organizations, 170–176

People
  blurring with nonhuman
      environment, 14–15, 17–
      18, 92
  creating technology in image
      of, 21–22
  reduction in interactions with,
      8–9, 24–25
  simulated, 14–15, 17–18
  vs. machines, 23
Persecutory anxiety, 43–51,
      218n.23
  defenses against, 68–71
  within organizations, 172–180
  responses to, 199–201
  splitting as defense against, 78,
      177, 186–187, 193, 196–197
Personal data, misuse of, 3–5
Personality, and mode of
      computer use, 65
Petot, J-M., 211n.11
Phillips, A., 83, 116, 120
Piontelli, A., 216n.16
Platt, C., 150
Postmodern world, 19
  attitudes in, 173, 175
  self creation in, 20, 22, 24
Potential space, 37–40, 194, 197–
      198, 205n.4, 217n.18
  and paranoid relatedness, 76–
      77, 79
  workplace as, 151–156, 187
Productivity
  effects of intranet system on,
      182–184
  effects of technology on, 145–
      146, 149

Projection, 178, 196, 207n.6,
      210n.9, 219n.25
Projective identification, 144,
      165–169, 205n.5
Provenzo, E. F., Jr., 9
Psychic reality, 69
  denying own, 55, 68, 70–71, 78,
      180, 200, 210n.11
  escape from, 186
  processes in, 60 (*See also* Logic,
      symmetrical and
      asymmetrical)
  triadic model of, 63, 68
Psychoanalysis, 19, 204n.3
  case study method in, 86–90
  individual *vs.* relational, 36–37
Psychologies, 213n.16
  individual *vs.* relational, 36–37

Racker, H., 148, 165, 206n.5
Reality, 34. *See also* Psychic
      reality
  and virtual reality, 94–107
  vs. virtual reality, 20, 136,
      219n.24
Reid, E., 102
Relatedness, 195, 207n.6
  in computer-mediated
      communications, 33–34,
      136
  enhanced through computer-
      mediated communications,
      52–56
  to nonhuman environment, 90–
      92
  paranoid, 71–79, 200–201,
      211n.12

Relatedness (*continued*)
  paranoid-schizoid, 170–187
  vs. insularity, 41–56
Relationships, 9–10, 218n.23. *See
    also* Computer-mediated
    relationships
  effects of technology on, 7–8,
    83–86
  in Freud's theories, 36–37
  maintaining distance in, 115–116
  need for, 20–21, 41, 132, 180–181
  partial, 25, 55, 151, 171, 187,
    193–194, 196
  withdrawal from, 19, 34, 121,
    132–134, 137, 177–179,
    181, 198
Reworking Authority (Hirschhorn),
    173
Rice, E., 4
Riegel, K. F., 214n.16
Risk, developmental need for,
    116–121
Roheim, G., 39, 42
Rosenwald, G. C., 214n.16
Roszak, T., 6
Rucker, N., 153

Schepper-Hughes, N., 153
Searle, J. R., 212n.14
Searles, H. F., 90–92, 136, 195,
    206n.5
Security, of corporate computers,
    150
Self, 36, 39, 75, 146, 215n.16
  conflicting views of, 34–35
  creation of, 24, 26, 120–121, 133–
    134, 136–37, 154–156

and false self, 114–115, 218n.20
  inside and outside, 37–38
  as realm of discourse, 19–20,
    22
  whole *vs.* part, 197, 208n.6
Self-expression, through
    cyberspace, 19–20
Self-knowledge, progression of,
    22
Separation, developmental need
    for, 116–121
Shopping, on-line, 8
Sleek, S., 83
Slippage, in relatedness and
    relationships, 19
Smircich, L., 141–142
Social involvement, effects of
    Internet use on, 83–85
Social saturation, 24
Social surround, of Internet users,
    83
Spears, R., 55, 86
Spitz, R. A., 121
Splitting, 211n.11, 217n.17
  as defense against persecutory
    anxiety, 78, 177, 186–187,
    193
  in paranoid-schizoid processes,
    196–197, 207n.6
Stalking, in computer-mediated
    relationships, 14
Star Trek: Insurrection, 7–8
Stern, D. N., 216n.16
Stimulation, social, 24
Stoll, C., 86
Stone, A. R., 26–27, 75, 86, 169,
    198

Stout, R., 149
Studies in Hysteria (Freud and
 Breuer), 87
Subjectivity, 71, 212n.14
Substance abuse, 110–113, 115
Sullivan, H. S., 147
Suspicion, 25. *See also* Paranoia

Technology
 adaptation to, 184, 186
 anxiety about, 74, 163–164,
  167–169
 effects of, 7–8, 31–33, 86, 155–
  159, 174, 193
 and identity, 24–25
 and productivity, 145–146
 reaction against, 5–6, 20–22,
  188, 203n.1
 role of nonhuman environment,
  90–92
Titchener, E., 213n.16
"Toading," in MUDs, 95–107
Tolstoy's Dictaphone (Birkerts), 6
Tracking protocols, 149
Transformational processes,
  213n.16, 217n.18
 in MUDs, 102–103
 between symmetrical and
  asymmetrical logic, 63–71,
  79, 105–107, 199–201
 through Internet relationships,
  121, 137
Transitional objects, 194,
  218n.22
 computers as, 39–40, 42
 Internet relationships as,
  115

Transitional processes, 136
 computer-mediated, 152–159,
  169–170, 194, 197–198,
  219n.24
 Internet relationships as, 121,
  133–135, 137
Transitional space. *See* Potential
 space
Turing, A., 18
Turing test, 18, 204n.2
Turkle, S., 4, 14, 52, 86, 107, 176,
  184
 on computer-mediated
  transitions, 42, 152– 153,
  169–170
 on creation of self, 75, 136–137
 on culture of calculation, 147,
  150, 187
 on cyberspace and self, 19–20, 22
 on potential space, 37–40, 197–
  198
Two-dimensionality, 59–60

Unconscious
 in cyberspace, 104–105
 of organizations, 142, 164–165
 symmetrical logic of, 60–71,
  199–201, 212n.15
"Use of an Object and Relating
 Through Identification, The"
 (Winnicott), 218n.21

Values, postmodern, 20, 22
Virtual reality, 20
 characteristics of, 27, 33
 compared to reality, 136, 219n.24
 in MUDs, 94–107

Wallace, J., 150
*War of Desire and Technology at the
    Close of the Mechanical Age,
    The* (Stone), 26–27
Winner, L., 143
Winnicott, D. W., 83, 120, 194,
    205n.4, 218n.21
  on false self, 114, 116,
    218n.20
  on potential space, 37–40,
    79, 152, 197– 198,
    217n.18

Wired Neighborhood, The (Doheny-
    Farina), 188–189
*Wisdom, Madness and Folly—The
    Philosophy of a Lunatic*
    (Custance), 52
Workplace
  computer-mediated
    communications in, 11, 16,
    141–189
  scrutiny of employees at, 219n.30
World Wide Web. *See* Computer-
    mediated communications

Also of interest from Other Press . . .

OTHER